THE ART OF DECEPTION

Controlling the Human Element of Security

KEVIN D. MITNICK
& William L. Simon

Wiley Publishing, Inc.

Publisher: Robert Ipsen
Editor: Carol Long
Developmental Editor: Nancy Stevenson
Managing Editor: John Atkins
Interior Design: Marie Kristine Parial-Leonardo
Text Design & Composition: Wiley Composition Services
Chart Design: Stacey Kirkland

Published by Wiley Publishing, Inc., Indianapolis, Indiana
Published simultaneously in Canada

For general information on our other products and services please contact our Customer Care Department within the United States at (800) 762-2974, outside the United States at (317) 572-3993 or fax (317) 572-4002.

Wiley also publishes its books in a variety of electronic formats. Some content that appears in print may not be available in electronic books.

ISBN: 0-471-23712-4

Printed in the United States of America

10 9 8 7 6 5 4 3 2

For Shelly Jaffe, Reba Vartanian, Chickie Leventhal, and Mitchell Mitnick, and for the late Alan Mitnick, Adam Mitnick, and Jack Biello

For Arynne, Victoria, and David, Sheldon, Vincent, and Elena

Social Engineering

Social engineering uses influence and persuasion to deceive people by convincing them that the social engineer is someone he is not, or by manipulation. As a result, the social engineer is able to take advantage of people to obtain information with or without the use of technology.

contents

Part 4   Raising the Bar   243

foreword

We humans are born with an inner drive to explore the nature of our surroundings. As young men, both Kevin Mitnick and I were intensely curious about the world and eager to prove ourselves. We were rewarded often in our attempts to learn new things, solve puzzles, and win at games. But at the same time, the world around us taught us rules of behavior that constrained our inner urge toward free exploration. For our boldest scientists and technological entrepreneurs, as well as for people like Kevin Mitnick, following this inner urge offers the greatest thrills, letting us accomplish things that others believe cannot be done.

Kevin Mitnick is one of the finest people I know. Ask him, and he will say forthrightly that what he used to do—social engineering—involves conning people. But Kevin is no longer a social engineer. And even when he was, his motive never was to enrich himself or damage others. That's not to say that there aren't dangerous and destructive criminals out there who use social engineering to cause real harm. In fact, that's exactly why Kevin wrote this book—to warn you about them.

The Art of Deception shows how vulnerable we all are—government, business, and each of us personally—to the intrusions of the social engineer. In this security-conscious era, we spend huge sums on technology to protect our computer networks and data. This book points out how easy it is to trick insiders and circumvent all this technological protection.

Whether you work in business or government, this book provides a powerful road map to help you understand how social engineers work and what you can do to foil them. Using fictionalized stories that are both entertaining and eye-opening, Kevin and coauthor Bill Simon bring to life the techniques of the social engineering underworld. After each story, they offer practical guidelines to help you guard against the breaches and threats they've described.

Technological security leaves major gaps that people like Kevin can help us close. Read this book and you may finally realize that we all need to turn to the Mitnick's among us for guidance.

— **Steve Wozniak**

preface

Some hackers destroy people's files or entire hard drives; they're called *crackers* or *vandals*. Some novice hackers don't bother learning the technology, but simply download hacker tools to break into computer systems; they're called *script kiddies*. More experienced hackers with programming skills develop hacker programs and post them to the Web and to bulletin board systems. And then there are individuals who have no interest in the technology, but use the computer merely as a tool to aid them in stealing money, goods, or services.

Despite the media-created myth of Kevin Mitnick, I am not a malicious hacker.

But I'm getting ahead of myself.

STARTING OUT

My path was probably set early in life. I was a happy-go-lucky kid, but bored. After my father split when I was three, my mother worked as a waitress to support us. To see me then—an only child being raised by a mother who put in long, harried days on a sometimes-erratic schedule—would have been to see a kid on his own almost all his waking hours. I was my own babysitter.

Growing up in a San Fernando Valley community gave me the whole of Los Angeles to explore, and by the age of twelve I had discovered a way to travel free throughout the whole greater L.A. area. I realized one day while riding the bus that the security of the bus transfer I had purchased relied on the unusual pattern of the paper-punch that the drivers used to mark day, time, and route on the transfer slips. A friendly driver, answering my carefully planted question, told me where to buy that special type of punch.

The transfers are meant to let you change buses and continue a journey to your destination, but I worked out how to use them to travel anywhere I wanted to go for free. Obtaining blank transfers was a walk in the park.

The trash bins at the bus terminals were always filled with only-partly-used books of transfers that the drivers tossed away at the end of their shifts. With a pad of blanks and the punch, I could mark my own transfers and travel anywhere that L.A. buses went. Before long, I had all but memorized the bus schedules of the entire system. (This was an early example of my surprising memory for certain types of information; I can still, today, remember phone numbers, passwords, and other seemingly trivial details as far back as my childhood.)

Another personal interest that surfaced at an early age was my fascination with performing magic. Once I learned how a new trick worked, I would practice, practice, and practice some more until I mastered it. To an extent, it was through magic that I discovered the enjoyment in gaining secret knowledge.

From Phone Phreak to Hacker

My first encounter with what I would eventually learn to call *social engineering* came about during my high school years when I met another student who was caught up in a hobby called *phone phreaking*. Phone phreaking is a type of hacking that allows you to explore the telephone network by exploiting the phone systems and phone company employees. He showed me neat tricks he could do with a telephone, like obtaining any information the phone company had on any customer, and using a secret test number to make long-distance calls for free. (Actually it was free only to us. I found out much later that it wasn't a secret test number at all. The calls were, in fact, being billed to some poor company's MCI account.)

That was my introduction to social engineering—my kindergarten, so to speak. My friend and another phone phreaker I met shortly thereafter let me listen in as they each made *pretext* calls to the phone company. I heard the things they said that made them sound believable; I learned about different phone company offices, lingo, and procedures. But that "training" didn't last long; it didn't have to. Soon I was doing it all on my own, learning as I went, doing it even better than my first teachers.

The course my life would follow for the next fifteen years had been set.

In high school, one of my all-time favorite pranks was gaining unauthorized access to the telephone switch and changing the class of service of a fellow phone phreak. When he'd attempt to make a call from home, he'd get a message telling him to deposit a dime because the telephone company switch had received input that indicated he was calling from a pay phone.

I became absorbed in everything about telephones, not only the electronics, switches, and computers, but also the corporate organization, the procedures, and the terminology. After a while, I probably knew more about the phone system than any single employee. And I had developed my social engineering skills to the point that, at seventeen years old, I was able to talk most telco employees into almost anything, whether I was speaking with them in person or by telephone.

My much-publicized hacking career actually started when I was in high school. While I cannot describe the detail here, suffice it to say that one of the driving forces in my early hacks was to be accepted by the guys in the hacker group.

Back then we used the term *hacker* to mean a person who spent a great deal of time tinkering with hardware and software, either to develop more efficient programs or to bypass unnecessary steps and get the job done more quickly. The term has now become a pejorative, carrying the meaning of "malicious criminal." In these pages I use the term the way I have always used it—in its earlier, more benign sense.

After high school I studied computers at the Computer Learning Center in Los Angeles. Within a few months, the school's computer manager realized I had found vulnerability in the operating system and gained full administrative privileges on their IBM minicomputer. The best computer experts on their teaching staff couldn't figure out how I had done this. In what may have been one of the earliest examples of "hire the hacker," I was given an offer I couldn't refuse: Do an honors project to enhance the school's computer security, or face suspension for hacking the system. Of course, I chose to do the honors project, and ended up graduating cum laude with honors.

Becoming a Social Engineer

Some people get out of bed each morning dreading their daily work routine at the proverbial salt mines. I've been lucky enough to enjoy my work. In particular, you can't imagine the challenge, reward, and pleasure I had in the time I spent as a private investigator. I was honing my talents in the performance art called *social engineering* (getting people to do things they wouldn't ordinarily do for a stranger) and being paid for it.

For me it wasn't difficult becoming proficient in social engineering. My father's side of the family had been in the sales field for generations, so the art of influence and persuasion might have been an inherited trait. When you combine that trait with an inclination for deceiving people, you have the profile of a typical social engineer.

You might say there are two specialties within the job classification of con artist. Somebody who swindles and cheats people out of their money belongs to one sub-specialty, the *grifter*. Somebody who uses deception, influence, and persuasion against businesses, usually targeting their information, belongs to the other sub-specialty, the *social engineer*. From the time of my bus-transfer trick, when I was too young to know there was anything wrong with what I was doing, I had begun to recognize a talent for finding out the secrets I wasn't supposed to have. I built on that talent by using deception, knowing the lingo, and developing a well-honed skill of manipulation.

One way I worked on developing the skills of my craft, if I may call it a craft, was to pick out some piece of information I didn't really care about and see if I could talk somebody on the other end of the phone into providing it, just to improve my skills. In the same way I used to practice my magic tricks, I practiced pretexting. Through these rehearsals, I soon found that I could acquire virtually any information I targeted.

As I described in Congressional testimony before Senators Lieberman and Thompson years later:

> *I have gained unauthorized access to computer systems at some of the largest corporations on the planet, and have successfully penetrated some of the most resilient computer systems ever developed. I have used both technical and nontechnical means to obtain the source code to various operating systems and telecommunications devices to study their vulnerabilities and their inner workings.*

All of this activity was really to satisfy my own curiosity; to see what I could do; and find out secret information about operating systems, cell phones, and anything else that stirred my curiosity.

FINAL THOUGHTS

I've acknowledged since my arrest that the actions I took were illegal, and that I committed invasions of privacy.

My misdeeds were motivated by curiosity. I wanted to know as much as I could about how phone networks worked and the ins-and-outs of computer security. I went from being a kid who loved to perform magic tricks to becoming the world's most notorious hacker, feared by corporations and the government. As I reflect back on my life for the last 30 years, I admit I made some extremely poor decisions, driven by my curiosity, the desire to learn about technology, and the need for a good intellectual challenge.

I'm a changed person now. I'm turning my talents and the extensive knowledge I've gathered about information security and social engineering tactics to helping government, businesses, and individuals prevent, detect, and respond to information-security threats.

This book is one more way that I can use my experience to help others avoid the efforts of the malicious information thieves of the world. I think you will find the stories enjoyable, eye-opening, and educational.

introduction

this book contains a wealth of information about information security and social engineering. To help you find your way, here's a quick look at how this book is organized:

In Part 1 I'll reveal security's weakest link and show you why you and your company are at risk from social engineering attacks.

In Part 2 you'll see how social engineers toy with your trust, your desire to be helpful, your sympathy, and your human gullibility to get what they want. Fictional stories of typical attacks will demonstrate that social engineers can wear many hats and many faces. If you think you've never encountered one, you're probably wrong. Will you recognize a scenario you've experienced in these stories and wonder if you had a brush with social engineering? You very well might. But once you've read Chapters 2 through 9, you'll know how to get the upper hand when the next social engineer comes calling.

Part 3 is the part of the book where you see how the social engineer ups the ante, in made-up stories that show how he can step onto your corporate premises, steal the kind of secret that can make or break your company, and thwart your hi-tech security measures. The scenarios in this section will make you aware of threats that range from simple employee revenge to cyber terrorism. If you value the information that keeps your business running and the privacy of your data, you'll want to read Chapters 10 through 14 from beginning to end.

It's important to note that unless otherwise stated, the anecdotes in this book are purely fictional.

In Part 4 I talk the corporate talk about how to prevent successful social engineering attacks on your organization. Chapter 15 provides a blueprint for a successful security-training program. And Chapter 16 might just save your neck—it's a complete security policy you can customize for your organization and implement right away to keep your company and information safe.

Finally, I've provided a Security at a Glance section, which includes checklists, tables, and charts that summarize key information you can use to help your employees foil a social engineering attack on the job. These tools also provide valuable information you can use in devising your own security-training program.

Throughout the book you'll also find several useful elements: Lingo boxes provide definitions of social engineering and computer hacker terminology; Mitnick Messages offer brief words of wisdom to help strengthen your security strategy; and notes and sidebars give interesting background or additional information.

part 1

behind the scenes

chapter

Security's Weakest Link

a company may have purchased the best security technologies that money can buy, trained their people so well that they lock up all their secrets before going home at night, and hired building guards from the best security firm in the business.

That company is still totally vulnerable.

Individuals may follow every best-security practice recommended by the experts, slavishly install every recommended security product, and be thoroughly vigilant about proper system configuration and applying security patches.

Those individuals are still completely vulnerable.

THE HUMAN FACTOR

Testifying before Congress not long ago, I explained that I could often get passwords and other pieces of sensitive information from companies by pretending to be someone else and *just asking for it*.

It's natural to yearn for a feeling of absolute safety, leading many people to settle for a false sense of security. Consider the responsible and loving homeowner who has a Medico, a tumbler lock known as being pickproof, installed in his front door to protect his wife, his children, and his home. He's now comfortable that he has made his family much safer against intruders. But what about the intruder who breaks a window, or cracks the code to the garage door opener? How about installing a robust security system? Better, but still no guarantee. Expensive locks or no, the homeowner remains vulnerable.

Why? Because the *human* factor is truly security's weakest link.

Security is too often merely an illusion, an illusion sometimes made even worse when gullibility, naïveté, or ignorance come into play. The world's most respected scientist of the twentieth century, Albert Einstein, is quoted as saying, "Only two things are infinite, the universe and human stupidity, and I'm not sure about the former." In the end, social engineering attacks can succeed when people are stupid or, more commonly, simply ignorant about good security practices. With the same attitude as our security-conscious homeowner, many information technology (IT) professionals hold to the misconception that they've made their companies largely immune to attack because they've deployed standard security products—firewalls, intrusion detection systems, or stronger authentication devices such as time-based tokens or biometric smart cards. Anyone who thinks that security products alone offer true security is settling for the *illusion* of security. It's a case of living in a world of fantasy: They will inevitably, later if not sooner, suffer a security incident.

As noted security consultant Bruce Schneier puts it, "Security is not a product, it's a process." Moreover, security is not a technology problem—it's a people and management problem.

As developers invent continually better security technologies, making it increasingly difficult to exploit technical vulnerabilities, attackers will turn more and more to exploiting the human element. Cracking the human firewall is often easy, requires no investment beyond the cost of a phone call, and involves minimal risk.

A CLASSIC CASE OF DECEPTION

What's the greatest threat to the security of your business assets? That's easy: the social engineer—an unscrupulous magician who has you watching his left hand while with his right he steals your secrets. This character is often so friendly, glib, and obliging that you're grateful for having encountered him.

Take a look at an example of social engineering. Not many people today still remember the young man named Stanley Mark Rifkin and his little adventure with the now defunct Security Pacific National Bank in Los Angeles. Accounts of his escapade vary, and Rifkin (like me) has never told his own story, so the following is based on published reports.

Code Breaking

One day in 1978, Rifkin moseyed over to Security Pacific's authorized-personnel-only wire-transfer room, where the staff sent and received transfers totaling several billion dollars every day.

He was working for a company under contract to develop a backup system for the wire room's data in case their main computer ever went down. That role gave him access to the transfer procedures, including how bank officials arranged for a transfer to be sent. He had learned that bank officers who were authorized to order wire transfers would be given a closely guarded daily code each morning to use when calling the wire room.

In the wire room the clerks saved themselves the trouble of trying to memorize each day's code: They wrote down the code on a slip of paper and posted it where they could see it easily. This particular November day Rifkin had a specific reason for his visit. He wanted to get a glance at that paper.

Arriving in the wire room, he took some notes on operating procedures, supposedly to make sure the backup system would mesh properly with the regular systems. Meanwhile, he surreptitiously read the security code from the posted slip of paper, and memorized it. A few minutes later he walked out. As he said afterward, he felt as if he had just won the lottery.

There's This Swiss Bank Account . . .

Leaving the room at about 3 o'clock in the afternoon, he headed straight for the pay phone in the building's marble lobby, where he deposited a coin and dialed into the wire-transfer room. He then changed hats, transforming himself from Stanley Rifkin, bank consultant, into Mike Hansen, a member of the bank's International Department.

According to one source, the conversation went something like this:

"Hi, this is Mike Hansen in International," he said to the young woman who answered the phone.

She asked for the office number. That was standard procedure, and he was prepared: "286," he said.

The girl then asked, "Okay, what's the code?"

Rifkin has said that his adrenaline-powered heartbeat "picked up its pace" at this point. He responded smoothly, "4789." Then he went on to give instructions for wiring "Ten million, two-hundred thousand dollars exactly" to the Irving Trust Company in New York, for credit of the Wozchod Handels Bank of Zurich, Switzerland, where he had already established an account.

The girl then said, "Okay, I got that. And now I need the interoffice settlement number."

Rifkin broke out in a sweat; this was a question he hadn't anticipated, something that had slipped through the cracks in his research. But he managed to stay in character, acted as if everything was fine, and on the spot answered without missing a beat, "Let me check; I'll call you right back." He changed hats once again to call another department at the bank, this time claiming to be an employee in the wire-transfer room. He obtained the settlement number and called the girl back.

She took the number and said, "Thanks." (Under the circumstances, her thanking him has to be considered highly ironic.)

Achieving Closure

A few days later Rifkin flew to Switzerland, picked up his cash, and handed over $8 million to a Russian agency for a pile of diamonds. He flew back, passing through U.S. Customs with the stones hidden in a money belt. He had pulled off the biggest bank heist in history—and done it without using a gun, even without a computer. Oddly, his caper eventually made it into the pages of the *Guinness Book of World Records* in the category of "biggest computer fraud."

Stanley Rifkin had used the art of deception—the skills and techniques that are today called social engineering. Thorough planning and a good gift of gab is all it really took.

And that's what this book is about—the techniques of social engineering (at which yours truly is proficient) and how to defend against their being used at your company.

THE NATURE OF THE THREAT

The Rifkin story makes perfectly clear how misleading our sense of security can be. Incidents like this—okay, maybe not $10 million heists, but harmful incidents nonetheless—are happening *every day*. You may be losing money right now, or somebody may be stealing new product plans, and you don't even know it. If it hasn't already happened to your company, it's not a question of *if* it will happen, but *when*.

A Growing Concern

The Computer Security Institute, in its 2001 survey of computer crime, reported that 85 percent of responding organizations had detected computer security breaches in the preceding twelve months. That's an astounding number: Only fifteen out of every hundred organizations responding were able to say that they had not had a security breach during the year. Equally astounding was the number of organizations that reported that they had experienced financial losses due to computer breaches: 64 percent. Well over half the organizations had suffered financially. *In a single year*.

My own experiences lead me to believe that the numbers in reports like this are somewhat inflated. I'm suspicious of the agenda of the people conducting the survey. But that's not to say that the damage isn't extensive; it is. Those who fail to plan for a security incident are planning for failure.

Commercial security products deployed in most companies are mainly aimed at providing protection against the amateur computer intruder, like the kids known as script kiddies. In fact, these wannabe hackers with downloaded software are mostly just a nuisance. The greater losses, the real threats, come from sophisticated attackers with well-defined targets who are motivated by financial gain. These people focus on one target at a time rather than, like the amateurs, trying to infiltrate as many systems as possible. While amateur computer intruders simply go for quantity, the professionals target information of quality and value.

Technologies like authentication devices (for proving identity), access control (for managing access to files and system resources), and intrusion detection systems (the electronic equivalent of burglar alarms) are necessary to a corporate security program. Yet it's typical today for a company to spend more money on coffee than on deploying countermeasures to protect the organization against security attacks.

Just as the criminal mind cannot resist temptation, the hacker mind is driven to find ways around powerful security technology safeguards. And in many cases, they do that by targeting the people who use the technology.

Deceptive Practices

There's a popular saying that a secure computer is one that's turned off. Clever, but false: The *pretexter* simply talks someone into going into the office and turning that computer on. An adversary who wants your information can obtain it, usually in any one of several different ways. It's just a matter of time, patience, personality, and persistence. That's where the art of deception comes in.

To defeat security measures, an attacker, intruder, or social engineer must find a way to deceive a trusted user into revealing information, or trick an unsuspecting mark into providing him with access. When trusted employees are deceived, influenced, or manipulated into revealing sensitive information, or performing actions that create a security hole for the attacker to slip through, no technology in the world can protect a business. Just as cryptanalysts are sometimes able to reveal the plain text of a coded message by finding a weakness that lets them bypass the encryption technology, social engineers use deception practiced on your employees to bypass security technology.

ABUSE OF TRUST

In most cases, successful social engineers have strong people skills. They're charming, polite, and easy to like—social traits needed for establishing rapid rapport and trust. An experienced social engineer is able to gain access to virtually any targeted information by using the strategies and tactics of his craft.

Savvy technologists have painstakingly developed information-security solutions to minimize the risks connected with the use of computers, yet left unaddressed the most significant vulnerability, the human factor. Despite our intellect, we humans—you, me, and everyone else—remain the most severe threat to each other's security.

Our National Character

We're not mindful of the threat, especially in the Western world. In the United States most of all, we're not trained to be suspicious of each other. We are taught to "love thy neighbor" and have trust and faith in each other. Consider how difficult it is for neighborhood watch organizations to get people to lock their homes and cars. This sort of vulnerability is obvious, and yet it seems to be ignored by many who prefer to live in a dream world—until they get burned.

We know that all people are not kind and honest, but too often we live as if they were. This lovely innocence has been the fabric of the lives of Americans and it's painful to give it up. As a nation we have built into our concept of freedom that the best places to live are those where locks and keys are the least necessary.

Most people go on the assumption that they will not be deceived by others, based upon a belief that the probability of being deceived is very low; the attacker, understanding this common belief, makes his request sound so reasonable that it raises no suspicion, all the while exploiting the victim's trust.

Organizational Innocence

That innocence that is part of our national character was evident back when computers were first being connected remotely. Recall that the ARPANet (the Defense Department's Advanced Research Projects Agency

Network), the predecessor of the Internet, was designed as a way of sharing research information between government, research, and educational institutions. The goal was information freedom, as well as technological advancement. Many educational institutions therefore set up early computer systems with little or no security. One noted software libertarian, Richard Stallman, even refused to protect his account with a password.

But with the Internet being used for electronic commerce, the dangers of weak security in our wired world have changed dramatically. Deploying more technology is not going to solve the human security problem.

Just look at our airports today. Security has become paramount, yet we're alarmed by media reports of travelers who have been able to circumvent security and carry potential weapons past checkpoints. How is this possible during a time when our airports are on such a state of alert? Are the metal detectors failing? No. The problem isn't the machines. The problem is the human factor: The people manning the machines. Airport officials can marshal the National Guard and install metal detectors and facial recognition systems, but educating the frontline security staff on how to properly screen passengers is much more likely to help.

The same problem exists within government, business, and educational institutions throughout the world. Despite the efforts of security professionals, information everywhere remains vulnerable and will continue to be seen as a ripe target by attackers with social engineering skills, until the weakest link in the security chain, the human link, has been strengthened.

Now more than ever we must learn to stop wishful thinking and become more aware of the techniques that are being used by those who attempt to attack the confidentiality, integrity, and availability of the information on our computer systems and networks. We've come to accept the need for defensive driving; it's time to accept and learn the practice of defensive computing.

The threat of a break-in that violates your privacy, your mind, or your company's information systems may not seem real until it happens. To avoid such a costly dose of reality, we all need to become aware, educated, vigilant, and aggressively protective of our information assets, our own personal information, and our nation's critical infrastructures. And we must implement those precautions today.

TERRORISTS AND DECEPTION

Of course, deception isn't an exclusive tool of the social engineer. Physical terrorism makes the biggest news, and we have come to realize as never before that the world is a dangerous place. Civilization is, after all, just a thin veneer.

The attacks on New York and Washington, D.C., in September 2001 infused sadness and fear into the hearts of every one of us—not just Americans, but well-meaning people of all nations. We're now alerted to the fact that there are obsessive terrorists located around the globe, well-trained and waiting to launch further attacks against us.

The recently intensified effort by our government has increased the levels of our security consciousness. We need to stay alert, on guard against all forms of terrorism. We need to understand how terrorists treacherously create false identities, assume roles as students and neighbors, and melt into the crowd. They mask their true beliefs while they plot against us—practicing tricks of deception similar to those you will read about in these pages.

And while, to the best of my knowledge, terrorists have not yet used social engineering ruses to infiltrate corporations, water-treatment plants, electrical generation facilities, or other vital components of our national infrastructure, the potential is there. It's just too easy. The security awareness and security policies that I hope will be put into place and enforced by corporate senior management because of this book will come none too soon.

ABOUT THIS BOOK

Corporate security is a question of balance. Too little security leaves your company vulnerable, but an overemphasis on security gets in the way of attending to business, inhibiting the company's growth and prosperity. The challenge is to achieve a balance between security and productivity.

Other books on corporate security focus on hardware and software technology, and do not adequately cover the most serious threat of all: human deception. The purpose of this book, in contrast, is to help you understand how you, your coworkers, and others in your company are being manipulated, and the barriers you can erect to stop being victims. The book focuses mainly on the non-technical methods that hostile intruders use to steal information, compromise the integrity of information that is believed to be safe but isn't, or destroy company work product.

My task is made more difficult by a simple truth: Every reader will have been manipulated by the grand experts of all time in social engineering—their parents. They found ways to get you—"for your own good"—to do what they thought best. Parents become great storytellers in the same way that social engineers skillfully develop very plausible stories, reasons, and justifications for achieving their goals. Yes, we were all molded by our parents: benevolent (and sometimes not so benevolent) social engineers.

Conditioned by that training, we have become vulnerable to manipulation. We would live a difficult life if we had to be always on our guard, mistrustful of others, concerned that we might become the dupe of someone trying to take advantage of us. In a perfect world we would implicitly trust others, confident that the people we encounter are going to be honest and trustworthy. But we do not live in a perfect world, and so we have to exercise a standard of vigilance to repel the deceptive efforts of our adversaries.

The main portions of this book, Parts 2 and 3, are made up of stories that show you social engineers in action. In these sections you'll read about:

- What phone phreaks discovered years ago: A slick method for getting an unlisted phone number from the telephone company.

- Several different methods used by attackers to convince even alert, suspicious employees to reveal their computer usernames and passwords.

- How an Operations Center manager cooperated in allowing an attacker to steal his company's most secret product information.

- The methods of an attacker who deceived a lady into downloading software that spies on every keystroke she makes and emails the details to him.

- How private investigators get information about your company, and about you personally, that I can practically guarantee will send a chill up your spine.

You might think as you read some of the stories in Parts 2 and 3 that they're not possible, that no one could really succeed in getting away with the lies, dirty tricks, and schemes described in these pages. The reality is that in every case, these stories depict events that can and do happen; many of them are happening every day somewhere on the planet, maybe even to your business as you read this book.

The material in this book will be a real eye-opener when it comes to protecting your business, but also personally deflecting the advances of a social engineer to protect the integrity of information in your private life.

In Part 4 of this book I switch gears. My goal here is to help you create the necessary business policies and awareness training to minimize the chances of your employees ever being duped by a social engineer. Understanding the strategies, methods, and tactics of the social engineer will help prepare you to deploy reasonable controls to safeguard your IT assets, without undermining your company's productivity.

In short, I've written this book to raise your awareness about the serious threat posed by social engineering, and to help you make sure that your company and its employees are less likely to be exploited in this way.

Or perhaps I should say, far less likely to be exploited *ever again*.

•••••●●●●●●•••••

part 2

the art of the attacker

chapter 2

When Innocuous Information Isn't

What do most people think is the real threat from social engineers? What should you do to be on your guard?

If the goal is to capture some highly valuable prize—say, a vital component of the company's intellectual capital—then perhaps what's needed is, figuratively, just a stronger vault and more heavily armed guards. Right?

But in reality penetrating a company's security often starts with the bad guy obtaining some piece of information or some document that seems so innocent, so everyday and unimportant, that most people in the organization wouldn't see any reason why the item should be protected and restricted.

THE HIDDEN VALUE OF INFORMATION

Much of the seemingly innocuous information in a company's possession is prized by a social engineering attacker because it can play a vital role in his effort to dress himself in a cloak of believability.

Throughout these pages, I'm going to show you how social engineers do what they do by letting you "witness" the attacks for yourself—sometimes presenting the action from the viewpoint of the people being victimized, allowing you to put yourself in their shoes and gauge how you yourself (or maybe one of your employees or coworkers) might have responded. In many cases you'll also experience the same events from the perspective of the social engineer.

The first story looks at a vulnerability in the financial industry.

CREDITCHEX

For a long time, the British put up with a very stuffy banking system. As an ordinary, upstanding citizen, you couldn't walk in off the street and open a bank account. No, the bank wouldn't consider accepting you as a customer unless some person already well established as a customer provided you with a letter of recommendation

Quite a difference, of course, in the seemingly egalitarian banking world of today. And our modern ease of doing business is nowhere more in evidence than in friendly, democratic America, where almost anyone can walk into a bank and easily open a checking account, right? Well, not exactly. The truth is that banks understandably have a natural reluctance to open an account for somebody who just might have a history of writing bad checks—that would be about as welcome as a rap sheet of bank robbery or embezzlement charges. So it's standard practice at many banks to get a quick thumbs-up or thumbs-down on a prospective new customer.

One of the major companies that banks contract with for this information is an outfit we'll call CreditChex. They provide a valuable service to their clients, but like many companies, can also unknowingly provide a handy service to knowing social engineers.

The First Call: Kim Andrews

"National Bank, this is Kim. Did you want to open an account today?"

"Hi, Kim. I have a question for you. Do you guys use CreditChex?"

"Yes."

"When you phone in to CreditChex, what do you call the number you give them—is it a 'Merchant ID'?"

A pause; she was weighing the question, wondering what this was about and whether she should answer.

The caller quickly continued without missing a beat: "Because, Kim, I'm working on a book. It deals with private investigations."

"Yes," she said, answering the question with new confidence, pleased to be helping a writer.

"So it's called a Merchant ID, right?"

"Uh huh."

"Okay, great. Because I wanted to make sure I had the lin
right. For the book. Thanks for your help. Good-bye,
Kim."

The Second Call: Chris Talbert

"National Bank, New Accounts, this is Chris."

"Hi, Chris. This is Alex," the caller said. "I'm a customer
service rep with CreditChex. We're doing a survey to
improve our services. Can you spare me a couple of
minutes?"

She was glad to, and the caller went on:

"Okay—what are the hours your branch is open for business?" She answered, and continued answering his
string of questions.

"How many employees at your branch use our service?"

"How often do you call us with an inquiry?"

"Which of our 800-numbers have we assigned you for calling us?"

"Have our representatives always been courteous?"

"How's our response time?"

"How long have you been with the bank?"

"What Merchant ID are you currently using?"

"Have you ever found any inaccuracies with the information
we've provided you?"

"If you had any suggestions for improving our service, what
would they be?"

And:

"Would you be willing to fill out periodic questionnaires if
we send them to your branch?"

She agreed, they chatted a bit, the caller rang off, and Chris
went back to work.

The Third Call: Henry McKinsey

"CreditChex, this is Henry McKinsey, how can I help you?"

The caller said he was from National Bank. He gave the
proper Merchant ID and then gave the name and social security number of the person he was looking for information on.
Henry asked for the birth date, and the caller gave that, too.

After a few moments, Henry read the listing from his computer screen.

"Wells Fargo reported NSF in 1998, one time, amount of $2,066." NSF—nonsufficient funds—is the familiar banking lingo for checks that have been written when there isn't enough money in the account to cover them.

"Any activities since then?"

"No activities."

"Have there been any other inquiries?"

"Let's see. Okay, two of them, both last month. Third United Credit Union of Chicago." He stumbled over the next name, Schenectady Mutual Investments, and had to spell it. "That's in New York State," he added.

Private Investigator at Work

All three of those calls were made by the same person: a private investigator we'll call Oscar Grace. Grace had a new client, one of his first. A cop until a few months before, he found that some of this new work came naturally, but some offered a challenge to his resources and inventiveness. This one came down firmly in the challenge category.

The hardboiled private eyes of fiction—the Sam Spades and the Philip Marlowes—spend long nighttime hours sitting in cars waiting to catch a cheating spouse. Real-life PIs do the same. They also do a less written about, but no less important kind of snooping for warring spouses, a method that leans more heavily on social engineering skills than on fighting off the boredom of nighttime vigils.

Grace's new client was a lady who looked as if she had a pretty comfortable budget for clothes and jewelry. She walked into his office one day and took a seat in the leather chair, the only one that didn't have papers piled on it. She settled her large Gucci handbag on his desk with the logo turned to face him and announced she was planning to tell her husband that she wanted a divorce, but admitted to "just a very little problem."

It seemed her hubby was one step ahead. He had already pulled the cash out of their savings account and an even larger sum from their brokerage account. She wanted to know where their assets had been squirreled away, and her divorce lawyer wasn't any help at all. Grace surmised the lawyer was one of those uptown, high-rise counselors who wouldn't get his hands dirty on something messy like where-did-the-money-go.

Could Grace help?

He assured her it would be a breeze, quoted a fee, expenses billed at cost, and collected a check for the first payment.

Then he faced his problem. What do you do if you've never handled a piece of work like this before and don't quite know how to go about tracking down a money trail? You move forward by baby steps. Here, according to our source, is Grace's story.

●••••●●●●●●●●•••●••

I knew about CreditChex and how banks used the outfit—my ex-wife used to work at a bank. But I didn't know the lingo and procedures, and trying to ask my ex- would be a waste of time.

Step one: Get the terminology straight and figure out how to make the request so it sounds like I know what I'm talking about. At the bank I called, the first young lady, Kim, was suspicious when I asked about how they identify themselves when they phone CreditChex. She hesitated; she didn't know whether to tell me. Was I put off by that? Not a bit. In fact, the hesitation gave me an important clue, a sign that I had to supply a reason she'd find believable. When I worked the con on her about doing research for a book, it relieved her suspicions. You say you're an author or a movie writer, and everybody opens up.

She had other knowledge that would have helped—things like what information CreditChex requires to identify the person you're calling about, what information you can ask for, and the big one, what was Kim's bank Merchant ID number. I was ready to ask those questions, but her hesitation sent up the red flag. She bought the book research story, but she already had a few niggling suspicions. If she'd been more willing right way, I would have asked her to reveal more details about their procedures.

You have to go on gut instinct, listen closely to what the mark is saying and how she's saying it. This lady sounded smart enough for alarm bells to start going off if I asked too many unusual questions. And even though she didn't know who I was or what number I was calling from, still in this

19

When Innocuous Information Isn't

lingo

MARK The victim of a con.

BURN THE SOURCE An attacker is said to have burned the source when he allows a victim to recognize that an attack has taken place. Once the victim becomes aware and notifies other employees or management of the attempt, it becomes extremely difficult to exploit the same source in future attacks.

business you never want anybody putting out the word to be on the look-out for someone calling to get information about the business. That's because you don't want to burn the source—you may want to call the same office back another time.

I'm always on the watch for little signs that give me a read on how cooperative a person is, on a scale that runs from "You sound like a nice person and I believe everything you're saying" to "Call the cops, alert the National Guard, this guy's up to no good."

I read Kim as a little bit on edge, so I just called somebody at a different branch. On my second call with Chris, the survey trick played like a charm. The tactic here is to slip the important questions in among inconsequential ones that are used to create a sense of believability. Before I dropped the question about the Merchant ID number with CreditChex, I ran a little last-minute test by asking her a personal question about how long she'd been with the bank.

A personal question is like a land mine—some people step right over it and never notice; for other people, it blows up and sends them scurrying for safety. So if I ask a personal question and she answers the question and the tone of her voice doesn't change, that means she probably isn't skeptical about the nature of the request. I can safely ask the sought-after question without arousing her suspicions, and she'll probably give me the answer I'm looking for.

One more thing a good PI knows: Never end the conversation after getting the key information. Another two or three questions, a little chat, and then it's okay to say good-bye. Later, if the victim remembers anything about what you asked, it will probably be the last couple of questions. The rest will usually be forgotten.

So Chris gave me their Merchant ID number, and the phone number they call to make requests. I would have been happier if I had gotten to ask some questions about how much information you can get from CreditChex. But it was better not to push my luck.

It was like having a blank check on CreditChex. I could now call and get information whenever I wanted. I didn't even have to pay for the service. As it turned out, the CreditChex rep was happy to share exactly the information I wanted: two places my client's husband had recently applied to open an account. So where were the assets his soon-to-be ex-wife was looking for? Where else but at the banking institutions the guy at CreditChex listed?

Analyzing the Con

This entire ruse was based on one of the fundamental tactics of social engineering: gaining access to information that a company employee treats as innocuous, when it isn't.

The first bank clerk confirmed the terminology to describe the identifying number used when calling CreditChex: the Merchant ID. The second provided the phone number for calling CreditChex, and the most vital piece of information, the bank's Merchant ID number. All this information appeared to the clerk to be innocuous. After all, the bank clerk thought she was talking to someone from CreditChex—so what could be the harm in disclosing the number?

All of this laid the groundwork for the third call. Grace had everything he needed to phone CreditChex, pass himself off as a rep from one of their customer banks, National, and simply ask for the information he was after.

With as much skill at stealing information as a good swindler has at stealing your money, Grace had well-honed talents for reading people. He knew the common tactic of burying the key questions among innocent ones. He knew a personal question would test the second clerk's willingness to cooperate, before innocently asking for the Merchant ID number.

The first clerk's error in confirming the terminology for the CreditChex ID number would be almost impossible to protect against. The information is so widely known within the banking industry that it appears to be unimportant—the very model of the innocuous. But the second clerk, Chris, should not have been so willing to answer questions without positively verifying that the caller was really who he claimed to be. She should, at the very least, have taken his name and number and called back; that way, if any questions arose later, she may have kept a record of what phone number the person had used. In this case, making a call like that would have made it much more difficult for the attacker to masquerade as a representative from CreditChex.

mitnick
message

A Merchant ID in this situation is analogous to a password. If bank personnel treated it like an ATM PIN, they might appreciate the sensitive nature of the information. Is there an internal code or number in your organization that people aren't treating with enough care?

Better still would have been a call to CreditChex using a number the bank already had on record—not a number provided by the caller—to verify that the person really worked there, and that the company was really doing a customer survey. Given the practicalities of the real world and the time pressures that most people work under today, though, this kind of verification phone call is a lot to expect, except when an employee is suspicious that some kind of attack is being made.

THE ENGINEER TRAP

It is widely known that head-hunter firms use social engineering tactics to recruit corporate talent. Here's an example of how it can happen.

In the late 1990s, a not very ethical employment agency signed a new client, a company looking for electrical engineers with experience in the telephone industry. The honcho on the project was a lady endowed with a throaty voice and sexy manner that she had learned to use to develop initial trust and rapport over the phone.

The lady decided to stage a raid on a cellular phone service provider, to see if she could locate some engineers who might be tempted to take a walk across the street to a competitor. She couldn't exactly call the switchboard and say, "Let me talk to anybody with five years of engineering experience." Instead, for reasons that will become clear in a moment, she began the talent assault by seeking a piece of information that appeared to have no sensitivity at all, information that company people give out to almost anybody who asks.

The First Call: The Receptionist

The attacker, using the name Didi Sands, placed a call to the corporate offices of the cellular phone service. In part, the conversation went like this:

Receptionist: Good afternoon. This is Marie, how may I help you?

Didi: Can you connect me to the Transportation Department?

R: I'm not sure if we have one, I'll look in my directory. Who's calling?

D: It's Didi.

R: Are you in the building, or . . . ?

D: No, I'm outside the building.

R: Didi who?

D: Didi Sands. I had the extension for Transportation, but I forgot what it was.

R: One moment.

To allay suspicions, at this point Didi asked a casual, just-making-conversation question designed to establish that she was on the "inside," familiar with company locations.

D: What building are you in—Lakeview or Main Place?

R: Main Place. *(pause)* It's 805 555 6469.

To provide herself with a backup in case the call to Transportation didn't provide what she was looking for, Didi said she also wanted to talk to Real Estate. The receptionist gave her that number, as well. When Didi asked to be connected to the Transportation number, the receptionist tried, but the line was busy.

At that point Didi asked for a *third* phone number, for Accounts Receivable, located at a corporate facility in Austin, Texas. The receptionist asked her to wait a moment, and went off the line. Reporting to Security that she had a suspicious phone call and thought there was something fishy going on? Not at all, and Didi didn't have the least bit of concern. She was being a bit of a nuisance, but to the receptionist it was all part of a typical workday. After about a minute, the receptionist came back on the line, looked up the Accounts Receivable number, tried it, and put Didi through.

The Second Call: Peggy

The next conversation went like this:

Peggy: Accounts Receivable, Peggy.

Didi: Hi, Peggy. This is Didi, in Thousand Oaks.

P: Hi, Didi.

D: How ya doing?

P: Fine.

Didi then used a familiar term in the corporate world that describes the charge code for assigning expenses against the budget of a specific organization or workgroup:

D: Excellent. I have a question for you. How do I find out the cost center for a particular department?

P: You'd have to get ahold of the budget analyst for the department.

D: Do you know who'd be the budget analyst for Thousand Oaks— headquarters? I'm trying to fill out a form and I don't know the proper cost center.

P: I just know when y'all need a cost center number, you call your budget analyst.

D: Do you have a cost center for your department there in Texas?

P: We have our own cost center but they don't give us a complete list of them.

D: How many digits is the cost center? For example, what's your cost center?

P: Well, like, are you with 9WC or with SAT?

Didi had no idea what departments or groups these referred to, but it didn't matter. She answered:

D: 9WC.

P: Then it's usually four digits. Who did you say you were with?

D: Headquarters—Thousand Oaks.

P: Well, here's one for Thousand Oaks. It's 1A5N, that's N like in Nancy.

By just hanging out long enough with somebody willing to be helpful, Didi had the cost center number she needed—one of those pieces of information that no one thinks to protect because it seems like something that couldn't be of any value to an outsider.

The Third Call: A Helpful Wrong Number

Didi's next step would be to parlay the cost center number into something of real value by using it as a poker chip.

She began by calling the Real Estate department, pretending she had reached a wrong number. Starting with a "Sorry to bother you, but . . . ," she claimed she was an employee who had lost her company directory, and asked who you were supposed to call to get a new copy. The man said the print copy was out of date because it was available on the company intranet site.

Didi said she preferred using a hard copy, and the man told her to call Publications, and then, without being asked— maybe just to keep the sexy-sounding lady on the phone a little longer—helpfully looked up the number and gave it to her.

In Publications, she spoke with a man named Bart. Didi said she was from Thousand Oaks, and they had a new consultant who needed a copy of the company directory. She told him a print copy would work better for the consultant, even if it was somewhat out of date. Bart told her she'd have to fill out a requisition form and send the form over to him.

Didi said she was out of forms and it was a rush, and could Bart be a sweetheart and fill out the form for her? He agreed with a little too much enthusiasm, and Didi gave him the details. For the address of the fictional contractor, she drawled the number of what social engineers call a *mail drop*, in this case a Mail Boxes Etc.-type of commercial business where her company rented boxes for situations just like this.

The earlier spadework now came in handy: There would be a charge for the cost and shipping of the directory. Fine—Didi gave the cost center for Thousand Oaks:

"1A5N, that's N like in Nancy."

A few days later, when the corporate directory arrived, Didi found it was an even bigger payoff than she had expected: It not only listed the names and phone numbers, but also showed who worked for whom—the corporate structure of the whole organization.

The lady of the husky voice was ready to start making her head-hunter, people-raiding phone calls. She had conned the information she needed to launch her raid using the gift of gab honed to a high polish by every skilled social engineer. Now she was ready for the payoff.

Analyzing the Con

In this social engineering attack, Didi started by getting phone numbers for three departments in the target company. This was easy, because the numbers she was asking for were no secret, especially to employees. A social engineer learns to sound like an insider, and Didi was skilled at this

lingo

MAIL DROP The social engineer's term for a rental mailbox, typically rented under an assumed name, which is used to deliver documents or packages the victim has been duped into sending.

> Just like pieces of a jigsaw puzzle, each piece of information may be irrelevant by itself. However, when the pieces are put together, a clear picture emerges. In this case, the picture the social engineer saw was the entire internal structure of the company

game. One of the phone numbers led her to a cost center number, which she then used to obtain a copy of the firm's employee directory.

The main tools she needed: sounding friendly, using some corporate lingo, and, with the last victim, throwing in a little verbal eyelash-batting.

And one more tool, an essential element not easily acquired—the manipulative skills of the social engineer, refined through extensive practice and the unwritten lessons of bygone generations of confidence men.

MORE "WORTHLESS" INFO

Besides a cost center number and internal phone extensions, what other seemingly useless information can be extremely valuable to your enemy?

Peter Abel's Phone Call

"Hi," the voice at the other end of the line says. "This is Tom at Parkhurst Travel. Your tickets to San Francisco are ready. Do you want us to deliver them, or do you want to pick them up?"

"San Francisco?" Peter says. "I'm not going to San Francisco."

"Is this Peter Abels?"

"Yes, but I don't have any trips coming up."

"Well," the caller says with a friendly laugh, "you sure you don't want to go to San Francisco?"

"If you think you can talk my boss into it . . ." Peter says, playing along with the friendly conversation.

"Sounds like a mix-up," the caller says. "On our system, we book travel arrangements under the employee number. Maybe somebody used the wrong number. What's your employee number?"

Peter obligingly recites his number. And why not? It goes on just about every personnel form he fills out, lots of people in the company have access to it—human resources, payroll, and, obviously, the outside travel agency. No one treats an employee number like some sort of secret. What difference could it make?

The answer isn't hard to figure out. Two or three pieces of information might be all it takes to mount an effective impersonation—the social engineer cloaking himself in someone else's identity. Get hold of an employee's name, his phone number, his employee number—and maybe, for good measure, his manager's name and phone number—and a halfway-competent social engineer is equipped with most of what he's likely to need to sound authentic to the next target he calls.

If someone who said he was from another department in your company had called yesterday, given a plausible reason, and asked for your employee number, would you have had any reluctance in giving it to him?

And by the way, what is your social security number?

mitnick message

The moral of the story is, don't give out any personal or internal company information or identifiers to anyone, unless his or her voice is recognizable and the requestor has a need to know.

PREVENTING THE CON

Your company has a responsibility to make employees aware of how a serious mistake can occur from mishandling nonpublic information. A well-thought-out information security policy, combined with proper education and training, will dramatically increase employee awareness about the proper handling of corporate business information. A data classification policy will help you to implement proper controls with respect to disclosing information. Without a data classification policy, all internal information must be considered confidential, unless otherwise specified.

Take these steps to protect your company from the release of seemingly innocuous information:

- The Information Security Department needs to conduct awareness training detailing the methods used by social engineers. One method, as described above, is to obtain seemingly nonsensitive information and use it as a poker chip to gain short-term trust. Each and every employee needs to be aware that when a caller has knowledge about company procedures, lingo, and internal identifiers it does not in any way, shape, or form authenticate the requestor or authorize him or her as having a need to know. A caller could be a former employee or contractor with the requisite insider information. Accordingly, each corporation has a responsibility to determine the appropriate authentication method to be used when employees interact with people they don't recognize in person or over the telephone.

- The person or persons with the role and responsibility of drafting a data classification policy should examine the types of details that may be used to gain access for legitimate employees that seem innocuous, but could lead to information that is sensitive. Though you'd never give out the access codes for your ATM card, would you tell somebody what server you use to develop company software products? Could that information be used by a person pretending to be somebody who has legitimate access to the corporate network?

- Sometimes just knowing inside terminology can make the social engineer appear authoritative and knowledgeable. The attacker often relies on this common misconception to dupe his or her victims into compliance. For example, a Merchant ID is an identifier that people in the New Accounts department of a bank casually use every day. But such an identifier is exactly the same as a password. If each and every employee understands the nature of this identifier—that it is used to positively authenticate a requestor—they might treat it with more respect.

- No companies—well, very few, at least—give out the direct-dial phone numbers of their CEO or board chairman. Most companies, though, have no concern about giving out phone numbers to most departments and workgroups in the organization—especially to someone who is, or appears to be, an employee. A possible countermeasure: Implement a policy

mitnick
message

As the old adage goes—even real paranoids probably have enemies. We must assume that every business has its enemies, too—attackers that target the network infrastructure to compromise business secrets. Don't end up being a statistic on computer crime—it's high time to shore up the necessary defenses by implementing proper controls through well-thought-out security policies and procedures.

that prohibits giving internal phone numbers of employees, contractors, consultants, and temps to outsiders. More importantly, develop a step-by-step procedure to positively identify whether a caller asking for phone numbers is really an employee.

- Accounting codes for workgroups and departments, as well as copies of the corporate directory (whether hard copy, data file, or electronic phone book on the intranet) are frequent targets of social engineers. Every company needs a written, well-publicized policy on disclosure of this type of information. The safeguards should include maintaining an audit log that records instances when sensitive information is disclosed to people outside of the company.

- Information such as an employee number, by itself, should not be used as any sort of authentication. Every employee must be trained to verify not just the identity of a requestor, but also the requestor's need to know.

- In your security training, consider teaching employees this approach: Whenever asked a question or asked for a favor by a stranger, learn first to politely decline until the request can be verified. Then—before giving in to the natural desire to be Mr. or Ms. Helpful—follow company policies and procedures with respect to verification and disclosure of nonpublic information. This style may go against our natural tendency to help others, but a little healthy paranoia may be necessary to avoid being the social engineer's next dupe.

As the stories in this chapter have shown, seemingly innocuous information can be the key to your company's most prized secrets.

•••••••••••••

chapter 3

The Direct Attack: Just Asking for It

many social engineering attacks are intricate, involving a number of steps and elaborate planning, combining a mix of manipulation and technological know-how.

But I always find it striking that a skillful social engineer can often achieve his goal with a simple, straightforward, direct attack. Just asking outright for the information may be all that's needed—as you'll see.

AN MLAC QUICKIE

Want to know someone's unlisted phone number? A social engineer can tell you half a dozen ways (and you'll find some of them described in other stories in these pages), but probably the simplest scenario is one that uses a single phone call, like this one.

Number, Please

The attacker dialed the private phone company number for the MLAC, the Mechanized Line Assignment Center. To the woman who answered, he said:

"Hey, this is Paul Anthony. I'm a cable splicer. Listen, a terminal box out here got fried in a fire. Cops think some creep tried to burn his own house down for the insurance. They got me out here alone trying to rewire this entire two hundred-pair terminal. I could really use some help right now. What facilities should be working at 6723 South Main?"

In other parts of the phone company, the person called would know that reverse lookup information on nonpub (nonpublished) numbers is supposed to be given out only to authorized phone company people. But MLAC is supposed to be known only to company employees. And while they'd never give out information to the public, who would want to refuse a little help to a company man coping with that heavy-duty assignment? She feels sorry for him, she's had bad days on the job herself, and she'll bend the rules a little to help out a fellow employee with a problem. She gives him the cable and pairs and each working number assigned to the address.

Analyzing the Con

As you'll notice repeatedly in these stories, knowledge of a company's lingo, and of its corporate structure—its various offices and departments, what each does and what information each has—is part of the essential bag of tricks of the successful social engineer.

mitnick message

It's human nature to trust our fellow man, especially when the request meets the test of being reasonable. Social engineers use this knowledge to exploit their victims and to achieve their goals.

YOUNG MAN ON THE RUN

A man we'll call Frank Parsons had been on the run for years, still wanted by the federal government for being part of an underground antiwar group in the 1960s. In restaurants he sat facing the door and he had a way of glancing over his shoulder every once in a while that other people found disconcerting. He moved every few years.

At one point Frank landed in a city he didn't know, and set about job hunting. For someone like Frank, with his well-developed computer skills (and social engineering skills as well, even though he never listed those on a job application), finding a good job usually wasn't a problem. Except in times when the economy is very tight, people with good technical computer knowledge usually find their talents in high demand and they have little problem landing on their feet. Frank quickly located a well-paying job opportunity at a large, upscale, long-term care facility near where he was living.

Just the ticket, he thought. But when he started plodding his way through the application forms, he came upon an uh-oh: The employer required the applicant to provide a copy of his state criminal history record, which he had to obtain himself from the state police. The stack of employment papers included a form to request this document, and the form had a little box for providing a fingerprint. Even though they were asking for a print of just the right index finger, if they matched his print with one in the FBI's database, he'd probably soon be working in food service at a federally funded resort.

On the other hand, it occurred to Frank that maybe, just maybe, he might still be able to get away with this. Perhaps the state didn't send those fingerprint samples to the FBI at all. How could he find out?

How? He was a social engineer—how do you *think* he found out? He placed a phone call to the state patrol: "Hi. We're doing a study for the State Department of Justice. We're researching the requirements to implement a new fingerprint identification system. Can I talk to somebody there that's really familiar with what you're doing who could maybe help us out?"

And when the local expert came on the phone, Frank asked a series of questions about what systems they were using, and the capabilities to search and store fingerprint data. Had they had any equipment problems? Were they tied into the National Crime Information Center's (NCIC) Fingerprint Search or just within the state? Was the equipment pretty easy for everybody to learn to use?

Slyly, he sneaked the key question in among the rest.

The answer was music to his ears: No, they weren't tied into the NCIC, they only checked against the state's Criminal Information Index (CII).

mitnick message

Savvy information swindlers have no qualms about ringing up federal, state, or local government officials to learn about the procedures of law enforcement. With such information in hand, the social engineer may be able to circumvent your company's standard security checks.

That was all Frank needed to know. He didn't have any record in that state, so he submitted his application, was hired for the job, and nobody ever showed up at his desk one day with the greeting, "These gentlemen are from the FBI and they'd like to have a little talk with you."

ON THE DOORSTEP

In spite of the myth of the paperless office, companies continue to print out reams of paper every day. Information in print at your company may be vulnerable, even if you use security precautions and stamp it confidential.

Here's one story that shows you how social engineers might obtain your most secret documents.

Loop-Around Deception

Every year the phone company publishes a volume called the Test Number Directory (or at least they used to, and because I am still on supervised release, I'm not going to ask if they still do). This document was highly prized by phone phreaks because it was packed with a list of all the closely guarded phone numbers used by company craftsmen, technicians, and others for things like trunk testing or checking numbers that always ring busy.

One of these test numbers, known in the lingo as a *loop-around*, was particularly useful. Phone phreaks used it as a way to find other phone phreaks to chat with, at no cost to them. Phone phreaks also used it as a way to create a callback number to give to, say, a bank. A social engineer would tell somebody at the bank the phone number to call to reach him at his office. When the bank called back to the test number (loop-around), the phone phreak would be able to receive the call, yet he had the protection of having used a phone number that could not be traced back to him.

A Test Number Directory provided a lot of neat information that could be used by any information-hungry phone phreak. So when the new directories were published each year, they were coveted by a lot of kids whose hobby was exploring the telephone network.

Security training with respect to company policy designed to protect information assets needs to be for everyone in the company, not just any employee who has electronic or physical access to the company's IT assets.

Stevie's Scam

Naturally phone companies don't make these books easy to get hold of, so phone phreaks have to be creative to get one. How can they do this? An eager kid with a mind bent on acquiring the directory might enact a scenario like this.

•••••••●●●●●•••••••

Late one day, a mild evening in the southern California autumn, a guy I'll call Stevie phones a small telephone company central office, which is the building from which phone lines run to all the homes and businesses in the established service area.

When the switchman on duty answers the call, Stevie announces that he's from the division of the phone company that publishes and distributes printed materials. "We have your new Test Number Directory," he says. "But for security reasons, we can't deliver your copy until we pick up the old one. And the delivery guy is running late. If you wanna leave your copy just outside your door, he can swing by, pick up yours, drop the new one, and be on his way."

The unsuspecting switchman seems to think that sounds reasonable. He does exactly as asked, putting out on the doorstep of the building his copy of the directory, its cover clearly marked in big red letters with the warning, "**COMPANY CONFIDENTIAL**—WHEN NO LONGER NEEDED, THIS DOCUMENT MUST BE SHREDDED."

Stevie drives by and looks around carefully to spot any cops or phone company security people who might be lurking behind trees or watching for him from parked cars. Nobody in sight. He casually picks up the coveted directory and drives away.

Here's just one more example of how easy it can be for a social engineer to get what he wants by following the simple principle of "just ask for it."

GAS ATTACK

Not only company assets are at risk in a social engineering scenario. Sometimes it's a company's customers who are the victims.

Working as a customer-service clerk brings its share of frustrations, its share of laughs, and its share of innocent mistakes—some of which can have unhappy consequences for a company's customers.

Janie Acton's Story

Janie Acton had been manning a cubicle as a customer service rep for Hometown Electric Power, in Washington, D.C., for just over three years. She was considered to be one of the better clerks, smart and conscientious.

••••••●●●●●●•••••

It was Thanksgiving week when this one particular call came in. The caller said, "This is Eduardo in the Billing Department. I've got a lady on hold, she's a secretary in the executive offices that works for one of the vice presidents, and she's asking for some information and I can't use my computer. I got an email from this girl in Human Resources that said 'ILOVEYOU,' and when I opened the attachment, I couldn't use my machine any more. A virus. I got caught by a stupid virus. Anyways, could you look up some customer information for me?"

"Sure," Janie answered. "It crashed your computer? That's terrible."

"Yeah."

"How can I help?" Janie asked.

Here the attacker called on information from his advance research to make himself sound authentic. He had learned that the information he wanted was stored in something called the Customer Billing Information System, and he had found out how employees referred to the system. He asked, "Can you bring up an account on CBIS?"

"Yes, what's the account number?"

"I don't have the number; I need you to bring it up by name."

"Okay, what's the name?"

"It's Heather Marning." He spelled the name, and Janie typed it in.

"Okay, I have it up."

"Great. Is the account current?"

"Uh huh, it's current."

"What's the account number?" he asked.

"Do you have a pencil?"

"Ready to write."

"Account number BAZ6573NR27Q."

He read the number back and then said, "And what's the service address?"

She gave him the address.

"And what's the phone?"

Janie obligingly read off that information, too.

The caller thanked her, said good-bye, and hung up. Janie went on to the next call, never thinking further about it.

Art Sealy's Research Project

Art Sealy had given up working as a freelance editor for small publishing houses when he found he could make more money doing research for writers and businesses. He soon figured out that the fee he could charge went up in proportion to how close the assignment took him to the sometimes hazy line between the legal and the illegal. Without ever realizing it, certainly without ever giving it a name, Art became a social engineer, using techniques familiar to every information broker. He turned out to have a native talent for the business, figuring out for himself techniques that most social engineers had to learn from others. After a while, he crossed the line without the least twinge of guilt.

•••••••●●●●●●••••••

A man contacted me who was writing a book about the Cabinet in the Nixon years, and was looking for a researcher who could get the inside scoop on William E. Simon, who had been Nixon's Treasury secretary. Mr. Simon had died, but the author had the name of a woman who had been on his staff. He was pretty sure she still lived in D.C., but hadn't been able to get an address. She didn't have a telephone in her name, or at least none that was listed. So that's when he called me. I told him, sure, no problem.

This is the kind of job you can usually bring off in a phone call or two, if you know what you're doing. Every local utility company can generally be counted on to give the information away. Of course, you have to BS a little. But what's a little white lie now and then—right?

I like to use a different approach each time, just to keep things interesting. "This is so-and-so in the executive offices" has always worked well for me. So has "I've got somebody on the line from Vice President Somebody's office," which worked this time, too.

Never think all social engineering attacks need to be elaborate ruses so complex that they're likely to be recognized before they can be completed. Some are in-and-out, strike-and-disappear, very simple attacks that are no more than . . . well, just asking for it.

You have to sort of develop the social engineer's instinct, get a sense of how cooperative the person on the other end is going to be with you. This time I lucked out with a friendly, helpful lady. In a single phone call, I had the address and phone number. Mission accomplished.

Analyzing the Con

Certainly Janie knew that customer information is sensitive. She would never discuss one customer's account with another customer, or give out private information to the public.

But naturally, for a caller from within the company, different rules apply. For a fellow employee it's all about being a team player and helping each other get the job done. The man from Billing could have looked up the details himself if his computer hadn't been down with a virus, and she was glad to be able to help a coworker.

Art built up gradually to the key information he was really after, asking questions along the way about things he didn't really need, such as the account number. Yet at the same time, the account number information provided a fallback: If the clerk had become suspicious, he'd call a second time and stand a better chance of success, because knowing the account number would make him sound all the more authentic to the next clerk he reached.

It never occurred to Janie that somebody might actually lie about something like this, that the caller might not really be from the billing department at all. Of course, the blame doesn't lie at Janie's feet. She wasn't well versed in the rule about making sure you know who you're talking to before discussing information in a customer's file. Nobody had ever told her about the danger of a phone call like the one from Art. It wasn't in the company policy, it wasn't part of her training, and her supervisor had never mentioned it.

PREVENTING THE CON

A point to include in your security training: Just because a caller or visitor knows the names of some people in the company, or knows some of the corporate lingo or procedures, doesn't mean he is who he claims to be. And it definitely doesn't establish him as anybody authorized to be given internal information, or access to your computer system or network.

Security training needs to emphasize: When in doubt, verify, verify, verify.

In earlier times, access to information within a company was a mark of rank and privilege. Workers stoked the furnaces, ran the machines, typed the letters, and filed the reports. The foreman or boss told them what to do, when, and how. It was the foreman or boss who knew how many widgets each worker should be producing on a shift, how many and in what colors and sizes the factory needed to turn out this week, next week, and by the end of the month.

Workers handled machines and tools and materials, and bosses handled information. Workers needed only the information specific to their specific jobs.

The picture is a little different today, isn't it? Many factory workers use some form of computer or computer-driven machine. For a large part of the workforce, critical information is pushed down to the users' desktops so that they can fulfill their responsibility to get their work done. In today's environment, almost everything employees do involves the handling of information.

That's why a company's security policy needs to be distributed enterprise-wide, regardless of position. Everybody must understand that it's not just the bosses and executives who have the information that an attacker might be after. Today, workers at every level, even those who don't use a computer, are liable to be targeted. The newly hired rep in the customer service group may be just the weak link that a social engineer breaks to achieve his objective.

Security training and corporate security policies need to strengthen that link.

chapter

Building Trust

Some of these stories might lead you to think that I believe everyone in business is a complete idiot, ready, even eager, to give away every secret in his or her possession. The social engineer knows that isn't true. Why are social engineering attacks so successful? It isn't because people are stupid or lack common sense. But we, as human beings, are all vulnerable to being deceived because people can misplace their trust if manipulated in certain ways.

The social engineer anticipates suspicion and resistance, and he's always prepared to turn distrust into trust. A good social engineer plans his attack like a chess game, anticipating the questions his target might ask so he can be ready with the proper answers.

One of his common techniques involves building a sense of trust on the part of his victim. How does a con man make you trust him? Trust me, he can.

TRUST: THE KEY TO DECEPTION

The more a social engineer can make his contact seem like business as usual, the more he allays suspicion. When people don't have a reason to be suspicious, it's easy for a social engineer to gain their trust.

Once he's got your trust, the drawbridge is lowered and the castle door thrown open so he can enter and take whatever information he wants.

You may notice I refer to social engineers, phone phreaks, and con-game operators as "he" through most of these stories. This is not chauvinism; it simply reflects the truth that most practitioners in these fields are male. But though there aren't many women social engineers, the number is growing. There are enough female social engineers out there that you shouldn't let your guard down just because you hear a woman's voice. In fact, female social engineers have a distinct advantage because they can use their sexuality to obtain cooperation. You'll find a small number of the so-called gentler sex represented in these pages.

The First Call: Andrea Lopez

Andrea Lopez answered the phone at the video rental store where she worked, and in a moment was smiling: It's always a pleasure when a customer takes the trouble to say he's happy about the service. This caller said he had had a very good experience dealing with the store, and he wanted to send the manager a letter about it.

He asked for the manager's name and the mailing address, and she told him it was Tommy Allison, and gave him the address. As he was about to hang up, he had another idea and said, "I might want to write to your company headquarters, too. What's your store number?" She gave him that information, as well. He said thanks, added something pleasant about how helpful she had been, and said good-bye.

"A call like that," she thought, "always seems to make the shift go by faster. How nice it would be if people did that more often."

The Second Call: Ginny

"Thanks for calling Studio Video. This is Ginny, how can I help you?"

"Hi, Ginny," the caller said enthusiastically, sounding as if he talked to Ginny every week or so. "It's Tommy Allison, manager at Forest Park, Store 863. We have a customer in here who wants to rent *Rocky 5* and we're all out of copies. Can you check on what you've got?"

She came back on the line after a few moments and said, "Yeah, we've got three copies."

"Okay, I'll see if he wants to drive over there. Listen, thanks. If you ever need any help from our store, just call and ask for Tommy. I'll be glad to do whatever I can for you."

Three or four times over the next couple of weeks, Ginny got calls from Tommy for help with one thing or another. They were seemingly legitimate requests, and he was always very friendly without sounding like he was trying to come on to her. He was a little chatty along the way, as well—"Did you hear about the big fire in Oak Park? Bunch of streets closed over there," and the like. The calls were a little break from the routine of the day, and Ginny was always glad to hear from him.

One day Tommy called sounding stressed. He asked, "Have you guys been having trouble with your computers?"

"No," Ginny answered. "Why?"

"Some guy crashed his car into a telephone pole, and the phone company repairman says a whole part of the city will lose their phones and Internet connection till they get this fixed."

"Oh, no. Was the man hurt?"

"They took him away in an ambulance. Anyway, I could use a little help. I've got a customer of yours here who wants to rent *Godfather II* and doesn't have his card with him. Could you verify his information for me?"

"Yeah, sure."

Tommy gave the customer's name and address, and Ginny found him in the computer. She gave Tommy the account number.

"Any late returns or balance owed?" Tommy asked.

"Nothing showing."

"Okay, great. I'll sign him up by hand for an account here and put it in our database later on when the computers come back up again. And he wants to put this charge on the Visa card he uses at your store, and he doesn't have it with him. What's the card number and expiration date?"

She gave it to him, along with the expiration date. Tommy said, "Hey, thanks for the help. Talk to you soon," and hung up.

Doyle Lonnegan's Story

Lonnegan is not a young man you would want to find waiting when you open your front door. A one-time collection man for bad gambling debts, he still does an occasional favor, if it doesn't put him out very much. In this case, he was offered a sizable bundle of cash for little more than making some phone calls to a video store. Sounds easy enough. It's just that none of his "customers" knew how to run this con; they needed somebody with Lonnegan's talent and know-how.

••••••••••••••••

People don't write checks to cover their bets when they're unlucky or stupid at the poker table. Everybody knows that. Why did these friends of mine keep on playing with a cheat that didn't have green out on the table? Don't ask. Maybe they're a little light in the IQ department. But they're friends of mine—what can you do?

This guy didn't have the money, so they took a check. I ask you! Should of drove him to an ATM machine, is what they should of done. But no, a check. For $3,230.

Naturally, it bounced. What would you expect? So then they call me; can I help? I don't close doors on people's knuckles any more. Besides, there are better ways nowadays. I told them, 30 percent commission, I'd see what I could do. So they give me his name and address, and I go up on the computer to see what's the closest video store to him.

I wasn't in a big hurry. Four phone calls to cozy up to the store manager, and then, bingo, I've got the cheat's Visa card number.

Another friend of mine owns a topless bar. For fifty bucks, he put the guy's poker money through as a Visa charge from the bar. Let the cheat explain that to his wife. You think he might try to tell Visa it's not his charge? Think again. He knows we know who he is. And if we could get his Visa number, he'll figure we could get a lot more besides. No worries on that score.

Analyzing the Con

Tommy's initial calls to Ginny were simply to build up trust. When time came for the actual attack, she let her guard down and accepted Tommy for who he claimed to be, the manager at another store in the chain.

And why *wouldn't* she accept him—she already knew him. She'd only met him over the telephone, of course, but they had established a business friendship that is the basis for trust. Once she had accepted him as an authority figure, a manager in the same company, the trust had been established and the rest was a walk in the park.

The sting technique of building trust is one of the most effective social engineering tactics. You have to think whether you really know the person you're talking to. In some rare instances, the person might not be who he claims to be. Accordingly, we all have to learn to observe, think, and question authority.

VARIATION ON A THEME: CARD CAPTURE

Building a sense of trust doesn't necessarily demand a series of phone calls with the victim, as suggested by the previous story. I recall one incident I witnessed where five minutes was all it took.

Surprise, Dad

I once sat at a table in a restaurant with Henry and his father. In the course of conversation, Henry scolded his father for giving out his credit card number as if it were his phone number. "Sure, you have to give your card number when you buy something," he said. "But giving it to a store that files your number in their records—that's real dumb."

"The only place I do that is at Studio Video," Mr. Conklin said, naming the same chain of video stores. "But I go over my Visa bill every month. If they started running up charges, I'd know it."

"Sure," said Henry, "but once they have your number, it's so easy for somebody to steal it."

"You mean a crooked employee."

"No, *anybody*—not just an employee. "

"You're talking through your hat," Mr. Conklin said.

"I can call up right now and get them to tell me your Visa number," Henry shot back.

"No, you *can't,* " his father said.

"I can do it in five minutes, right here in front of you without ever leaving the table."

Mr. Conklin looked tight around the eyes, the look of somebody feeling sure of himself, but not wanting to show it. "I say you don't know what you're talking about," he barked, taking out his wallet and slapping a fifty dollar bill down on the table. "If you can do what you say, that's yours."

"I don't want your money, Dad," Henry said.

He pulled out his cell phone, asked his father which branch he used, and called Directory Assistance for the phone number, as well as the number of the store in nearby Sherman Oaks.

He then called the Sherman Oaks store. Using pretty much the same approach described in the previous story, he quickly got the manager's name and the store number.

Then he called the store where his father had an account. He pulled the old impersonate-the-manager trick, using the manager's name as his own and giving the store number he had just obtained. Then he used the same ruse: "Are your computers working okay? Ours have been up and down." He listened to her reply and then said, "Well, look, I've got one of your customers here who wants to rent a video, but our computers are down right now. I need you to look up the customer account and make sure he's a customer at your branch."

Henry gave him his father's name. Then, using only a slight variation in technique, he made the request to read off the account information: address, phone number, and date the account was opened. And then he said, "Hey, listen, I'm holding up a long line of customers here. What's the credit card number and expiration date?"

Henry held the cell phone to his ear with one hand while he wrote on a paper napkin with the other. As he finished the call, he slid the napkin in front of his father, who stared at it with his mouth hanging open. The poor guy looked totally shocked, as if his whole system of trust had just gone down the drain.

Analyzing the Con

Think of your own attitude when somebody you don't know asks you for something. If a shabby stranger comes to your door, you're not likely to let him in; if a stranger comes to your door nicely dressed, shoes shined, hair perfect, with polite manner and a smile, you're likely to be much less suspicious. Maybe he's really Jason from the *Friday the 13th* movies, but you're willing to start out trusting that person as long as he looks normal and doesn't have a carving knife in his hand.

What's less obvious is that we judge people on the telephone the same way. Does this person sound like he's trying to sell me something? Is he friendly and outgoing or do I sense some kind of hostility or pressure? Does he or she have the speech of an educated person? We judge these things and perhaps a dozen others unconsciously, in a flash, often in the first few moments of the conversation.

It's human nature to think that it's unlikely you're being deceived in any particular transaction, at least until you have some reason to believe otherwise. We weigh the risks and then, most of the time, give people the benefit of the doubt. That's the natural behavior of civilized people . . . at least civilized people who have never been conned or manipulated or cheated out of a large amount of money.

As children our parents taught us not to trust strangers. Maybe we should all heed this age-old principle in today's workplace.

At work, people make requests of us all the time. Do you have an email address for this guy? Where's the latest version of the customer list? Who's the subcontractor on this part of the project? Please send me the latest project update. I need the new version of the source code.

And guess what: Sometimes people who make those requests are people you don't personally know, folks who work for some other part of the company, or claim they do. But if the information they give checks out, and they appear to be in the know ("Marianne said . . ."; "It's on the K-16 server . . ."; ". . . revision 26 of the new product plans"), we extend our circle of trust to include them, and blithely give them what they're asking for.

Sure, we may stumble a little, asking ourselves "Why does somebody in the Dallas plant need to see the new product plans?" or "Could it hurt anything to give out the name of the server it's on?" So we ask another question or two. If the answers appear reasonable and the person's manner is reassuring, we let down our guard, return to our natural inclination to trust our fellow man or woman, and do (within reason) whatever it is we're being asked to do.

And don't think for a moment that the attacker will only target people who use company computer systems. What about the guy in the mail room? "Will you do me a quick favor? Drop this into the intracompany mail pouch?" Does the mail room clerk know it contains a floppy disk with a special little program for the CEO's secretary? Now that attacker gets his own personal copy of the CEO's email. Wow! Could that really happen at your company? The answer is, absolutely.

THE ONE-CENT CELL PHONE

Many people look around until they find a better deal; social engineers don't look for a better deal, they find a way to make a deal better. For example, sometimes a company launches a marketing campaign that's so good you can hardly bear to pass it up, while the social engineer looks at the offer and wonders how he can sweeten the deal.

Not long ago, a nationwide wireless company had a major promotion underway offering a brand-new phone for one cent when you signed up for one of their calling plans.

As lots of people have discovered too late, there are a good many questions a prudent shopper should ask before signing up for a cell phone calling plan—whether the service is analog, digital, or a combination; the number of anytime minutes you can use in a month; whether roaming charges are included . . . and on, and on. Especially important to understand up front is the contract term of commitment—how many months or years will you have to commit to?

Picture a social engineer in Philadelphia who is attracted by a cheap phone model offered by a cellular phone company on sign-up, but he hates the calling plan that goes with it. Not a problem. Here's one way he might handle the situation.

The First Call: Ted

First, the social engineer dials an electronics chain store on West Girard.

"Electron City. This is Ted."

"Hi, Ted. This is Adam. Listen, I was in a few nights ago talking to a sales guy about a cell phone. I said I'd call him back when I decided on the plan I wanted, and I forgot his name. Who's the guy who works in that department on the night shift?"

"There's more than one. Was it William?"

"I'm not sure. Maybe it was William. What's he look like?"

"Tall guy. Kind of skinny."

"I think that's him. What's his last name, again?

"Hadley. H—A—D—L—E— Y."

"Yeah, that sounds right. When's he going to be on?"

"Don't know his schedule this week, but the evening people come in about five."

"Good. I'll try him this evening, then. Thanks, Ted."

The Second Call: Katie

The next call is to a store of the same chain on North Broad Street.

"Hi, Electron City. Katie speaking, how can I help you?"

"Katie, hi. This is William Hadley, over at the West Girard store. How're you today?"

"Little slow, what's up?"

"I've got a customer who came in for that one-cent cell phone program. You know the one I mean?"

"Right. I sold a couple of those last week."

"You still have some of the phones that go with that plan?"

"Got a stack of them."

"Great. 'Cause I just sold one to a customer. The guy passed credit; we signed him up on the contract. I checked the damned inventory and we don't have any phones left. I'm so embarrassed. Can you do me a favor? I'll send him over to your store to pick up a phone. Can you sell him the phone for one cent and write him up a receipt? And he's supposed to call me back once he's got the phone so I can talk him through how to program it."

"Yeah, sure. Send him over."

"Okay. His name is Ted. Ted Yancy."

When the guy who calls himself Ted Yancy shows up at the North Broad St. store, Katie writes up an invoice and sells him the cell phone for one cent, just as she had been asked to do by her "coworker." She fell for the con hook, line, and sinker.

When it's time to pay, the customer doesn't have any pennies in his pocket, so he reaches into the little dish of pennies at the cashier's counter, takes one out, and gives it to the girl at the register. He gets the phone without paying even the one cent for it.

He's then free to go to another wireless company that uses the same model of phone, and choose any service plan he likes. Preferably one on a month-to-month basis, with no commitment required.

Analyzing the Con

It's natural for people to have a higher degree of acceptance for anyone who *claims* to be a fellow employee, and who knows company procedures and lingo. The social engineer in this story took advantage of that by finding out the details of a promotion, identifying himself as a company employee, and asking for a favor from another branch. This happens between branches of retail stores and between departments in a company, where people are physically separated and deal with fellow employees whom they have never actually met day in and day out.

HACKING INTO THE FEDS

People often don't stop to think about what materials their organization is making available on the Web. For my weekly show on KFI Talk Radio in Los Angeles, the producer did a search on line and found a copy of an instruction manual for accessing the database of the National Crime Information Center. Later he found the actual NCIC manual itself on line, a sensitive document that gives all the instructions for retrieving information from the FBI's national crime database.

The manual is a handbook for law enforcement agencies that gives the formatting and codes for retrieving information on criminals from the national database. Agencies all over the country can search the same database for information to help solve crimes in their own jurisdiction. The manual contains the codes used in the database for designating everything from different kinds of tattoos, to different boat hulls, to denominations of stolen money and bonds.

Anybody with access to the manual can look up the syntax and the commands to extract information from the national database. Then, following instructions from the procedures guide, with a little nerve, anyone can extract information from the database. The manual also gives phone numbers to call for support in using the system. You may have similar manuals in your company offering product codes or codes for retrieving sensitive information.

The FBI almost certainly has never discovered that their sensitive manual and procedural instructions are available to anyone on line, and I don't think they'd be very happy about it if they knew. One copy was posted by a government department in Oregon, the other by a law enforcement agency in Texas. Why? In each case, somebody probably thought the information was of no value and posting it couldn't do any harm. Maybe somebody posted it on their intranet just as a convenience to their own employees, never realizing that it made the information available to everyone on the Internet who has access to a good search engine such as Google—including the just-plain-curious, the wannabe cop, the hacker, and the organized crime boss.

Tapping into the System

The principle of using such information to dupe someone in the government or a business setting is the same: Because a social engineer knows how to access specific databases or applications, or knows the names of a company's computer servers, or the like, he gains credibility. Credibility leads to trust.

Once a social engineer has such codes, getting the information he needs is an easy process. In this example, he might begin by calling a clerk in a local state police Teletype office, and asking a question about one of the codes in the manual—for example, the offense code. He might say something like, "When I do an OFF inquiry in the NCIC, I'm getting a 'System is down' error. Are you getting the same thing when you do an OFF? Would you try it for me?" Or maybe he'd say he was trying to look up a *wpf*—police talk for a wanted person's file.

The Teletype clerk on the other end of the phone would pick up the cue that the caller was familiar with the operating procedures and the commands to query the NCIC database. Who else other than someone trained in using NCIC would know these procedures?

After the clerk has confirmed that her system is working okay, the conversation might go something like this:

"I could use a little help."

"What're you looking for?"

"I need you to do an OFF command on Reardon, Martin. DOB 10/18/66."

"What's the sosh?" (Law enforcement people sometimes refer to the social security number as the *sosh*.)

"700-14-7435."

After looking for the listing, she might come back with something like, "He's got a 2602."

The attacker would only have to look at the NCIC on line to find the meaning of the number: The man has a case of swindling on his record.

Analyzing the Con

An accomplished social engineer wouldn't stop for a minute to ponder ways of breaking into the NCIC database. Why should he, when a simple call to his local police department, and some smooth talking so he sounds convincingly like an insider, is all it takes to get the information he wants? And the next time, he just calls a different police agency and uses the same pretext.

lingo

SOSH   Law enforcement slang for a social security number.

You might wonder, isn't it risky to call a police department, a sheriff's station, or a highway patrol office? Doesn't the attacker run a huge risk?

The answer is no . . . and for a specific reason. People in law enforcement, like people in the military, have ingrained in them from the first day in the academy a respect for rank. As long as the social engineer is posing as a sergeant or lieutenant—a higher rank than the person he's talking to—the victim will be governed by that well-learned lesson that says you don't question people who are in a position of authority over you. Rank, in other words, has its privileges, in particular the privilege of not being challenged by people of lower rank.

But don't think law enforcement and the military are the only places where this respect for rank can be exploited by the social engineer. Social engineers often use authority or rank in the corporate hierarchy as a weapon in their attacks on businesses—as a number of the stories in these pages demonstrate.

PREVENTING THE CON

What are some steps your organization can take to reduce the likelihood that social engineers will take advantage of your employees' natural instinct to trust people? Here are some suggestions.

Protect Your Customers

In this electronic age many companies that sell to the consumer keep credit cards on file. There are reasons for this: It saves the customer the nuisance of having to provide the credit card information each time he visits the store or the Web site to make a purchase. However, the practice should be discouraged.

If you must keep credit card numbers on file, that process needs to be accompanied by security provisions that go beyond encryption or using access control. Employees need to be trained to recognize social engineering scams like the ones in this chapter. That fellow employee you've never met in person but who has become a telephone friend may not be who he or she claims to be. He may not have the "need to know" to access

mitnick
message

> Everyone should be aware of the social engineer's modus operandi: Gather as much information about the target as possible, and use that information to gain trust as an insider. Then go for the jugular!

sensitive customer information, because he may not actually work for the company at all.

Trust Wisely

It's not just the people who have access to clearly sensitive information—the software engineers, the folks in R&D, and so on—who need to be on the defensive against intrusions. Almost everyone in your organization needs training to protect the enterprise from industrial spies and information thieves.

Laying the groundwork for this should begin with a survey of enterprise-wide information assets, looking separately at each sensitive, critical, or valuable asset, and asking what methods an attacker might use to compromise those assets through the use of social engineering tactics. Appropriate training for people who have trusted access to such information should be designed around the answers to these questions.

When anyone you don't know personally requests some information or material, or asks you to perform any task on your computer, have your employees ask themselves some questions. If I gave this information to my worst enemy, could it be used to injure me or my company? Do I completely understand the potential effect of the commands I am being asked to enter into my computer?

We don't want to go through life being suspicious of every new person we encounter. Yet the more trusting we are, the more likely that the next social engineer to arrive in town will be able to deceive us into giving up our company's proprietary information.

What Belongs on Your Intranet?

Parts of your intranet may be open to the outside world, other parts restricted to employees. How careful is your company in making sure sensitive information isn't posted where it's accessible to audiences you meant to protect it from? When is the last time anyone in your organization checked to see if any sensitive information on your company's intranet had inadvertently been made available through the public-access areas of your Web site?

If your company has implemented proxy servers as intermediaries to protect the enterprise from electronic security threats, have those servers been checked recently to be sure they're configured properly?

In fact, has anyone *ever* checked the security of your intranet?

chapter 5

"Let Me Help You"

We're all grateful when we're plagued by a problem and somebody with the knowledge, skill, and willingness comes along offering to lend us a hand. The social engineer understands that, and knows how to take advantage of it.

He also knows how to *cause* a problem for you . . . then make you grateful when he resolves the problem . . . and finally play on your gratitude to extract some information or a small favor from you that will leave your company (or maybe you, individually) very much worse off for the encounter. And you may never even know you've lost something of value.

Here are some typical ways that social engineers step forward to "help."

THE NETWORK OUTAGE

Day/Time: Monday, February 12, 3:25 p.m.
Place: Offices of Starboard Shipbuilding

The First Call: Tom DeLay

"Tom DeLay, Bookkeeping."

"Hey, Tom, this is Eddie Martin from the Help Desk. We're trying to troubleshoot a computer networking problem. Do you know if anyone in your group has been having trouble staying on line?"

"Uh, not that I know of."

"And you're not having any problems yourself."

"No, everything seems fine."

"Okay, that's good. Listen, we're calling people who might be affected 'cause it's important you let us know right away if you lose your network connection."

"That doesn't sound good. You think it might happen?"

"We hope not, but you'll call if it does, right?"

"You better believe it."

"Listen, sounds like having your network connection go down would be a problem for you . . ."

"You *bet* it would."

". . . so while we're working on this, let me give you my cell phone number. Then you can reach me directly if you need to."

"That'd be great. Go ahead."

"It's 555 867 5309."

"555 867 5309. Got it. Hey, thanks. What was your name again?"

"It's Eddie. Listen, one other thing—I need to check which port your computer is connected to. Take a look on your computer and see if there's a sticker somewhere that says something like 'Port Number'."

"Hang on. . . . No, don't see anything like that."

"Okay, then in the back of the computer, can you recognize the network cable."

"Yeah."

"Trace it back to where it's plugged in. See if there's a label on the jack it's plugged into."

"Hold on a second. Yeah, wait a minute—I have to squat down here so I can get close enough to read it. Okay—it says Port 6 dash 47."

"Good—that's what we had you down as, just making sure."

The Second Call: The IT Guy

Two days later, a call came through to the same company's Network Operations Center.

"Hi, this is Bob; I'm in Tom DeLay's office in Bookkeeping. We're trying to troubleshoot a cabling problem. I need you to disable Port 6-47."

The IT guy said it would be done in just a few minutes, and to let them know when he was ready to have it enabled.

The Third Call: Getting Help from the Enemy

About an hour later, the guy who called himself Eddie Martin was shopping at Circuit City when his cell phone rang. He checked the caller ID, saw the call was from the shipbuilding company, and hurried to a quiet spot before answering.

"Help Desk, Eddie."

"Oh, hey, Eddie. You've got an echo, where are you?"

"I'm, uh, in a cabling closet. Who's this?

"It's Tom DeLay. Boy, am I glad I got ahold of you. Maybe you remember you called me the other day? My network connection just went down like you said it might, and I'm a little panicky here."

"Yeah, we've got a bunch of people down right now. We should have it taken care of by the end of the day. That okay?"

"NO! Damn, I'll get way behind if I'm down that long. What's the best you can do for me?"

"How pressed are you?"

"I could do some other things for right now. Any chance you could take care of it in half an hour?"

"HALF AN HOUR! You don't want much. Well, look, I'll drop what I'm doing and see if I can tackle it for you."

"Hey, I really appreciate that, Eddie."

The Fourth Call: Gotcha!

Forty-five minutes later . . .

"Tom? It's Eddie. Go ahead and try your network connection."

After a couple of moments:

"Oh, good, it's working. That's just great."

"Good, glad I could take care of it for you."

"Yeah, thanks a lot."

"Listen, if you want to make sure your connection doesn't go down again, there's some software you oughta be running. Just take a couple of minutes."

"Now's not the best time."

"I understand . . . It could save us both big headaches the next time this network problem happens."

"Well . . . if it's only a few minutes."

"Here's what you do . . ."

Eddie then took Tom through the steps of downloading a small application from a Web site. After the program had downloaded, Eddie told Tom to double-click on it. He tried, but reported:

"It's not working. It's not doing anything."

"Oh, what a pain. Something must be wrong with the program. Let's just get rid of it, we can try again another time." And he talked Tom through the steps of deleting the program so it couldn't be recovered.

Total elapsed time, twelve minutes.

The Attacker's Story

Bobby Wallace always thought it was laughable when he picked up a good assignment like this one and his client pussyfooted around the unasked but obvious question of why they wanted the information. In this case he could only think of two reasons. Maybe they represented some outfit that was interested in buying the target company, Starboard Shipbuilding, and wanted to know what kind of financial shape they were really in— especially all the stuff the target might want to keep hidden from a potential buyer. Or maybe they represented investors who thought there was something fishy about the way the money was being handled and wanted to find out whether some of the executives had a case of hands-in-the-cookie-jar.

And maybe his client also didn't want to tell him the real reason because, if Bobby knew how valuable the information was, he'd probably want more money for doing the job.

····•••●●●●●●•••····

There are a lot of ways to crack into a company's most secret files. Bobby spent a few days mulling over the choices and doing a little checking around before he decided on a plan. He settled on one that called for an approach he especially liked, where the target is set up so that he asks the attacker for help.

For starters, Bobby picked up a $39.95 prepaid cell phone at a convenience store. He placed a call to the man he had chosen as his target, passed himself off as being from the company help desk, and set things up so the man would call Bobby's cell phone any time he found a problem with his network connection.

He left a pause of two days so as not to be too obvious, and then made a call to the network operations center (NOC) at the company. He claimed he was trouble-shooting a problem for Tom, the target, and asked to have Tom's network connection disabled. Bobby knew this was the trickiest part of the whole escapade—in many companies, the help desk people work closely with the NOC; in fact, he knew the help desk is often part of the IT organization. But the indifferent NOC guy he spoke with treated the call as routine, didn't ask for the name of the help desk person who was supposedly working on the networking problem, and agreed to disable the target's network port. When done, Tom would be totally isolated from the company's intranet, unable to retrieve files from the server, exchange files with his coworkers, download his email, or even send a page of data to the printer. In today's world, that's like living in a cave.

As Bobby expected, it wasn't long before his cell phone rang. Of course he made himself sound eager to help this poor "fellow employee" in distress. Then he called the NOC and had the man's network connection turned back on. Finally, he called the man and manipulated him once again, this time making him feel guilty for saying no after Bobby had done him a favor. Tom agreed to the request that he download a piece of software to his computer.

Of course, what he agreed to wasn't exactly what it seemed. The software that Tom was told would keep his network connection from going down was really a *Trojan Horse,* a software application that did for Tom's computer what the original deception did for the Trojans: It brought the enemy inside the camp. Tom reported that nothing happened when he double-clicked on the software icon; the fact was that, by design, he couldn't see anything happening, even though the small application was installing a secret program that would allow the infiltrator covert access to Tom's computer.

With the software running, Bobby was provided with complete control over Tom's computer, an arrangement known as a *remote command shell.* When Bobby accessed Tom's computer, he could look for the accounting

lingo

TROJAN HORSE A program containing malicious or harmful code, designed to damage the victim's computer or files, or obtain information from the victim's computer or network. Some Trojans are designed to hide within the computer's operating system and spy on every keystroke or action, or accept instructions over a network connection to perform some function, all without the victim being aware of its presence.

files that might be of interest and copy them. Then, at his leisure, he'd examine them for the information that would give his clients what they were looking for.

And that wasn't all. He could go back at any time to search through the email messages and private memos of the company's executives, running a text search for words that might reveal any interesting tidbits of information.

Late on the night that he conned his target into installing the Trojan Horse software, Bobby threw the cell phone into a Dumpster. Of course he was careful to clear the memory first and pull the battery out before he tossed it—the last thing he wanted was for somebody to call the cell phone's number by mistake and have the phone start ringing!

Analyzing the Con

The attacker spins a web to convince the target he has a problem that, in fact, doesn't really exist—or, as in this case, a problem that hasn't happened yet, but that the attacker knows *will* happen because he's going to cause it. He then presents himself as the person who can provide the solution.

The setup in this kind of attack is particularly juicy for the attacker: Because of the seed planted in advance, when the target discovers he has a problem, he himself makes the phone call to plead for help. The attacker just sits and waits for the phone to ring, a tactic fondly known in the trade as *reverse social engineering*. An attacker who can make the target call *him* gains instant credibility: If I place a call to someone I think is on the help

> ## lingo
>
> **REMOTE COMMAND SHELL** A nongraphical interface that accepts text-based commands to perform certain functions or run programs. An attacker who exploits technical vulnerabilities or is able to install a Trojan Horse program on the victim's computer may be able to obtain remote access to a command shell.
>
> **REVERSE SOCIAL ENGINEERING** A social engineering attack in which the attacker sets up a situation where the victim encounters a problem and contacts the attacker for help. Another form of reverse social engineering turns the tables on the attacker. The target recognizes the attack, and uses psychological principles of influence to draw out as much information as possible from the attacker so that the business can safeguard targeted assets.

> If a stranger does you a favor, then asks you for a favor, don't reciprocate without thinking carefully about what he's asking for.

desk, I'm not going to start asking him to prove his identity. That's when the attacker has it made.

In a con like this one, the social engineer tries to pick a target who is likely to have limited knowledge of computers. The more he knows, the more likely that he'll get suspicious, or just plain figure out that he's being manipulated. What I sometimes call the computer-challenged worker, who is less knowledgeable about technology and procedures, is more likely to comply. He's all the more likely to fall for a ruse like "Just download this little program," because he has no idea of the potential damage a software program can inflict. What's more, there's a much smaller chance he'll understand the value of the information on the computer network that he's placing at risk.

A LITTLE HELP FOR THE NEW GAL

New employees are a ripe target for attackers. They don't know many people yet, they don't know the procedures or the dos and don'ts of the company. And, in the name of making a good first impression, they're eager to show how cooperative and quick to respond they can be.

Helpful Andrea

"Human Resources, Andrea Calhoun."

"Andrea, hi, this is Alex, with Corporate Security."

"Yes?"

"How're you doing today?"

"Okay. What can I help you with?"

"Listen, we're developing a security seminar for new employees and we need to round up some people to try it out on. I want to get the name and phone number of all the new hires in the past month. Can you help me with that?"

"I won't be able to get to it 'til this afternoon. Is that okay? What's your extension?"

"Sure, okay, it's 52 . . . oh, uh, but I'll be in meetings most of today. I'll call you when I'm back in my office, probably after four."

When Alex called about 4:30, Andrea had the list ready, and read him the names and extensions.

A Message for Rosemary

Rosemary Morgan was delighted with her new job. She had never worked for a magazine before and was finding the people much friendlier than she expected, a surprise because of the never-ending pressure most of the staff was always under to get yet another issue finished by the monthly deadline. The call she received one Thursday morning reconfirmed that impression of friendliness.

"Is that Rosemary Morgan?"

"Yes."

"Hi, Rosemary. This is Bill Jorday, with the Information Security group."

"Yes?"

"Has anyone from our department discussed best security practices with you?"

"I don't think so."

"Well, let's see. For starters, we don't allow anybody to install software brought in from outside the company. That's because we don't want any liability for unlicensed use of software. And to avoid any problems with software that might have a worm or a virus."

"Okay."

"Are you aware of our email policies?"

"No."

"What's your current email address?"

"Rosemary@ttrzine.net."

"Do you sign in under the username Rosemary?"

"No, it's R-underscore-Morgan."

"Right. We like to make all our new employees aware that it can be dangerous to open any email attachment you aren't expecting. Lots of viruses and worms get sent around and they come in emails that seem to be from people you know. So if you get an email with an attachment you weren't expecting you should always check to be sure the person listed as sender really did send you the message. You understand?"

"Yes, I've heard about that."

"Good. And our policy is that you change your password every ninety days. When did you last change your password?"

"I've only been here three weeks; I'm still using the one I first set."

"Okay, that's fine. You can wait the rest of the ninety days. But we need to be sure people are using passwords that aren't too easy to guess. Are you using a password that consists of both letters and numbers?"

"No."

We need to fix that. What password are you using now?"

"It's my daughter's name—Annette."

"That's really not a secure password. You should never choose a password that's based on family information. Well, let's see . . . you could do the same thing I do. It's okay to use what you're using now as the first part of the password, but then each time you change it, add a number for the current month."

"So if I did that now, for March, would I use three, or ohthree."

"That's up to you. Which would you be more comfortable with?"

"I guess Annette-three."

"Fine. Do you want me to walk you through how to make the change?"

"No, I know how."

"Good. And one more thing we need to talk about. You have antivirus software on your computer and it's important to keep it up to date. You should never disable the automatic update even if your computer slows down every once in a while. Okay?"

"Sure."

"Very good. And do you have our phone number over here, so you can call us if you have any computer problems?"

She didn't. He gave her the number, she wrote it down carefully, and went back to work, once again, pleased at how well taken care of she felt.

Analyzing the Con

This story reinforces an underlying theme you'll find throughout this book: The most common information that a social engineer wants from an employee, regardless of his ultimate goal, is the target's authentication credentials. With an account name and password in hand from a single employee in the right area of the company, the attacker has what he needs

> Before new employees are allowed access to any company computer systems, they must be trained to follow good security practices, especially policies about never disclosing their passwords.

to get inside and locate whatever information he's after. Having this information is like finding the keys to the kingdom; with them in hand, he can move freely around the corporate landscape and find the treasure he seeks.

NOT AS SAFE AS YOU THINK

"The company that doesn't make an effort to protect its sensitive information is just plain negligent." A lot of people would agree with that statement. And the world would be a better place if life were so obvious and so simple. The truth is that even those companies that do make an effort to protect confidential information may be at serious risk.

Here's a story that illustrates once again how companies fool themselves every day into thinking their security practices, designed by experienced, competent, professionals, cannot be circumvented.

Steve Cramer's Story

It wasn't a big lawn, not one of those expensively seeded spreads. It garnered no envy. And it certainly wasn't big enough to give him an excuse for buying a sit-down mower, which was fine because he wouldn't have used one anyway. Steve enjoyed cutting the grass with a hand-mower because it took longer, and the chore provided a convenient excuse to focus on his own thoughts instead of listening to Anna telling him stories about the people at the bank where she worked or explaining errands for him to do. He hated those honey-do lists that had become an integral part of his weekends. It flashed though his mind that 12-year-old Pete was damn smart to join the swimming team. Now he'd have to be at practice or a meet every Saturday so he wouldn't get stuck with Saturday chores.

Some people might think Steve's job designing new devices for GeminiMed Medical Products was boring; Steve knew he was saving lives. Steve thought of himself as being in a creative line of work. Artist, music composer, engineer—in Steve's view they all faced the same kind of challenge he did: They created something that no one had ever done before. And his latest, an intriguingly clever new type of heart stent, would be his proudest achievement yet.

It was almost 11:30 on this particular Saturday, and Steve was annoyed because he had almost finished cutting the grass and hadn't made any real progress in figuring out how to reduce the power requirement on the heart stent, the last remaining hurdle. A perfect problem to mull over while mowing, but no solution had come.

●●●●●●●●●●●●●

Anna appeared at the door, her hair covered in the red paisley cowboy scarf she always wore when dusting. "Phone call," she shouted to him. "Somebody from work."

"Who?" Steve shouted back.

"Ralph something. I think."

Ralph? Steve couldn't remember anybody at GeminiMed named Ralph who might be calling on a weekend. But Anna probably had the name wrong.

"Steve, this is Ramon Perez in Tech Support." Ramon—how in the world did Anna get from a Hispanic name to Ralph, Steve wondered.

"This is just a courtesy call," Ramon was saying. "Three of the servers are down, we think maybe a worm, and we have to wipe the drives and restore from backup. We should be able to have your files up and running by Wednesday or Thursday. If we're lucky."

"Absolutely unacceptable," Steve said firmly, trying not to let his frustration take over. How could these people be so stupid? Did they really think he could manage without access to his files all weekend and most of next week? "No way. I'm going to sit down at my home terminal in just about two hours and I will need access to my files. Am I making this clear?"

"Yeah, well, everybody I've called so far wants to be at the top of the list. I gave up my weekend to come in and work on this and it's no fun having everybody I talk to get pissed at me."

"I'm on a tight deadline, the company is counting on this; I've got to get work done this afternoon. What part of this do you not understand?"

"I've still got a lot of people to call before I can even get started," Ramon said. "How about we say you'll have your files by Tuesday?"

"Not Tuesday, not Monday, today. NOW!" Steve said, wondering who he was going to call if he couldn't get his point through this guy's thick skull.

"Okay, okay," Ramon said, and Steve could hear him breathe a sigh of annoyance. "Let me see what I can do to get you going. You use the RM22 server, right?"

"RM22 and the GM16. Both."

"Right. Okay, I can cut some corners, save some time—I'll need your username and password."

Uh oh, Steve thought. *What's going on here? Why would he need my password? Why would IT, of all people, ask for it?*

"What did you say your last name was? And who's your supervisor?"

"Ramon Perez. Look, I tell you what, when you were hired, there was a form you had to fill out to get your user account, and you had to put down a password. I could look that up and show you we've got it on file here. Okay?"

Steve mulled that over for a few moments, then agreed. He hung on with growing impatience while Ramon went to retrieve documents from a file cabinet. Finally back on the phone, Steve could hear him shuffling through a stack of papers.

"Ah, here it is," Ramon said at last. "You put down the password 'Janice.'"

Janice, Steve thought. It was his mother's name, and he had indeed sometimes used it as a password. He might very well have put that down for his password when filling out his new-hire papers.

"Yes, that's right," he acknowledged.

"Okay, we're wasting time here. You know I'm for real, you want me to use the shortcut and get your files back in a hurry, you're gonna have to help me out here."

"My ID is s, d, underscore, cramer—c-r-a-m-e-r. The password is 'pelican1.'"

"I'll get right on it," Ramon said, sounding helpful at last. "Give me a couple of hours."

Steve finished the lawn, had lunch, and by the time he got to his computer found that his files had indeed been restored. He was pleased with himself for handling that uncooperative IT guy so forcefully, and hoped Anna had heard how assertive he was. Would be good to give the guy or his boss an attaboy, but he knew it was one of those things he'd never get around to doing.

Craig Cogburne's Story

Craig Cogburne had been a salesman for a high-tech company, and done well at it. After a time he began to realize he had a skill for reading a customer, understanding where the person was resistant and recognizing some weakness or vulnerability that made it easy to close the sale. He began to think about other ways to use this talent, and the path eventually led him into a far more lucrative field: corporate espionage.

•••••••●●●●••••••

This one was a hot assignment. Didn't look to take me very long and worth enough to pay for a trip to Hawaii. Or maybe Tahiti.

The guy that hired me, he didn't tell me the client, of course, but it figured to be some company that wanted to catch up with the competition in one quick, big, easy leap. All I'd have to do is get the designs and product specs for a new gadget called a heart stent, whatever that was. The company was called GeminiMed. Never heard of it, but it was a Fortune 500 outfit with offices in half a dozen locations—which makes the job easier than a smaller company where there's a fair chance the guy you're talking to knows the guy you're claiming to be and knows you're not him. This, like pilots say about a midair collision, can ruin your whole day.

My client sent me a fax, a bit from some doctor's magazine that said GeminiMed was working on a stent with a radical new design and it would be called the STH-100. For crying out loud, some reporter has already done a big piece of the legwork for me. I had one thing I needed even before I got started, the new product name.

First problem: Get names of people in the company who worked on the STH-100 or might need to see the designs. So I called the switchboard operator and said, "I promised one of the people in your engineering group I'd get in touch with him and I don't remember his last name, but his first name started with an S." And she said, "We have a Scott Archer and a Sam Davidson." I took a long shot. "Which one works in the STH-100 group?" She didn't know, so I just picked Scott Archer at random, and she rang his phone.

When he answered, I said, "Hey, this is Mike, in the mail room. We've got a FedEx here that's for the Heart Stent STH-100 project team. Any idea who that should go to?" He gave me the name of the project leader, Jerry Mendel. I even got him to look up the phone number for me.

I called. Mendel wasn't there but his voice mail message said he'd be on vacation till the thirteenth, which meant he had another week left for skiing or whatever, and anybody who needed something in the meantime should call Michelle on 9137. Very helpful, these people. Very helpful.

I hung up and called Michelle, got her on the phone and said, "This is Bill Thomas. Jerry told me I should call you when I had the spec ready that he wanted the guys on his team to review. You're working on the heart stent, right?" She said they were.

Now we were getting to the sweaty part of the scam. If she started sounding suspicious, I was ready to play the card about how I was just trying to do a favor Jerry had asked me for. I said, "Which system are you on?"

"System?"

"Which computer servers does your group use?"

"Oh," she said, "RM22. And some of the group also use GM16."

Good. I needed that, and it was a piece of information I could get from her without making her suspicious. Which softened her up for the next bit, done as casually as I could manage. "Jerry said you could give me a list of email addresses for people on the development team," I said, and held my breath.

"Sure. The distribution list is too long to read off, can I email it to you?"

Oops. Any email address that didn't end in GeminiMed.com would be a huge red flag. "How about you fax it to me?" I said.

She had no problem with doing that.

"Our fax machine is on the blink. I'll have to get the number of another one. Call you back in a bit," I said, and hung up.

Now, you might think I was saddled with a sticky problem here, but it's just another routine trick of the trade. I waited a while so my voice wouldn't sound familiar to the receptionist, then called her and said, "Hi, it's Bill Thomas, our fax machine isn't working up here, can I have a fax sent to your machine?" She said sure, and gave me the number.

Then I just walk in and pick up the fax, right? Of course not. First rule: Never visit the premises unless you absolutely have to. They have a hard time identifying you if you're just a voice on the telephone. And if they can't identify you, they can't arrest you. It's hard to put handcuffs around a voice. So I called the receptionist back after a little while and asked her, did my fax come? "Yes," she said.

"Look," I told her, "I've got to get that to a consultant we're using. Could you send it out for me?" She agreed. And why not—how could any receptionist be expected to recognize sensitive data? While she sent the fax out to the "consultant," I had my exercise for the day walking over to a stationery store near me, the one with the sign out front "Faxes Sent/Rcvd." My fax was supposed to arrive before I did, and as expected, it was there waiting for me when I walked in. Six pages at $1.75. For a $10 bill and change, I had the group's entire list of names and email addresses.

Getting Inside

Okay, so I had by now talked to three or four different people in only a few hours and was already one giant step closer to getting inside the company's computers. But I'd need a couple more pieces before I was home.

Number one was the phone number for dialing into the Engineering server from outside. I called GeminiMed again and asked the switchboard operator for the IT Department, and asked the guy who answered for somebody who could give me some computer help. He transferred me, and I put on an act of being confused and kind of stupid about anything technical. "I'm at home, just bought a new laptop, and I need to set it up so I can dial in from outside."

The procedure was obvious but I patiently let him talk me through it until he got to the dial-in phone number. He gave me the number like it was just another routine piece of information. Then I made him wait while I tried it. Perfect.

So now I had passed the hurdle of connecting to the network. I dialed in and found they were set up with a terminal server that would let a caller connect to any computer on their internal network. After a bunch of tries I stumbled across somebody's computer that had a guest account with no password required. Some operating systems, when first installed, direct the user to set up an ID and password, but also provide a guest account. The user is supposed to set his or her own password for the guest account or disable it, but most people don't know about this, or just don't bother. This system was probably just set up and the owner hadn't bothered to disable the guest account.

Thanks to the guest account, I now had access to one computer, which turned out to be running an older version of the UNIX operating system. Under UNIX, the operating system maintains a password file which contains the encrypted passwords of everybody authorized to access that computer. The password file contains the one-way *hash* (that is, a form of encryption that is irreversible) of every user's password. With a one-way hash an actual password such as, say, "justdoit" would be represented by a

lingo

PASSWORD HASH A string of gibberish that results from processing a password through a one-way encryption process. The process is supposedly irreversible; that is, it's believed that it is not possible to reconstruct the password from the hash.

hash in encrypted form; in this case the hash would be converted by UNIX to thirteen alphanumeric characters.

When Billy Bob down the hall wants to transfer some files to a computer, he's required to identify himself by providing a username and password. The system program that checks his authorization encrypts the password he enters, and then compares the result to the encrypted password (the hash) contained in the password file; if the two match, he's given access.

Because the passwords in the file were encrypted, the file itself was made available to any user on the theory that there's no known way to decrypt the passwords. That's a laugh—I downloaded the file, ran a dictionary attack on it (see Chapter 12 for more about this method) and found that one of the engineers on the development team, a guy named Steven Cramer, currently had an account on the computer with the password "Janice." Just on the chance, I tried entering his account with that password on one of the development servers; if it had worked, it would have saved me some time and a little risk. It didn't.

That meant I'd have to trick the guy into telling me his username and password. For that, I'd wait until the weekend.

You already know the rest. On Saturday I called Cramer and walked him through a ruse about a worm and the servers having to be restored from backup to overcome his suspicions.

What about the story I told him, the one about listing a password when he filled out his employee papers? I was counting on him not remembering that had never happened. A new employee fills out so many forms that, years later, who would remember? And anyway, if I had struck out with him, I still had that long list of other names.

With his username and password, I got into the server, fished around for a little while, and then located the design files for the STH-100. I wasn't exactly sure which ones were key, so I just transferred all the files to a *dead drop*, a free FTP site in China, where they could be stored without anybody getting suspicious. Let the client sort through the junk and find what he wants.

lingo

> **DEAD DROP** A place for leaving information where it is unlikely to be found by others. In the world of traditional spies, this might be behind a loose stone in a wall; in the world of the computer hacker, it's commonly an Internet site in a remote country.

Analyzing the Con

For the man we're calling Craig Cogburne, or anyone like him equally skilled in the larcenous-but-not-always-illegal arts of social engineering, the challenge presented here was almost routine. His goal was to locate and download files stored on a secure corporate computer, protected by a firewall and all the usual security technologies.

Most of his work was as easy as catching rainwater in a barrel. He began by posing as somebody from the mail room and furnished an added sense of urgency by claiming there was a FedEx package waiting to be delivered. This deception produced the name of the team leader for the heart-stent engineering group, who was on vacation, but—convenient for any social engineer trying to steal information—he had helpfully left the name and phone number of his assistant. Calling her, Craig defused any suspicions by claiming that he was responding to a request from the team leader. With the team leader out of town, Michelle had no way to verify his claim. She accepted it as the truth and had no problem providing a list of people in the group—for Craig, a necessary and highly prized set of information.

She didn't even get suspicious when Craig wanted the list sent by fax instead of by email, ordinarily more convenient on both ends. Why was she so gullible? Like many employees, she didn't want her boss to return to town and find she had stonewalled a caller who was just trying to do something the boss had asked him for. Besides, the caller said that the boss had not just authorized the request, but asked for his assistance. Once again, here's an example of someone displaying the strong desire to be a team player, which makes most people susceptible to deception.

Craig avoided the risk of physically entering the building simply by having the fax sent to the receptionist, knowing she was likely to be helpful. Receptionists are, after all, usually chosen for their charming personalities and their ability to make a good impression. Doing small favors like receiving a fax and sending it on comes with the receptionist's territory, a fact that Craig was able to take advantage of. What she was sending out happened to be information that might have raised alarm bells with anyone knowing the value of the information—but how could a receptionist be expected to know which information is benign and which sensitive?

Using a different style of manipulation, Craig acted confused and naïve to convince the guy in computer operations to provide him with the dial-up access number to the company's terminal server, the hardware used as a connection point to other computer systems within the internal network.

Everybody's first priority at work is to get the job done. Under that pressure, security practices often take second place and are overlooked or ignored. Social engineers rely on this when practicing their craft.

Craig was able to connect easily by trying a default password that had never been changed, one of the glaring, wide-open gaps that exist throughout many internal networks that rely on firewall security. In fact, the default passwords for many operating systems, routers, and other types of products, including PBXs, are made available on line. Any social engineer, hacker, or industrial spy, as well as the just plain curious, can find the list at http://www.phenoelit.de/dpl/dpl.html. (It's absolutely incredible how easy the Internet makes life for those who know where to look. And now *you* know, too.)

Cogburne then actually managed to convince a cautious, suspicious man ("What did you say your last name was? Who's your supervisor?") to divulge his username and password so that he could access servers used by the heart-stent development team. This was like leaving Craig with an open door to browse the company's most closely guarded secrets and download the plans for the new product.

What if Steve Cramer had continued to be suspicious about Craig's call? It was unlikely he would do anything about reporting his suspicions until he showed up at work on Monday morning, which would have been too late to prevent the attack.

One key to the last part of the ruse: Craig at first made himself sound lackadaisical and uninterested in Steve's concerns, then changed his tune and sounded as if he was trying to help so Steve could get his work done. Most of the time, if the victim believes you're trying to help him or do him some kind of favor, he will part with confidential information that he would have otherwise protected carefully.

PREVENTING THE CON

One of the most powerful tricks of the social engineer involves turning the tables. That's what you've seen in this chapter. The social engineer creates the problem, and then magically solves the problem, deceiving the victim into providing access to the company's most guarded secrets. Would your employees fall for this type of ruse? Have you bothered to draft and distribute specific security rules that could help to prevent it?

Educate, Educate, and Educate . . .

There's an old story about a visitor to New York who stops a man on the street and asks, "How do I get to Carnegie Hall?" The man answers, "Practice, practice, practice." Everyone is so vulnerable to social engineering attacks that a company's only effective defense is to educate and train your people, giving them the practice they need to spot a social engineer. And then keep reminding people on a consistent basis of what they learned in the training, but are all too apt to forget.

Everyone in the organization must be trained to exercise an appropriate degree of suspicion and caution when contacted by someone he or she doesn't personally know, especially when that someone is asking for any sort of access to a computer or network. It's human nature to want to trust others, but as the Japanese say, business is war. Your business cannot afford to let down its guard. Corporate security policy must clearly define appropriate and inappropriate behavior.

Security is not one-size-fits-all. Business personnel usually have disparate roles and responsibilities and each position has associated vulnerabilities. There should be a base level of training that everyone in the company is required to complete, and then people must also be trained according to their job profile to adhere to certain procedures that will reduce the chance that they will become part of the problem. People who work with sensitive information or are placed in positions of trust should be given additional specialized training.

Keeping Sensitive Information Safe

When people are approached by a stranger offering to help, as seen in the stories in this chapter, they have to fall back on corporate security policy that is tailored as appropriate to the business needs, size, and culture of your company.

Never cooperate with a stranger who asks you to look up information, enter unfamiliar commands into a computer, make changes to software settings or—the most potentially disastrous of all—open an email attachment

> **note**
>
> Personally, I don't believe any business should allow any exchange of passwords. It's much easier to establish a hard rule that forbids personnel from ever sharing or exchanging confidential passwords. It's safer, too. But each business has to assess its own culture and security concerns in making this choice.

or download unchecked software. Any software program—even one that appears to do nothing at all—may not be as innocent as it appears to be.

There are certain procedures that, no matter how good our training, we tend to grow careless about over time. Then we forget about that training at crunch time, just when we need it. You would think that not giving out your account name and password is something that just about everybody knows (or should know) and hardly needs to be told: it's simple common sense. But in fact, every employee needs to be reminded frequently that giving out the account name and password to their office computer, their home computer, or even the postage machine in the mail room is equivalent to giving out the PIN number for their ATM card.

There is occasionally—*very* occasionally—a quite valid circumstance when it's necessary, perhaps even important, to give someone else confidential information. For that reason, it's not appropriate to make an absolute rule about "never." Still, your security policies and procedures do need to be very specific about circumstances under which an employee may give out his or her password and—most importantly—who is authorized to ask for the information.

Consider the Source

In most organizations, the rule should be that any information that can possibly cause harm to the company or to a fellow employee may be given only to someone who is known on a face-to-face basis, or whose voice is so familiar that you recognize it without question.

In high-security situations, the only requests that should be granted are ones delivered in person or with a strong form of authentication—for example, two separate items such as a shared secret and a time-based token.

Data classification procedures must designate that *no* information be provided from a part of the organization involved with sensitive work to anyone not personally known or vouched for in some manner.

So how do you handle a legitimate-sounding request for information from another company employee, such as the list of names and email addresses of people in your group? In fact, how do you raise awareness so that an item like this, which is clearly less valuable than, say, a spec sheet for a product under development, is recognized as something for internal use only? One major part of the solution: Designate employees in each department who will handle all requests for information to be sent outside the group. An advanced security-training program must then be

Incredibly, even looking up the name and phone number of the caller in the company's employee database and calling him back is not an absolute guarantee—social engineers know ways of planting names in a corporate database or redirecting telephone calls.

provided to make these designated employees aware of the special verification procedures they should follow.

Forget Nobody

Anyone can quickly rattle off the identity of organizations within her company that need a high degree of protection against malicious attacks. But we often overlook other places that are less obvious, yet highly vulnerable. In one of these stories, the request for a fax to be sent to a phone number within the company seemed innocent and secure enough, yet the attacker took advantage of this security loophole. The lesson here: Everybody from secretaries and administrative assistants to company executives and high-level managers needs to have special security training so that they can be alert to these types of tricks. And don't forget to guard the front door: Receptionists, too, are often prime targets for social engineers and must also be made aware of the deceptive techniques used by some visitors and callers.

Corporate security should establish a single point of contact as a kind of central clearinghouse for employees who think they may have been the target of a social engineering ruse. Having a single place to report security incidents will provide an effective early-warning system that will make it clear when a coordinated attack is under way, so that any damage can be controlled immediately.

chapter

"Can You Help Me?"

You've seen how social engineers trick people by offering to help. Another favorite approach turns the tables: The social engineer manipulates by pretending he needs the other person to help him. We can all sympathize with people in a tight spot, and the approach proves effective over and over again in allowing a social engineer to reach his goal.

THE OUT-OF-TOWNER
A story in Chapter 3 showed how an attacker can talk a victim into revealing his employee number. This one uses a different approach for achieving the same result, and then shows how the attacker can make use of that information.

Keeping Up with the Joneses
In Silicon Valley there is a certain global company that shall be nameless. The scattered sales offices and other field installations around the world are all connected to that company's headquarters over a WAN, a wide area network. The intruder, a smart, feisty guy named Brian Atterby, knew it was almost always easier to break into a network at one of the remote sites, where security is practically guaranteed to be more lax than at headquarters.

• • • • • • • • • • • • • • •

The intruder phoned the Chicago office and asked to speak with Mr. Jones. The receptionist asked if he knew Mr. Jones's first name; he answered, "I had it here, I'm looking for it. How many Joneses do you have?" She said, "Three. Which department would he be in?"

He said, "If you read me the names, maybe I'll recognize it." So she did: "Barry, Joseph, and Gordon."

"Joe. I'm pretty sure that was it," he said. "And he was in . . . which department?"

"Business Development."

"Fine. Can you connect me, please?"

She put the call through. When Jones answered, the attacker said, "Mr. Jones? Hi, this is Tony in Payroll. We just put through your request to have your paycheck deposited directly to your credit union account."

"WHAT???!!! You've got to be kidding. I didn't make any request like that. I don't even have an account at a credit union."

"Oh, damn, I already put it through."

Jones was more than a little upset at the idea that his paycheck might be going to someone else's account, and he was beginning to think the guy on the other end of the phone must be a little slow. Before he could even reply, the attacker said, "I better see what happened. Payroll changes are entered by employee number. What's your employee number?"

Jones gave the number. The caller said, "No, you're right, the request wasn't from you, then." They get more stupid every year, Jones thought.

"Look, I'll see it's taken care of. I'll put in a correction right now. So don't worry—you'll get your next paycheck okay," the guy said reassuringly.

A Business Trip

Not long after, the system administrator in the company's Austin, Texas, sales office received a phone call. "This is Joseph Jones," the caller announced. "I'm in Business Development at corporate. I'll be in town for the week, at the Driskill Hotel. I'd like to have you set me up with a temporary account so I can access my email without making a long distance call."

"Let me get that name again, and give me your employee number," the sys admin said. The false Jones gave the number and went on, "Do you have any high speed dial-up numbers?"

"Hold on, buddy. I gotta verify you in the database." After a bit, he said, "Okay, Joe. Tell me, what's your building number?" The attacker had done his homework and had the answer ready.

"Okay," the sys admin told him, "you convinced me."

It was as simple as that. The sys admin had verified the name Joseph Jones, the department, and the employee number, and "Joe" had given the right answer to the test question. "Your username's going to be the same as your corporate one, jbjones," the sys admin said, "and I'm giving you an initial password of 'changeme.'"

Analyzing the Con

With a couple of phone calls and fifteen minutes of time, the attacker had gained access to the company's wide area network. This was a company that, like many, had what I refer to as *candy security*, after a description first used by two Bell Labs researchers, Steve Bellovin and Steven Cheswick. They described such security as "a hard crunchy shell with a soft chewy center"—like an M&M candy. The outer shell, the firewall, Bellovin and Cheswick argued, is not sufficient protection, because once an intruder is able to circumvent it, the internal computer systems have soft, chewy security. Most of the time, they are inadequately protected.

This story fits the definition. With a dial-up number and an account, the attacker didn't even have to bother trying to defeat an Internet firewall, and, once inside, he was easily able to compromise most of the systems on the internal network.

Through my sources, I understand a similar ruse was worked on one of the largest computer software manufacturers in the world. You would think the systems administrators in such a company would be trained to detect this type of ruse. But in my experience, nobody is completely safe if a social engineer is clever and persuasive enough.

lingo

CANDY SECURITY A term coined by Bellovin and Cheswick of Bell Labs to describe a security scenario where the outer perimeter, such as a firewall, is strong, but the infrastructure behind it is weak. The term refers to M&M candy, which has a hard outer shell and soft center.

> **SPEAKEASY SECURITY**   Security that relies on knowing where desired information is, and using a word or name to gain access to that information or computer system.

SPEAKEASY SECURITY

In the old days of speakeasies—those Prohibition-era nightclubs where so-called bathtub gin flowed—a would-be customer gained admission by showing up at the door and knocking. After a few moments, a small flap in the door would swing open and a tough, intimidating face would peer out. If the visitor was in the know, he would speak the name of some frequent patron of the place ("Joe sent me" was often enough), whereupon the bouncer inside would unlatch the door and let him in.

The real trick lay in knowing the location of the speakeasy because the door was unmarked, and the owners didn't exactly hang out neon signs to mark their presence. For the most part, just showing up at the right place was about all it took to get in. The same degree of safekeeping is, unhappily, practiced widely in the corporate world, providing a level of nonprotection that I call *speakeasy security*.

I Saw It at the Movies

Here's an illustration from a favorite movie that many people will remember. In *Three Days of the Condor* the central character, Turner (played by Robert Redford), works for a small research firm contracted by the CIA. One day he comes back from a lunch run to find that all his coworkers have been gunned down. He's left to figure out who has done this and why, all the while knowing that the bad guys, whoever they are, are looking for him.

Late in the story, Turner manages to get the phone number of one the bad guys. But who is this person, and how can Turner pin down his location? He's in luck: The screenwriter, David Rayfiel, has happily given Turner a background that includes training as a telephone lineman with the Army Signal Corps, making him knowledgeable about techniques and practices of the phone company. With the bad guy's phone number in hand, Turner knows exactly what to do. In the screenplay, the scene reads like this:

TURNER RECONNECTS and TAPS OUT ANOTHER NUMBER.
     RING! RING! Then:

WOMAN'S VOICE *(FILTER)*

CNA, Mrs. Coleman speaking.

TURNER *(into test set)*

This is Harold Thomas, Mrs. Coleman. Customer Service.
     CNA on 202-555-7389, please.

WOMAN'S VOICE *(FILTER)*

One moment, please.

(almost at once)

Leonard Atwood, 765 MacKensie Lane, Chevy Chase,
     Maryland.

Ignoring the fact that the screenwriter mistakenly uses a Washington, D.C., area code for a Maryland address, can you spot what just happened here?

Turner, because of his training as a telephone lineman, knew what number to dial in order to reach a phone company office called CNA, the Customer Name and Address bureau. CNA is set up for the convenience of installers and other authorized phone company personnel. An installer could call CNA, and give them a phone number. The CNA clerk would respond by providing the name of the person the phone belongs to and his address.

Fooling the Phone Company

In the real world, the phone number for CNA is a closely guarded secret. Although the phone companies finally caught on and these days are less generous about handing out information so readily, at the time they operated on a variation of speakeasy security that security professionals call *security through obscurity*. They presumed that anybody who called CNA and knew the proper lingo ("Customer service. CNA on 555-1234, please," for example) was a person authorized to have the information.

lingo

> **SECURITY THROUGH OBSCURITY** An ineffective method of computer security that relies on keeping secret the details of how the system works (protocols, algorithms, and internal systems). Security through obscurity relies on the false assumption that no one outside a trusted group of people will be able to circumvent the system.

> Security through obscurity does not have *any* effect in blocking social engineering attacks. Every computer system in the world has at least one human that uses it. So, if the attacker is able to manipulate people who use the systems, the obscurity of the system is irrelevant.

There was no need to verify or identify oneself, no need to give an employee number, no need for a password that was changed daily. If you knew the number to call and you sounded authentic, then you must be entitled to the information.

That was not a very solid assumption on the part of the telephone company. Their only effort at security was to change the phone number on a periodic basis, at least once a year. Even so, the current number at any particular moment was very widely known among phone phreaks, who delighted in taking advantage of this convenient source of information, and in sharing the how-to-do-it with their fellow phreaks. The CNA Bureau trick was one of the first things I learned when I was introduced to the hobby of phone phreaking as a teenager.

Throughout the world of business and government, speakeasy security is still prevalent. It's likely that any semiskilled intruder can pass himself off as an authorized person just by putting together enough information about your company's departments, people, and lingo. Sometimes less than that: Sometimes an internal phone number is all it takes.

THE CARELESS COMPUTER MANAGER

Though many employees in organizations are negligent, unconcerned, or unaware of security dangers, you'd expect someone with the title of manager in the computer center of a Fortune 500 corporation to be thoroughly knowledgeable about best security practices, right?

You would not expect a computer center manager—someone who is part of his company's Information Technology department—to fall victim to a simplistic and obvious social engineering con game. *Especially* not if the social engineer is hardly more than a kid, barely out of his teens. But sometimes your expectations can be wrong.

Tuning In

Years ago it was an amusing pastime for many people to keep a radio tuned to the local police or fire department frequencies, listening in on the occasional highly charged conversations about a bank robbery in progress, an office building on fire, or a high-speed chase as the event unfolded. The radio frequencies used by law enforcement agencies and fire departments used to be available in books at the corner bookstore; today they're provided in listings on the Web, and from a book you can buy at Radio Shack—frequencies for local, county, state, and, in some cases, even federal agencies.

Of course, it wasn't just the curious who were listening in. Crooks robbing a store in the middle of the night could tune in to hear if a police car was being dispatched to the location. Drug dealers could keep a check on activities of the local Drug Enforcement Agency agents. An arsonist could enhance his sick pleasure by lighting a blaze and then listening to all the radio traffic while firemen struggled to put it out.

Over recent years developments in computer technology have made it possible to encrypt voice messages. As engineers found ways to cram more and more computing power onto a single microchip, they began to build small, encrypted radios for law enforcement that kept the bad guys and the curious from listening in.

Danny the Eavesdropper

A scanner enthusiast and skilled hacker we'll call Danny decided to see if he couldn't find a way to get his hands on the super-secret encryption software—the source code—from one of the top manufacturers of secure radio systems. He was hoping a study of the code would enable him to learn how to eavesdrop on law enforcement, and possibly also use the technology so that even the most powerful government agencies would find it difficult to monitor his conversations with his friends.

The Dannys of the shadowy world of hackers belong to a special category that falls somewhere in between the merely-curious-but-entirely-benign and the dangerous. Dannys have the knowledge of the expert, combined with the mischievous hacker's desire to break into systems and networks for the intellectual challenge and for the pleasure of gaining insight into how technology works. But their electronic breaking-and-entering stunts are just that—stunts. These folks, these benign hackers, illegally enter sites for the sheer fun and exhilaration of proving they can do it. They don't steal anything, they don't make any money from their exploits; they don't destroy any files, disrupt any network connections, or crash any computer system. The mere fact of their being there, snaring copies of files and searching emails for passwords behind the backs of security and network administrators, tweaks the noses of the people responsible for keeping out intruders like them. The one-upmanship is a big part of the satisfaction.

In keeping with this profile, our Danny wanted to examine the details of his target company's most closely guarded product just to satisfy his own burning curiosity and to admire whatever clever innovations the manufacturer might have come up with.

The product designs were, needless to say, carefully guarded trade secrets, as precious and protected as just about anything in the company's possession. Danny knew that. And he didn't care a bit. After all, it was just some big, nameless company.

But how to get the software source code? As it turned out, grabbing the crown jewels of the company's Secure Communications Group proved to be all too easy, even though the company was one of those that used *two-factor authentication*, an arrangement under which people are required to use not one but two separate identifiers to prove their identity.

Here's an example you're probably already familiar with. When your renewal credit card arrives, you're asked to phone the issuing company to let them know that the card is in possession of the intended customer, and not somebody who stole the envelope from the mail. The instructions with the card these days generally tell you to call *from home*. When you call, software at the credit card company analyzes the *ANI*, the automatic number identification, which is provided by the telephone switch on toll-free calls that the credit card company is paying for.

A computer at the credit card company uses the calling party's number provided by the ANI, and matches that number against the company's database of cardholders. By the time the clerk comes on the line, her or his display shows information from the database giving details about the customer. So the clerk already knows the call is coming from the home of a customer; that's one form of authentication.

The clerk then picks an item from the information displayed about you—most often social security number, date of birth, or mother's maiden name—and asks you for this piece of information. If you give the right

lingo

TWO-FACTOR AUTHENTICATION   The use of two different types of authentication to verify identity. For example, a person might have to identify himself by calling from a certain identifiable location and knowing a password.

answer, that's a second form of authentication—based on information you should know.

At the company manufacturing the secure radio systems in our story, every employee with computer access had their usual account name and password, but in addition was provided with a small electronic device called Secure ID. This is what's called a time-based token. These devices come in two types: One is about half the size of a credit card but a little thicker; another is small enough that people simply attach it to their key chains.

Derived from the world of cryptography, this particular gadget has a small window that displays a series of six digits. Every sixty seconds, the display changes to show a different six-digit number. When an authorized person needs to access the network from offsite, she must first identify herself as an authorized user by typing in her secret PIN and the digits displayed on her token device. Once verified by the internal system, she then authenticates with her account name and password.

For the young hacker Danny to get at the source code he so coveted, he would have to not only compromise some employee's account name and password (not much of a challenge for the experienced social engineer) but also get around the time-based token.

Defeating the two-factor authentication of a time-based token combined with a user's secret PIN code sounds like a challenge right out of *Mission Impossible*. But for social engineers, the challenge is similar to that faced by a poker player who has more than the usual skill at reading his opponents. With a little luck, when he sits down at a table he knows he's likely to walk away with a large pile of other people's money.

Storming the Fortress

Danny began by doing his homework. Before long he had managed to put together enough pieces to masquerade as a real employee. He had an employee's name, department, phone number, and employee number, as well as the manager's name and phone number.

Now was the calm before the storm. Literally. Going by the plan he had worked out, Danny needed one more thing before he could take the next step, and it was something he had no control over: He needed a snowstorm. Danny needed a little help from Mother Nature in the form of weather so bad that it would keep workers from getting into the office.

In the winter in South Dakota, where the manufacturing plant in question was located, anyone hoping for bad weather did not have very long to wait. On Friday night, a storm arrived. What had begun as snow quickly turned to freezing rain so that, by morning, the roads were coated with a slick, dangerous sheet of ice. For Danny, this was a perfect opportunity.

He telephoned the plant, asked for the computer room and reached one of the worker bees of IT, a computer operator who announced himself as Roger Kowalski.

Giving the name of the real employee he had obtained, Danny said, "This is Bob Billings. I work in the Secure Communications Group. I'm at home right now and I can't drive in because of the storm. And the problem is that I need to access my workstation and the server from home, and I left my Secure ID in my desk. Can you go fetch it for me? Or can somebody? And then read off my code when I need to get in? Because my team has a critical deadline and there's no way I can get my work done. And there's no way I can get to the office—the roads are much too dangerous up my way."

The computer operator said, "I can't leave the Computer Center."

Danny jumped right in: "Do you have a Secure ID yourself?"

"There's one here in the Computer Center," he said. "We keep one for the operators in case of an emergency."

"Listen," Danny said. "Can you do me a big favor? When I need to dial into the network, can you let me borrow your Secure ID? Just until it's safe to drive in."

"Who are you again?" Kowalski asked.

"Bob Billings."

"Who do you work for?"

"For Ed Trenton."

"Oh, yeah, I know him."

When he's liable to be faced with tough sledding, a good social engineer does more than the usual amount of research. "I'm on the second floor," Danny went on. "Next to Roy Tucker."

He knew that name, as well. Danny went back to work on him. "It'd be much easier just to go to my desk and fetch my Secure ID for me."

Danny was pretty certain the guy would not buy into this. First of all, he would not want to leave in the middle of his shift to go traipsing down corridors and up staircases to some distant part of the building. He would also not want to have to paw through someone else's desk, violating somebody's personal space. No, it was a safe bet he wouldn't want to do that.

Kowalski didn't want to say no to a guy who needed some help, but he didn't want to say yes and get in trouble, either. So he sidestepped the decision: "I'll have to ask my boss. Hang on." He put the phone down, and Danny could hear him pick up another phone, put in the call, and explain the request. Kowalski then did something unexplainable: He actually vouched for the man using the name Bob Billings. "I know him," he told his manager. "He works for Ed Trenton. Can we let him use the Secure ID in the Computer Center?" Danny, holding on to the phone, was amazed to overhear this extraordinary and unexpected support for his cause. He couldn't believe his ears or his luck.

After another couple of moments, Kowalski came back on the line and said, "My manager wants to talk to you himself," and gave him the man's name and cell phone number.

Danny called the manager and went through the whole story one more time, adding details about the project he was working on and why his product team needed to meet a critical deadline. "It'd be easier if someone just goes and fetches my card," he said. "I don't think the desk is locked, it should be there in my upper left drawer."

"Well," said the manager, "just for the weekend, I think we can let you use the one in the Computer Center. I'll tell the guys on duty that when you call, they should read off the random-access code for you," and he gave him the PIN number to use with it.

For the whole weekend, every time Danny wanted to get into the corporate computer system, he only had to call the Computer Center and ask them to read off the six digits displayed on the Secure ID token.

An Inside Job

Once he was inside the company's computer system, then what? How would Danny find his way to the server with the software he wanted?

He had already prepared for this.

Many computer users are familiar with newsgroups, that extensive set of electronic bulletin boards where people can post questions that other people answer, or find virtual companions who share an interest in music, computers, or any of hundreds of other topics.

What few people realize when they post any message on a newsgroup site is that their message remains on line and available for years. Google, for example, now maintains an archive of seven hundred million messages, some dating back twenty years! Danny started by going to the Web address http://groups.google.com.

As search terms, Danny entered "encryption radio communications" and the name of the company, and found a years-old message on the subject from an employee. It was a posting that had been made back when the company was first developing the product, probably long before police departments and federal agencies had considered scrambling radio signals.

The message contained the sender's signature, giving not just the man's name, Scott Baker, but his phone number and even the name of his workgroup, the Secure Communications Group.

Danny picked up the phone and dialed the number. It seemed like a long shot—would he still be working in the same organization years later? Would he be at work on such a stormy weekend? The phone rang once, twice, three times, and then a voice came on the line. "This is Scott," he said.

Claiming to be from the company's IT Department, Danny manipulated Baker (in one of the ways now familiar to you from earlier chapters) into revealing the names of the servers he used for development work. These were the servers that could be expected to hold the source code containing the proprietary encryption algorithm and firmware used in the company's secure radio products.

Danny was moving closer and closer, and his excitement was building. He was anticipating the rush, the great high he always felt when he succeeded at something he knew only a very limited number of people could accomplish.

Still, he wasn't home free yet. For the rest of the weekend he'd be able to get into the company's network whenever he wanted to, thanks to that cooperative computer center manager. And he knew which servers he wanted to access. But when he dialed in, the terminal server he logged on to would not permit him to connect to the Secure Communications Group development systems. There must have been an internal firewall or router protecting the computer systems of that group. He'd have to find some other way in.

The next step took nerve: Danny called back to Kowalski in Computer Operations and complained "My server won't let me connect," and told the IT guy, "I need you to set me up with an account on one of the computers in your department so I can use Telnet to connect to my system."

The manager had already approved disclosing the access code displayed on the time-based token, so this new request didn't seem unreasonable. Kowalski set up a temporary account and password on one of the Operation Center's computers, and told Danny to "call me back when you don't need it any more and I'll remove it."

Once logged into the temporary account, Danny was able to connect over the network to the Secure Communications Group's computer systems. After an hour of on-line searching for a technical vulnerability that would give him access to a main development server, he hit the jackpot. Apparently the system or network administrator wasn't vigilant in keeping up with the latest news on security bugs in the operating system that allowed remote access. But Danny was.

Within a short time he had located the source code files that he was after and was transferring them remotely to an e-commerce site that offered free storage space. On this site, even if the files were ever discovered, they would never be traced back to him.

He had one final step before signing off: the methodical process of erasing his tracks. He finished before the Jay Leno show had gone off the air for the night. Danny figured this had been one very good weekend's work. And he had never had to put himself personally at risk. It was an intoxicating thrill, even better than snowboarding or skydiving.

Danny got drunk that night, not on scotch, gin, beer, or sake, but on his sense of power and accomplishment as he poured through the files he had stolen, closing in on the elusive, extremely secret radio software.

Analyzing the Con

As in the previous story, this ruse only worked because one company employee was all too willing to accept at face value that a caller was really the employee he claimed to be. That eagerness to help out a coworker with a problem is, on the one hand, part of what greases the wheels of industry, and part of what makes the employees of some companies more pleasant to work with than employees of others. But on the other hand, this helpfulness can be a major vulnerability that a social engineer will attempt to exploit.

One bit of manipulation Danny used was delicious: When he made the request that someone get his Secure ID from his desk, he kept saying he wanted somebody to "fetch" it for him. Fetch is a command you give your dog. Nobody wants to be told to fetch something. With that one word, Danny made it all the more certain the request would be refused and some other solution accepted instead, which was exactly what he wanted.

The Computer Center operator, Kowalski, was taken in by Danny dropping the names of people Kowalski happened to know. But why would Kowalski's *manager*—an IT manager, no less—allow some stranger access to the company's internal network? Simply because the call for help can be a powerful, persuasive tool in the social engineer's arsenal.

This story goes to show that time-based tokens and similar forms of authentication are not a defense against the wily social engineer. The only defense is a conscientious employee who follows security policies and understands how others can maliciously influence his behavior.

Could something like that ever happen in *your* company? Has it already?

PREVENTING THE CON

It seems to be an often-repeated element in these stories that an attacker arranges to dial in to a computer network from outside the company, without the person who helps him taking sufficient measures to verify that the caller is really an employee and entitled to the access. Why do I return to this theme so often? Because it truly is a factor in so many social engineering attacks. For the social engineer, it's the easiest way to reach his goal. Why should an attacker spend hours trying to break in, when he can do it instead with a simple phone call?

One of the most powerful methods for the social engineer to carry out this kind of attack is the simple ploy of pretending to need help—an approach frequently used by attackers. You don't want to stop your employees from being helpful to coworkers or customers, so you need to arm them with specific verification procedures to use with anybody making a request for computer access or confidential information. That way they can be helpful to those who deserve to be helped, but at the same time protect the organization's information assets and computer systems.

Company security procedures need to spell out in detail what kind of verification mechanisms should be used in various circumstances. Chapter 17 provides a detailed list of procedures, but here are some guidelines to consider:

- One good way to verify the identity of a person making a request is to call the phone number listed in the company directory for that person. If the person making the request is actually an attacker, the verification call will either let you speak to the real person on the phone while the imposter is on hold, or you will reach the employee's voice mail so that you can listen to the sound of his voice, and compare it to the speech of the attacker.

- If employee numbers are used in your company for verifying identity, then those numbers have to be treated as sensitive information, carefully guarded and not given out to strangers. The same goes for all other kinds of internal identifiers, such as internal telephone numbers, departmental billing identifiers, and even email addresses.

- Corporate training should call everyone's attention to the common practice of accepting unknown people as legitimate employees on the grounds that they sound authoritative or knowledgeable. Just because somebody knows a company practice or uses internal terminology is no reason to assume that his identity doesn't need to be verified in other ways.

- Security officers and system administrators must not narrow their focus so that they are only alert to how security-conscious everyone *else* is being. They also need to make sure they themselves are following the same rules, procedures, and practices.

- Passwords and the like must, of course, never be shared, but the restriction against sharing is even more important with time-based tokens and other secure forms of authentication. It should be a matter of common sense that sharing any of these items violates the whole point of the company's having installed the systems. Sharing means there can be no accountability. If a security incident takes place or something goes wrong, you won't be able to determine who the responsible party is.

- As I reiterate throughout this book, employees need to be familiar with social engineering strategies and methods to thoughtfully analyze requests they receive. Consider using role-playing as a standard part of security training, so that employees can come to a better understanding of how the social engineer works.

••••••●●●●●●••••

chapter 7

Phony Sites and Dangerous Attachments

there's an old saying that you never get something for nothing. Still, the ploy of offering something for free continues to be a big draw for both legitimate ("But wait—there's more! Call right now and we'll throw in a set of knives and a popcorn popper!") and not-so-legitimate ("Buy one acre of swampland in Florida and get a second acre free!") businesses.

And most of us are so eager to get something free that we may be distracted from thinking clearly about the offer or the promise being made. We know the familiar warning, "buyer beware," but it's time to heed another warning: Beware of come-on email attachments and free software. The savvy attacker will use nearly any means to break into the corporate network, including appealing to our natural desire to get a free gift. Here are a few examples.

"WOULDN'T YOU LIKE A FREE (BLANK)?"

Just as viruses have been a curse to mankind and medical practitioners since the beginning of time, so the aptly named computer virus represents a similar curse to users of technology. The computer viruses that get most of the attention and end up in the spotlight, not coincidentally, do the most damage. These are the product of computer vandals.

Computer nerds turned malicious, computer vandals strive to show off how clever they are. Sometimes their acts are like a rite of initiation, meant to impress older and more experienced hackers. These people are motivated to create a worm or virus intended to inflict damage. If their work destroys files, trashes entire hard drives, and emails itself to thousands of unsuspecting people, vandals puff with pride at their accomplishment. If the virus causes enough chaos that newspapers write about it and the network news broadcasts warn against it, so much the better.

Much has been written about vandals and their viruses; books, software programs, and entire companies have been created to offer protection, and we won't deal here with the defenses against their technical attacks. Our interest at the moment is less in the destructive acts of the vandal than in the more targeted efforts of his distant cousin, the social engineer.

It Came in the Email

You probably receive unsolicited emails every day that carry advertising messages or offer a free something-or-other that you neither need nor want. You know the kind. They promise investment advice, discounts on computers, televisions, cameras, vitamins, or travel, offers for credit cards you don't need, a device that will let you receive pay television channels free, ways to improve your health or your sex life, and on and on.

But every once in a while an offer pops up in your electronic mailbox for something that catches your eye. Maybe it's a free game, an offer of photos of your favorite star, a free calendar program, or inexpensive shareware that will protect your computer against viruses. Whatever the offer, the email directs you to download the file with the goodies that the message has convinced you to try.

Or maybe you receive a message with a subject line that reads "Don, I miss you," or "Anna, why haven't you written me," or "Hi, Tim, here's the sexy photo I promised you." This couldn't be junk advertising mail, you think, because it has your own name on it and sounds so personal. So you open the attachment to see the photo or read the message.

All of these actions—downloading software you learned about from an advertising email, clicking on a link that takes you to a site you haven't heard of before, opening an attachment from someone you don't really know—are invitations to trouble. Sure, most of the time what you get is exactly what you expected, or at worst something disappointing or offensive, but harmless. But sometimes what you get is the handiwork of a vandal.

Sending malicious code to your computer is only a small part of the attack. The attacker needs to persuade you to download the attachment for the attack to succeed.

The most damaging forms of malicious code—worms with names like Love Letter, SirCam, and Anna Kournikiva, to name a few—have all relied on social engineering techniques of deception and taking advantage of our desire to get something for nothing in order to be spread. The worm arrives as an attachment to an email that offers something tempting, such as confidential information, free pornography, or—a very clever ruse—a message saying that the attachment is the receipt for some expensive item you supposedly ordered. This last ploy leads you to open the attachment for fear your credit card has been charged for an item you didn't order.

It's astounding how many people fall for these tricks; even after being told and told again about the dangers of opening email attachments, awareness of the danger fades over time, leaving each of us vulnerable.

Spotting Malicious Software

Another kind of *malware*—short for *malicious software*—puts a program onto your computer that operates without your knowledge or consent, or performs a task without your awareness. Malware may look innocent enough, may even be a Word document or PowerPoint presentation, or any program that has macro functionality, but it will secretly install an unauthorized program. For example, malware may be a version of the Trojan Horse talked about in Chapter 6. Once this software is installed on your machine, it can feed every keystroke you type back to the attacker, including all your passwords and credit card numbers.

There are two other types of malicious software you may find shocking. One can feed the attacker every word you speak within range of your computer microphone, *even when you think the microphone is turned off.* Worse, if you have a Web cam attached to your computer, an attacker using a variation of this technique may be able to capture everything that takes place in front of your terminal, even when you think the camera is off, day or night.

> Beware of geeks bearing gifts, otherwise your company might endure the same fate as the city of Troy. When in doubt, to avoid an infection, use protection.

A hacker with a malicious sense of humor might try to plant a little program designed to be wickedly annoying on your computer. For example, it might make your CD drive tray keep popping open, or the file you're working on keep minimizing. Or it might cause an audio file to play a scream at full volume in the middle of the night. None of these is much fun when you're trying to get sleep or get work done . . . but at least they don't do any lasting damage.

MESSAGE FROM A FRIEND

The scenarios can get even worse, despite your precautions. Imagine: You've decided not to take any chances. You will no longer download any files except from secure sites that you know and trust, such as SecurityFocus.com or Amazon.com. You no longer click on links in email from unknown sources. You no longer open attachments in any email that you were not expecting. And you check your browser page to make sure there is a secure site symbol on every site you visit for e-commerce transactions or to exchange confidential information.

And then one day you get an email from a friend or business associate that carries an attachment. Couldn't be anything malicious if it comes from someone you know well, right? Especially since you would know who to blame if your computer data were damaged.

You open the attachment, and . . . BOOM! You just got hit with a worm or Trojan Horse. Why would someone you know do this to you? Because some things are not as they appear. You've read about this: the worm that gets onto someone's computer, and then emails itself to everyone in that person's address book. Each of those people gets an email from someone he knows and trusts, and each of those trusted emails contains the worm, which propagates itself like the ripples from a stone thrown into a still pond.

The reason this technique is so effective is that it follows the theory of killing two birds with one stone: The ability to propagate to other unsuspecting victims, and the appearance that it originated from a trusted person.

> Man has invented many wonderful things that have changed the world and our way of life. But for every good use of technology, whether a computer, telephone, or the Internet, someone will always find a way to abuse it for his or her own purposes.

It's a sad fact of life in the current state of technology that you may get an email from someone close to you and still have to wonder if it's safe to open.

VARIATIONS ON A THEME

In this era of the Internet, there is a kind of fraud that involves misdirecting you to a Web site that is not what you expected. This happens regularly, and it takes a variety of forms. This example, which is based on an actual scam perpetrated on the Internet, is representative.

Merry Christmas . . .

A retired insurance salesman named Edgar received an email one day from PayPal, a company that offers a fast and convenient way of making on-line payments. This kind of service is especially handy when a person in one part of the country (or the world, for that matter) is buying an item from an individual he doesn't know. PayPal charges the purchaser's credit card and transfers the money directly to the seller's account.

As a collector of antique glass jars Edgar did a lot of business through the on-line auction company eBay. He used PayPal often, sometimes several times a week. So Edgar was interested when he received an email in the holiday season of 2001 that seemed to be from PayPal, offering him a reward for updating his PayPal account. The message read:

> Season's Greetings Valued PayPal Customer;
>
> As the New Year approaches and as we all get ready to move a year ahead, PayPal would like to give you a $5 credit to your account!
>
> All you have to do to claim your $5 gift from us is update your information on our secure Pay Pal site by January 1st, 2002. A year brings a lot of changes, by updating your information with us you will allow for us to continue providing you and our valued customer service with excellent service and in the meantime, keep our records straight!

To update your information now and to receive $5 in your PayPal account instantly, click this link:

`http://www.paypal-secure.com/cgi-bin`

Thank you for using PayPal.com and helping us grow to be the largest of our kind!

Sincerely wishing you a very "Merry Christmas and Happy New Year,"

PayPal Team

A Note about E-commerce Web Sites

You probably know people who are reluctant to buy goods on line, even from brand-name companies such as Amazon and eBay, or the Web sites of Old Navy, Target, or Nike. In a way, they're right to be suspicious. If your browser uses today's standard of 128-bit encryption, the information you send to any secure site goes out from your computer encrypted. This data could be unencrypted with a lot of effort, but probably is not breakable in a reasonable amount of time, except perhaps by the National Security Agency (and the NSA, so far as we know, has not shown any interest in stealing credit card numbers of American citizens or trying to find out who is ordering sexy videotapes or kinky underwear).

These encrypted files could actually be broken by anyone with the time and resources. But really, what fool would go to all that effort to steal *one* credit card number when many e-commerce companies make the mistake of storing all their customer financial information unencrypted in their databases? Worse, a number of e-commerce companies that use a particular SQL database software badly compound the problem: They have never changed the default system administrator password for the program. When they took the software out of the box, the password was "null," and it's still "null" today. So the contents of the database are available to anyone on the Internet who decides to try to connect to the database server. These sites are under attack all the time and information does get stolen, without anyone being the wiser.

On the other hand, the same people who won't buy on the Internet because they're afraid of having their credit card information stolen have no problem buying with that same credit card in a brick-and-mortar store, or paying for lunch, dinner, or drinks with the card—even in a back-street bar or restaurant they wouldn't take their mother to. Credit card receipts get stolen from these places all the time, or fished out of trash bins in the back alley. And any unscrupulous clerk or waiter can jot down your name and card info, or use a gadget readily available on the Internet, a card-swiping device that stores data from any credit card passed through it, for later retrieval.

There are some hazards to shopping on line, but it's probably as safe as shopping in a bricks-and-mortar store. And the credit card companies offer you the same protection when using your card on line—if any fraudulent charges get made to the account, you're only responsible for the first $50.

So in my opinion, fear of shopping online is just another misplaced worry.

Edgar didn't notice any of the several tell-tale signs that something was wrong with this email (for example, the semicolon after the greeting line, and the garbled text about "our valued customer service with excellent service"). He clicked on the link, entered the information requested—name, address, phone number, and credit card information—and sat back to wait for the five-dollar credit to show up on his next credit-card bill. What showed up instead was a list of charges for items he never purchased.

Analyzing the Con

Edgar had been taken in by a commonplace Internet scam. It's a scam that comes in a variety of forms. One of them (detailed in Chapter 9) involves a decoy login screen created by the attacker that looks identical to the real thing. The difference is that the phony screen doesn't give access to the computer system that the user is trying to reach, but instead feeds his username and password to the hacker.

Edgar had been taken in by a scam in which the crooks had registered a Web site with the name "paypal-secure.com"—which sounds as if it should have been a secure page on the legitimate PayPal site, but it isn't. When he entered information on that site, the attackers got just what they wanted.

VARIATIONS ON THE VARIATION

How many other ways are there to deceive computer users into going to a bogus Web site where they provide confidential information? I don't suppose anyone has a valid, accurate answer, but "lots and lots" will serve the purpose.

The Missing Link

One trick pops up regularly: Sending out an email that offers a tempting reason to visit a site, and provides a link for going directly to it. Except that the link doesn't take you to the site you think you're going to, because the link actually only resembles a link for that site. Here's another example that has actually been used on the Internet, again involving misuse of the name PayPal:

`www.PayPai.com`

At a quick glance, this looks as if it says PayPal. Even if the victim notices, he may think it's just a slight defect in the text that makes the "l" of Pal look like an "i." And who would notice at a glance that:

`www.PayPal.com`

uses the number 1 instead of a lowercase letter L? There are enough people who accept misspellings and other misdirection to make this gambit continually popular with credit card bandits. When people go to the phony site, it looks like the site they expected to go to, and they blithely enter their credit card information. To set up one of these scams, an attacker only needs to register the phony domain name, send out his emails, and wait for suckers to show up, ready to be cheated.

In mid-2002, I received an email, apparently part of a mass mailing that was marked as being from "Ebay@ebay.com." The message is shown in Figure 8.1.

msg: Dear eBay User,

It has become very noticeable that another party has been corrupting your eBay account and has violated our User Agreement policy listed:

4. Bidding and Buying

You are obligated to complete the transaction with the seller if you purchase an item through one of our fixed price formats or are the highest bidder as described below. If you are the highest bidder at the end of an auction (meeting the applicable minimum bid or reserve requirements) and your bid is accepted by the seller, you are obligated to complete the transaction with the seller, or the transaction is prohibited by law or by this Agreement.

You received this notice from eBay because it has come to our attention that your current account has caused interruptions with other eBay members and eBay requires immediate verification for your account. Please verify your account or the account may become disabled. Click Here To Verify Your Account – http://error_ebay.tripod.com

****

Designated trademarks and brands are the property of their respective owners. eBay and the eBay logo are trademarks of eBay Inc.

Figure 8.1 The link in this or any other email should be used with caution.

Victims who clicked on the link went to a Web page that looked very much like an eBay page. In fact, the page was well designed, with an authentic eBay logo, and "Browse," "Sell" and other navigation links that, if clicked, took the visitor to the actual eBay site. There was also a security logo in the bottom right corner. To deter the savvy victim, the designer had even used HTML encryption to mask where the user-provided information was being sent.

It was an excellent example of a malicious computer-based social engineering attack. Still, it was not without several flaws.

The email message was not well written; in particular, the paragraph beginning "You received this notice" is clumsy and inept (the people responsible for these hoaxes never hire a professional to edit their copy, and it always shows). Also, anybody who was paying close attention would have become suspicious about eBay asking for the visitor's PayPal information; there is no reason eBay would ask a customer for this private information involving a different company.

And anyone knowledgeable about the Internet would probably recognize that the hyperlink connects not to the eBay domain but to

> Why are people allowed to register deceptive or inappropriate domain names? Because under the current law and on-line policy, anyone can register any site name that's not already in use.
>
> Companies try to fight this use of copycat addresses, but consider what they're up against. General Motors filed suit against a company that registered f**kgeneralmotors.com (but without the asterisks) and pointed the URL to General Motor's Web site. GM lost.

tripod.com, which is a free Web hosting service. This was a dead giveaway that the email was not legitimate. Still, I bet a lot of people entered their information, including a credit card number, onto this page.

Be Alert

As individual users of the Internet, we all need to be alert, making a conscious decision about when it's okay to enter personal information, passwords, account numbers, PINs, and the like.

How many people do you know who could tell you whether a particular Internet page they're looking at meets the requirements of a secure page? How many employees in your company know what to look for?

Everyone who uses the Internet should know about the little symbol that often appears somewhere on a Web page and looks like a drawing of a padlock. They should know that when the hasp is closed, the site has been certified as being secure. When the hasp is open or the lock icon is missing, the Web site is not authenticated as genuine, and any information transmitted is in the clear—that is, unencrypted.

However, an attacker who manages to compromise administrative privileges on a company computer may be able to modify or patch the operating system code to change the user's perception of what is really happening. For example, the programming instructions in the browser software that indicate a Web site's digital certificate is invalid can be modified to bypass the check. Or the system could be modified with something called a root kit, installing one or more *back doors* at the operating system level, which are harder to detect.

A secure connection authenticates the site as genuine, and encrypts the information being communicated, so an attacker cannot make use of any data that is intercepted. Can you trust any Web site, even one that uses a secure connection? No, because the site owner may not be vigilant about applying all the necessary security patches, or forcing users or

lingo

BACK DOOR   A covert entry point that provides a secret way into a user's computer that is unknown to the user. Also used by programmers while developing a software program so that they can go into the program to fix problems.

administrators to respect good password practices. So you can't assume that any supposedly secure site is invulnerable to attack.

Secure HTTP (*hypertext transfer protocol*) or SSL (*secure sockets layer*) provides an automatic mechanism that uses digital certificates not only to encrypt information being sent to the distant site, but also to provide authentication (an assurance that you are communicating with the genuine Web site). However, this protection mechanism does not work for users who fail to pay attention to whether the site name displayed in the address bar is in fact the correct address of the site they're trying to access.

Another security issue, mostly ignored, appears as a warning message that says something like "This site is not secure or the security certificate has expired. Do you want to go to the site anyway?" Many Internet users don't understand the message, and when it appears, they simply click Okay or Yes and go on with their work, unaware that they may be on quicksand. Be warned: On a Web site that does not use a secure protocol, you should never enter any confidential information such as your address or phone number, credit card or bank account numbers, or anything else you want to keep private.

Thomas Jefferson said maintaining our freedom required "eternal vigilance." Maintaining privacy and security in a society that uses information as currency requires no less.

Becoming Virus Savvy

A special note about virus software: It is essential for the corporate intranet, but also essential for every employee who uses a computer. Beyond just having antivirus software installed on their machines, users obviously need to have the software turned on (which many people don't like because it inevitably slows down some computer functions).

With antivirus software there's another important procedure to keep in mind, as well: Keeping the virus definitions up to date. Unless your company is set up to distribute software or updates over the network to every user, each individual user must carry the responsibility of downloading the

lingo

SECURE SOCKETS LAYER   A protocol developed by Netscape that provides authentication of both client and server in a secure communication on
the Internet.

latest set of virus definitions on his own. My personal recommendation is
to have everyone set the virus software preferences so that new virus definitions are automatically updated every day.

Simply put, you're vulnerable unless the virus definitions are updated
regularly. And even so, you're still not completely safe from viruses or
worms that the antivirus software companies don't yet know about or
haven't yet published a detection pattern file for.

All employees with remote access privileges from their laptops or home
computers need to have updated virus software and a personal firewall on
those machines at a minimum. A sophisticated attacker will look at the
big picture to seek out the weakest link, and that's where he'll attack.
Reminding people with remote computers regularly about the need for
personal firewalls and updated, active virus software is a corporate responsibility, because you can't expect that individual workers, managers, sales
people, and others remote from an IT department will remember the dangers of leaving their computers unprotected.

Beyond these steps, I strongly recommend use of the less common, but
no less important, software packages that guard against Trojan Horse
attacks, so-called anti-Trojan software. At the time of this writing, two of
the better-known programs are The Cleaner (www.moosoft.com), and
Trojan Defence Suite (www.diamondcs.com.au).

Finally, what is probably the most important security message of all for
companies that do not scan for dangerous emails at the corporate gateway:
Since we all tend to be forgetful or negligent about things that seem
peripheral to getting our jobs done, employees need to be reminded over
and over again, in different ways, about not opening email attachments
unless they are certain that the source is a person or organization they can
trust. And management also needs to remind employees that they must
use active virus software and anti-Trojan software that provides invaluable
protection against the seemingly trustworthy email that may contain a
destructive payload.

chapter 8

Using Sympathy, Guilt, and Intimidation

as discussed in Chapter 15, a social engineer uses the psychology of influence to lead his target to comply with his request. Skilled social engineers are very adept at developing a ruse that stimulates emotions, such as fear, excitement, or guilt. They do this by using psychological triggers—automatic mechanisms that lead people to respond to requests without in-depth analysis of all the available information.

We all want to avoid difficult situations for ourselves and others. Based on this positive impulse, the attacker can play on a person's sympathy, make his victim feel guilty, or use intimidation as a weapon.

Here are some graduate-school lessons in popular tactics that play on the emotions.

A VISIT TO THE STUDIO

Have you ever noticed how some people can walk up to the guard at the door of, say, a hotel ballroom where some meeting, private party, or book-launching function is under way, and just walk past that person without being asked for his ticket or pass?

In much the same way, a social engineer can talk his way into places that you would not have thought possible—as the following story about the movie industry makes clear.

"Ron Hillyard's office, this is Dorothy."

"Dorothy, hi. My name is Kyle Bellamy. I've just come on board to work in Animation Development on Brian Glassman's staff. You folks sure do things different over here."

"I guess. I never worked on any other movie lot so I don't really know. What can I do for you?"

"To tell you the truth, I'm feeling sort of stupid. I've got a writer coming over this afternoon for a pitch session and I don't know who I'm supposed to talk to about getting him onto the lot. The people over here in Brian's office are really nice but I hate to keep bothering them, how do I do this, how do I do that. It's like I just started junior high and can't find my way to the bathroom. You know what I mean?"

Dorothy laughed.

"You want to talk to Security. Dial 7, and then 6138. If you get Lauren, tell her Dorothy said she should take good care of you."

"Thanks, Dorothy. And if I can't find the men's room, I may call you back!"

They chuckled together over the idea, and hung up.

David Harold's Story

I love the movies and when I moved to Los Angeles, I thought I'd get to meet all kinds of people in the movie business and they'd take me along to parties and have me over to lunch at the studios. Well, I was there for a year, I was turning twenty-six years old, and the closest I got was going on the Universal Studios tour with all the nice people from Phoenix and Cleveland. So finally it got to the point where I figured, if they won't invite me in, I'll invite myself. Which is what I did.

I bought a copy of the *Los Angeles Times* and read the entertainment column for a couple of days, and wrote down the names of some producers at different studios. I decided I'd try hitting on one of the big studios first.

So I called the switchboard and asked for the office of this producer I had read about in the paper. The secretary that answered sounded like the motherly type, so I figured I had gotten lucky; if it was some young girl who was just there hoping she'd be discovered, she probably wouldn't have given me the time of day.

But this Dorothy, she sounded like somebody that would take in a stray kitten, somebody who'd feel sorry for the new kid that was feeling a little overwhelmed on the new job. And I sure got just the right touch with her. It's not every day you try to trick somebody and they give you even more than you asked for. Out of pity, she not only gave me the name of one of the people in Security, but said I should tell the lady that Dorothy wanted her to help me.

Of course I had planned to use Dorothy's name anyway. This made it even better. Lauren opened right up and never even bothered to look up the name I gave to see if it was really in the employee database.

When I drove up to the gate that afternoon, they not only had my name on the visitor's list, they even had a parking space for me. I had a late lunch at the commissary, and wandered the lot until the end of the day. I even sneaked into a couple of sound stages and watched them shooting movies. Didn't leave till 7 o'clock. It was one of my most exciting days ever.

Analyzing the Con

Everybody was a new employee once. We all have memories of what that first day was like, especially when we were young and inexperienced. So when a new employee asks for help, he can expect that many people— especially entry-level people—will remember their own new-kid-on-the-block feelings and go out of their way to lend a hand. The social engineer knows this, and he understands that he can use it to play on the sympathies of his victims.

We make it too easy for outsiders to con their way into our company plants and offices. Even with guards at entrances and sign-in procedures for anyone who isn't an employee, any one of several variations on the ruse used in this story will allow an intruder to obtain a visitor's badge and walk right in. And if your company requires that visitors be escorted? That's a good rule, but it's only effective if your employees are truly conscientious about stopping anyone with or without a visitor's badge who is on his own, and questioning him. And then, if the answers aren't satisfactory, your employees have to be willing to contact security.

Making it too easy for outsiders to talk their way into your facilities endangers your company's sensitive information. In today's climate, with the threat of terrorist attacks hanging over our society, it's more than just information that could be at risk.

"DO IT NOW"

Not everyone who uses social engineering tactics is a polished social engineer. Anybody with an insider's knowledge of a particular company can turn dangerous. The risk is even greater for any company that holds in its files and databases any personal information about its employees, which, of course, most companies do.

When workers are not educated or trained to recognize social engineering attacks, determined people like the jilted lady in the following story can do things that most honest people would think impossible.

Doug's Story

Things hadn't been going all that well with Linda anyway, and I knew as soon as I met Erin that she was the one for me. Linda is, like, a little bit . . . well, sort of not exactly unstable but she can sort of go off the deep end when she gets upset.

I told her as gentle as I could that she had to move out, and I helped her pack and even let her take a couple of the Queensryche CDs that were really mine. As soon as she was gone I went to the hardware store for a new Medico lock to put on the front door and put it on that same night. The next morning I called the phone company and had them change my phone number, and made it unpublished.

That left me free to pursue Erin.

Linda's Story

I was ready to leave, anyway, I just hadn't decided when. But nobody likes to feel rejected. So it was just a question of, what could I do to let him know what a jerk he was?

It didn't take long to figure out. There had to be another girl, otherwise he wouldn't of sent me packing in such a hurry. So I'd just wait a bit and then start calling him late in the evening. You know, around the time they would least want to be called.

I waited till the next weekend and called around 11 o'clock on Saturday night. Only he had changed his phone number. And the new number was unlisted. That just shows what kind of SOB the guy was.

It wasn't that big of a setback. I started rummaging through the papers I had managed to take home just before I left my job at the phone company. And there it was—I had saved a repair ticket from once when there was a problem with the telephone line at Doug's, and the printout listed the cable and pair for his phone. See, you can change your phone number all you want, but you still have the same pair of copper wires running from your house to the telephone company switching office, called the Central Office, or CO. The set of copper wires from every house and apartment is identified by these numbers, called the cable and pair. And if you know how the phone company does things, which I do, knowing the target's cable and pair is all you need to find out the phone number.

I had a list giving all the COs in the city, with their addresses and phone numbers. I looked up the number for the CO in the neighborhood where I used to live with Doug the jerk, and called, but naturally nobody was there. Where's the switchman when you really need him? Took me all of about twenty seconds to come up with a plan. I started calling around to the other COs and finally located a guy. But he was miles away and he was probably sitting there with his feet up. I knew he wouldn't want to do what I needed. I was ready with my plan.

"This is Linda, Repair Center," I said. "We have an emergency. Service for a paramedic unit has gone down. We have a field tech trying to restore service but he can't find the problem. We need you to drive over to the Webster CO immediately and see if we have dial tone leaving the central office."

And then I told him, "I'll call you when you get there," because of course I couldn't have him calling the Repair Center and asking for me.

I knew he wouldn't want to leave the comfort of the central office to bundle up and go scrape ice off his windshield and drive through the slush late at night. But it was an "emergency," so he couldn't exactly say he was too busy.

When I reached him forty-five minutes later at the Webster CO, I told him to check cable 29 pair 2481, and he walked over to the frame and checked and said, Yes, there was dial tone. Which of course I already knew.

So then I said, "Okay, I need you to do an LV," which means line verification, which is asking him to identify the phone number. He does this by dialing a special number that reads back the number he called from. He doesn't know anything about if it's an unlisted number or that it's just been changed, so he did what I asked and I heard the number being announced over his lineman's test set. Beautiful. The whole thing had worked like a charm.

I told him, "Well, the problem must be out in the field," like I knew the number all along. I thanked him and told him we'd keep working on it, and said good night.

Once a social engineer knows how things work inside the targeted company, it becomes easy to use that knowledge to develop rapport with legitimate employees. Companies need to prepare for social engineering attacks from current or former employees who may have an axe to grind. Background checks may be helpful to weed out prospects who may have a propensity toward this type of behavior. But in most cases, these people will be extremely difficult to detect. The only reasonable safeguard in these cases is to enforce and audit procedures for verifying identity, including the person's employment status, prior to disclosing any information to anyone not personally known to still be with the company.

So much for that Doug and trying to hide from me behind an unlisted number. The fun was about to begin.

Analyzing the Con

The young lady in this story was able to get the information she wanted to carry out her revenge because she had inside knowledge: the phone numbers, procedures, and lingo of the telephone company. With it she was not only able to find out a new, unlisted phone number, but was able to do it in the middle of a wintry night, sending a telephone switchman chasing across town for her.

"MR. BIGG WANTS THIS"

A popular and highly effective form of intimidation—popular in large measure because it's so simple—relies on influencing human behavior by using authority.

Just the name of the assistant in the CEO's office can be valuable. Private investigators and even head-hunters do this all the time. They'll call the switchboard operator and say they want to be connected to the CEO's office. When the secretary or executive assistant answers, they'll say they have a document or package for the CEO, or if they send an email attachment, would she print it out? Or else they'll ask, what's the fax number? And by the way, what's your name?

Then they call the next person, and say, "Jeannie in Mr. Bigg's office told me to call you so you can help me with something."

The technique is called name-dropping, and it's usually used as a method to quickly establish rapport by influencing the target to believe that the attacker is connected with somebody in authority. A target is more likely to do a favor for someone who knows somebody he knows.

If the attacker has his eyes set on highly sensitive information, he may use this kind of approach to stir up useful emotions in the victim, such as fear of getting into trouble with his superiors. Here's an example.

Scott's Story

"Scott Abrams."

"Scott, this is Christopher Dalbridge. I just got off the phone with Mr. Biggley, and he's more than a little unhappy. He says he sent a note ten days ago that you people were to get copies of all your market penetration research over to us for analysis. We never got a thing."

"Market penetration research? Nobody said anything to me about it. What department are you in?"

"We're a consulting firm he hired, and we're already behind schedule."

"Listen, I'm just on my way to a meeting. Let me get your phone number and . . ."

The attacker now sounded just short of truly frustrated: "Is that what you want me to tell Mr. Biggley?! Listen, he expects our analysis by tomorrow morning and we have to work on it tonight. Now, do you want *me* to tell him we couldn't do it 'cause we couldn't get the report from you, or do you want to tell him that yourself?"

An angry CEO can ruin your week. The target is likely to decide that maybe this is something he better take care of before he goes into that meeting. Once again, the social engineer has pressed the right button to get the response he wanted.

Analyzing the Con

The ruse of intimidation by referencing authority works especially well if the other person is at a fairly low level in the company. The use of an important person's name not only overcomes normal reluctance or suspicion, but often makes the person eager to please; the natural instinct of wanting to be helpful is multiplied when you think that the person you're helping is important or influential.

The social engineer knows, though, that it's best when running this particular deceit to use the name of someone at a higher level than the person's own boss. And this gambit is tricky to use within a small organization: The attacker doesn't want his victim making a chance comment to the VP of marketing. "I sent out the product marketing plan you had that guy call me about," can too easily produce a response of "What

Intimidation can create a fear of punishment, influencing people to cooperate. Intimidation can also raise the fear of embarrassment or of being disqualified from that new promotion.

People must be trained that it's not only acceptable but expected to challenge authority when security is at stake. Information security training should include teaching people how to challenge authority in customer-friendly ways, without damaging relationships. Moreover, this expectation must be supported from the top down. If an employee is not going to be backed up for challenging people regardless of their status, the normal reaction is to stop challenging—just the opposite of what you want.

marketing plan? What guy?" And that could lead to the discovery that the company has been victimized.

WHAT THE SOCIAL SECURITY ADMINISTRATION KNOWS ABOUT YOU

We like to think that government agencies with files on us keep the information safely locked away from people without an authentic need to know. The reality is that even the federal government isn't as immune to penetration as we would like to imagine.

May Linn's Phone Call

Place: A regional office of the Social Security Administration
Time: 10:18 A.M., Thursday morning

"Mod Three. This is May Linn Wang."

The voice on the other end of the phone sounded apologetic, almost timid.

"Ms. Wang, this is Arthur Arondale, in the Office of the Inspector General. Can I call you 'May'?

"It's 'May Linn'," she said.

"Well, it's like this, May Linn. We've got a new guy in here who there's no computer for yet, and right now he's got a priority project and he's using mine. We're the government of the United States, for cryin' out loud, and they say they don't have enough money in the budget to buy a computer for this guy to use. And now my boss thinks I'm falling behind and doesn't want to hear any excuses, you know?"

"I know what you mean, all right."

"Can you help me with a quick inquiry on MCS?" he asked, using the name of the computer system for looking up taxpayer information.

"Sure, what'cha need?"

"The first thing I need you to do is an alphadent on Joseph Johnson, DOB 7/4/69." (Alphadent means to have the computer search for an account alphabetically by tax-payer name, further identified by date of birth.)

After a brief pause, she asked:

"What do you need to know?"

"What's his account number?" he said, using the insider's shorthand for the social security number. She read it off.

"Okay, I need you to do a numident on that account number," the caller said.

That was a request for her to read off the basic taxpayer data, and May Linn responded by giving the taxpayer's place of birth, mother's maiden name, and father's name. The caller listened patiently while she also gave him the month and year the card was issued, and the district office it was issued by.

He next asked for a DEQY. (Pronounced "DECK-wee," it's short for "detailed earnings query.")

The DEQY request brought the response, "For what year?" The caller replied, "Year 2001."

May Linn said, "The amount was $190,286, the payer was Johnson MicroTech."

"Any other wages?"

"No."

"Thanks," he said. "You've been very kind."

Then he tried to arrange to call her whenever he needed information and couldn't get to his computer, again using the favorite trick of social engineers of always trying to establish a connection so that he can keep going back to the same person, avoiding the nuisance of having to find a new mark each time.

"Not next week," she told him, because she was going to Kentucky for her sister's wedding. Any other time, she'd do whatever she could.

When she put the phone down, May Linn felt good that she had been able to offer a little help to a fellow unappreciated public servant.

Keith Carter's Story

To judge from the movies and from best-selling crime novels, a private investigator is short on ethics and long on knowledge of how to get the juicy facts on people. They do this by using thoroughly illegal methods, while just barely managing to avoid getting arrested. The truth, of course, is that most PIs run entirely legitimate businesses. Since many of them started their working lives as sworn law enforcement officers, they know perfectly well what's legal and what isn't, and most are not tempted to cross the line.

There are, however, exceptions. Some PIs—more than a few—do indeed fit the mold of the guys in the crime stories. These guys are known in the trade as information brokers, a polite term for people who are willing to break the rules. They know they can get any assignment done a good deal faster and a good deal easier if they take some shortcuts. That these short-cuts happen to be potential felonies that might land them behind bars for a few years doesn't seem to deter the more unscrupulous ones.

Meanwhile the upscale PIs—the ones who work out of a fancy office suite in a high-rent part of town—don't do this kind of work themselves. They simply hire some information broker to do it for them.

The guy we'll call Keith Carter was the kind of private eye unencumbered by ethics.

•••••••••●●●●••••••

It was a typical case of "Where's he hiding the money?" Or sometimes it's "Where's she hiding the money?" Sometimes it was a rich lady who wanted to know where her husband had hidden her money (though why a woman with money ever marries a guy without was a riddle Keith Carter wondered about now and then but had never found a good answer for).

In this case the husband, whose name was Joe Johnson, was the one keeping the money on ice. He was a very smart guy who had started a high-tech company with ten thousand dollars he borrowed from his wife's family and built into a hundred-million dollar firm. According to her divorce lawyer, he had done an impressive job of hiding his assets, and the lawyer wanted a complete rundown.

Keith figured his starting point would be the Social Security Administration, targeting their files on Johnson, which would be packed with highly useful information for a situation like this. Armed with their info, Keith could pretend to be the target and get the banks, brokerage firms, and offshore institutions to tell him everything.

His first phone call was to a local district office, using the same 800-number that any member of the public uses, the number listed in the local phone book. When a clerk came on the line, Keith asked to be connected to someone in Claims. Another wait, and then a voice. Now Keith shifted gears; "Hi," he began. "This is Gregory Adams, District Office 329. Listen, I'm trying to reach a claims adjuster that handles an account number that ends in 6363, and the number I have goes to a fax machine."

"That's Mod 2," the man said. He looked up the number and gave it to Keith.

Next he called Mod 2. When May Linn answered, he switched hats and went through the routine about being from the Office of the Inspector General, and the problem about somebody else having to use his computer. She gave him the information he was looking for, and agreed to do whatever she could when he needed help in the future.

Analyzing the Con

What made this approach effective was the play on the employee's sympathy with the story about someone else using his computer and "my boss is not happy with me." People don't show their emotions at work very often; when they do, it can roll right over someone else's ordinary defenses against social engineering attacks. The emotional ploy of "I'm in trouble, won't you help me?" was all it took to win the day.

Social Insecurity

Incredibly, the Social Security Administration has posted a copy of their entire Program Operations Manual on the Web, crammed with information that's useful for their people, but also incredibly valuable to social engineers. It contains abbreviations, lingo, and instructions for how to request what you want, as described in this story.

Want to learn more inside information about the Social Security Administration? Just search on Google or enter the following address into your browser: http://policy.ssa.gov/poms.nsf/. Unless the agency has already read this story and removed the manual by the time you read this, you'll find on-line instructions that even give detailed information on what data an SSA clerk is allowed to give to the law enforcement community. In practical terms, that community includes any social engineer who can convince an SSA clerk that he is from a law enforcement organization.

The attacker could not have been successful in obtaining this information from one of the clerks who handles phone calls from the general public. The kind of attack Keith used only works when the person on the receiving end of the call is someone whose phone number is unavailable to the public, and who therefore has the expectation that anyone calling must be somebody on the inside—another example of speakeasy security.

The elements that helped this attack to work included:

- Knowing the phone number to the Mod.
- Knowing the terminology they used—numident, alphadent, and DEQY.
- Pretending to be from the Office of the Inspector General, which every federal government employee knows as a government-wide investigative agency with broad powers. This gives the attacker an aura of authority.

One interesting sidelight: Social engineers seem to know how to make requests so that hardly anyone ever thinks, "Why are you calling *me?*"— even when, logically, it would have made more sense if the call had gone to some other person in some completely different department. Perhaps it simply offers such a break in the monotony of the daily grind to help the caller that the victim discounts how unusual the call seems.

Finally, the attacker in this incident, not satisfied with getting the information just for the case at hand, wanted to establish a contact he could call on regularly. He might otherwise have been able to use a common ploy for the sympathy attack—"I spilled coffee on my keyboard." That was no good here, though, because a keyboard can be replaced in a day. Hence he used the story about somebody else using his computer, which he could reasonably string out for weeks: "Yep, I thought he'd have his own computer yesterday, but one came in and another guy pulled some kind of deal and got it instead. So this joker is still showing up in my cubicle." And so on.

Poor me, I need help. Works like a charm.

ONE SIMPLE CALL

One of an attacker's main hurdles is to make his request sound *reasonable*— something typical of requests that come up in the victim's workday, something that doesn't put the victim out too much. As with a lot of other things in life, making a request sound logical may be a challenge one day, but the next, it may be a piece of cake.

Mary H's Phone Call

Date/Time: Monday, November 23, 7:49 A.M.
Place: Mauersby & Storch Accounting, New York

To most people, accounting work is number crunching and bean count-ing, generally viewed as being about as enjoyable as having a root canal. Fortunately, not everyone sees the work that way. Mary Harris, for example, found her work as a senior accountant absorbing, part of the reason she was one of the most dedicated accounting employees at her firm.

On this particular Monday, Mary arrived early to get a head start on what she expected to be a long day, and was surprised to find her phone ringing. She picked it up and gave her name.

"Hi, this is Peter Sheppard. I'm with Arbuckle Support, the company that does tech support for your firm. We logged a couple of complaints over the weekend from people having problems with the computers there. I thought I could troubleshoot before everybody comes into work this morning. Are you having any problems with your computer or connect-ing to the network?"

She told him she didn't know yet. She turned her computer on and while it was booting, he explained what he wanted to do.

"I'd like to run a couple of tests with you," he said. "I'm able to see on my screen the keystrokes you type, and I want to make sure they're going across the network correctly. So every time you type a stroke, I want you to tell me what it is, and I'll see if the same letter or number is appearing here. Okay?"

With nightmare visions of her computer not working and a frustrating day of not being able to get any work done, she was more than happy to have this man help her. After a few moments, she told him, "I have the login screen, and I'm going to type in my ID. I'm typing it now— M . . . A . . . R . . . Y . . . D."

"Great so far," he said. "I'm seeing that here. Now, go ahead and type your password but don't tell me what it is. You should never tell anybody your password, not even tech support. I'll just see asterisks here—your password is protected so I can't see it." None of this was true, but it made sense to Mary. And then he said, "Let me know once your computer has started up."

When she said it was running, he had her open two of her applications, and she reported that they launched "just fine."

Mary was relieved to see that everything seemed to be working normally. Peter said, "I'm glad I could make sure you'll be able to use your computer okay. And listen," he went on, "we just installed an update that allows people to change their passwords. Would you be willing to take a couple of minutes with me so I can see if we got it working right?

She was grateful for the help he had given her and readily agreed. Peter talked her through the steps of launching the application that allows a user to change passwords, a standard element of the Windows 2000 operating system. "Go ahead and enter your password," he told her. "But remember not to say it out loud."

When she had done that, Peter said, "Just for this quick test, when it asks for your new password, enter 'test123.' Then type it again in the Verification box, and click Enter."

He walked her through the process of disconnecting from the server. He had her wait a couple of minutes, then connect again, this time trying to log on with her new password. It worked like a charm, Peter seemed very pleased, and talked her through changing back to her original password or choosing a new one—once more cautioning her about not saying the password out loud.

"Well, Mary," Peter told her. "We didn't find any trouble, and that's great. Listen, if any problems do come up, just call us over here at Arbuckle. I'm usually on special projects but anybody here who answers can help you." She thanked him and they said good-bye.

Peter's Story

The word had gotten around about Peter—a number of the people in his community who had gone to school with him had heard he turned into some kind of a computer whiz who could often find out useful information that other people couldn't get. When Alice Conrad came to him to ask a favor, he said no at first. Why should he help? When he ran into her once and tried to ask for a date, she had turned him down cold.

But his refusal to help didn't seem to surprise her. She said she didn't think it was something he could do anyway. That was like a challenge, because of course he was sure he could. And that was how he came to agree.

Alice had been offered a contract for some consulting work for a marketing company, but the contract terms didn't seem very good. Before she went back to ask for a better deal, she wanted to know what terms other consultants had on their contracts.

This is how Peter tells the story.

· · · ● ● ● ● ● ● ● ● · · ·

I wouldn't tell Alice but I got off on people wanting me to do something they didn't think I could, when I knew it would be easy. Well, not easy, exactly, not this time. It would take a bit of doing. But that was okay.

I could show her what smart was really all about.

A little after 7:30 Monday morning, I called the marketing company's offices and got the receptionist, said that I was with the company that handled their pension plans and I need to talk to somebody in Accounting. Had she noticed if any of the Accounting people had come in yet? She said, "I think I saw Mary come in a few minutes ago, I'll try her for you."

When Mary picked up the phone, I told her my little story about computer problems, which was designed to give her the jitters so she'd be glad to cooperate. As soon as I had talked her through changing her password, I then quickly logged onto the system with the same temporary password I had asked her to use, test123.

Here's where the mastery comes in—I installed a small program that allowed me to access the company's computer system whenever I wanted, using a secret password of my own. After I hung up with Mary, my first step was to erase the audit trail so no one would even know I had been on his or her system. It was easy. After elevating my system privileges, I was able to download a free program called *clearlogs* that I found on a security-related Web site at www.ntsecurity.nu.

Time for the real job. I ran a search for any documents with the word "contract" in the filename, and downloaded the files. Then I searched some more and came on the mother lode—the directory containing all the consultant payment reports. So I put together all the contract files and a list of payments.

Alice could pore through the contracts and see how much they were paying other consultants. Let her do the donkeywork of poring through all those files. I had done what she asked me to.

From the disks I put the data onto, I printed out some of the files so I could show her the evidence. I made her meet me and buy dinner. You should have seen her face when she thumbed through the stack of papers. "No way," she said. "No way."

I didn't bring the disks with me. They were the bait. I said she'd have to come over to get them, hoping maybe she'd want to show her gratitude for the favor I just did her.

It's amazing how easy it is for a social engineer to get people to do things based on how he structures the request. The premise is to trigger an automatic response based on psychological principles, and rely on the mental shortcuts people take when they perceive the caller as an ally.

Analyzing the Con

Peter's phone call to the marketing company represented the most basic form of social engineering—a simple attempt that needed little preparation, worked on the first attempt, and took only a few minutes to bring off.

Even better, Mary, the victim, had no reason to think that any sort of trick or ruse had been played on her, no reason to file a report or raise a ruckus.

The scheme worked through Peter's use of three social engineering tactics. First he got Mary's initial cooperation by generating fear—making her think that her computer might not be usable. Then he took the time to have her open two of her applications so she could be sure they were working okay, strengthening the rapport between the two of them, a sense of being allies. Finally, he got her further cooperation for the essential part of his task by playing on her gratitude for the help he had provided in making sure her computer was okay.

By telling her she shouldn't ever reveal her password, should not reveal it even to him, Peter did a thorough but subtle job of convincing her that he was concerned about the security of her company's files. This boosted her confidence that he must be legitimate because he was protecting her and the company.

THE POLICE RAID

Picture this scene: The government has been trying to lay a trap for a man named Arturo Sanchez, who has been distributing movies free over the Internet. The Hollywood studios say he's violating their copyrights, he says he's just trying to nudge them to recognize an inevitable market so they'll start doing something about making new movies available for download. He points out (correctly) that this could be a huge source of revenue for the studios that they seem to be completely ignoring.

Search Warrant, Please

Coming home late one night, he checks the windows of his apartment from across the street and notices the lights are off, even though he always leaves one on when he goes out.

He pounds and bangs on a neighbor's door until he wakes the man up, and learns that there was indeed a police raid in the building. But they made the neighbors stay downstairs, and he still isn't sure what apartment they went into. He only knows they left carrying some heavy things, only they were wrapped up and he couldn't tell what they were. And they didn't take anybody away in handcuffs.

Arturo checks his apartment. The bad news is that there's a paper from the police requiring that he call immediately and set up an appointment for an interview within three days. The worse news is that his computers are missing.

Arturo vanishes into the night, going to stay with a friend. But the uncertainty gnaws at him. How much do the police know? Have they caught up with him at last, but left him a chance to flee? Or is this about something else entirely, something he can clear up without having to leave town?

Before you read on, stop and think for a moment: Can you imagine any way you could find out what the police know about you? Assuming you don't have any political contacts or friends in the police department or the prosecutor's office, do you imagine there's any way that you, as an ordinary citizen, could get this information? Or that even someone with social engineering skills could?

Scamming the Police

Arturo satisfied his need to know like this: To start with, he got the phone number for a nearby copy store, called them, and asked for their fax number.

Then he called the district attorney's office, and asked for Records. When he was connected with the records office, he introduced himself as an investigator with Lake County, and said he needed to speak with the clerk who files the active search warrants.

"I do," the lady said. "Oh, great," he answered. "Because we raided a suspect last night and I'm trying to locate the affidavit."

"We file them by address," she told him.

He gave his address, and she sounded almost excited. "Oh, yeah," she bubbled, "I know about *that* one. 'The Copyright Caper.'"

"That's the one," he said. "I'm looking for the affidavit and copy of the warrant."

"Oh, I have it right here."

"Great," he said. "Listen, I'm out in the field and I have a meeting with the Secret Service on this case in fifteen minutes. I've been so absent-minded lately, I left the file at home, and I'll never make it there and back in time. Could I get copies from you?"

"Sure, no problem. I'll make copies; you can come right over and pick them up."

"Great," he said. "That's great. But listen, I'm on the other side of town. Is it possible you could fax them to me?"

That created a small problem, but not insurmountable. "We don't have a fax up here in Records," she said. "But they have one downstairs in the Clerk's office they might let me use."

He said, "Let me call the Clerk's office and set it up."

The lady in the Clerk's office said she'd be glad to take care of it but wanted to know "Who's going to pay for it?" She needed an accounting code.

"I'll get the code and call you back," he told her.

He then called the DA's office, again identified himself as a police officer and simply asked the receptionist, "What's the accounting code for the DA's office?" Without hesitation, she told him.

Calling back to the Clerk's office to provide the accounting number gave him the excuse for manipulating the lady a little further: He talked her into walking upstairs to get the copies of the papers to be faxed.

Covering His Tracks

Arturo still had another couple of steps to take. There was always a possibility that someone would smell something fishy, and he might arrive at the copy store to find a couple of detectives, casually dressed and trying to

> **note**
>
> How does a social engineer know the details of so many operations—police departments, prosecutor's offices, phone company practices, the organization of specific companies that are in fields useful in his attacks, such as telecommunications and computers? Because it's his business to find out. This knowledge is a social engineer's stock in trade because information can aid him in his efforts to deceive.

look busy until somebody showed up asking for that particular fax. He waited a while, and then called the Clerk's office back to verify that the lady had sent the fax. Fine so far.

He called another copy store in the same chain across town and used the ruse about how he was "pleased with your handling of a job and want to write the manager a letter of congratulations, what's her name?" With that essential piece of information, he called the first copy store again and said he wanted to talk to the manager. When the man picked up the phone, Arturo said, "Hi, this is Edward at store 628 in Hartfield. My manager, Anna, told me to call you. We've got a customer who's all upset—somebody gave him the fax number of the wrong store. He's here waiting for an important fax, only the number he was given is for your store." The manager promised to have one of his people locate the fax and send it on to the Hartfield store immediately.

Arturo was already waiting at the second store when the fax arrived there. Once he had it in hand, he called back to the Clerk's office to tell the lady thanks, and "It's not necessary to bring those copies back upstairs, you can just throw them away now." Then he called the manager at the first store and told him, too, to throw away their copy of the fax. This way there wouldn't be any record of what had taken place, just in case somebody later came around asking questions. Social engineers know you can never be too careful.

Arranged this way, Arturo didn't even have to pay charges at the first copy store for receiving the fax and for sending it out again to the second store. And if it turned out that the police did show up at the first store, Arturo would already have his fax and be long gone by the time they could arrange to get people to the second location.

The end of the story: The affidavit and warrant showed that the police had well-documented evidence of Arturo's movie-copying activities. That was what he needed to know. By midnight, he had crossed the state line. Arturo was on the way to a new life, somewhere else with a new identity, ready to get started again on his campaign.

Analyzing the Con

The people who work in any district attorney's office, anywhere, are in constant contact with law enforcement officers—answering questions, making arrangements, taking messages. Anybody gutsy enough to call and claim to be a police officer, sheriff's deputy, or whatever will likely be taken at his word. Unless it's obvious that he doesn't know the terminology, or if he's nervous and stumbles over his words, or in some other way doesn't sound authentic, he may not even be asked a single question to verify his claim. That's exactly what happened here, with two different workers.

Obtaining a needed charge code was handled with a single phone call. Then Arturo played the sympathy card with the story about "a meeting with the Secret Service in fifteen minutes, I've been absent-minded and left the file at home." She naturally felt sorry for him, and went out of her way to help.

Then by using not one but two copy stores, Arturo made himself extra safe when he went to pick up the fax. A variation on this that makes the fax even more difficult to trace: Instead of having the document sent to another copy store, the attacker can give what appears to be a fax number, but is really an address at a free Internet service that will receive a fax for you and automatically forward it to your email address. That way it can be downloaded directly to the attacker's computer, and he never has to show his face anyplace where someone might later be able to identify him. And the email address and electronic fax number can be abandoned as soon as the mission has been accomplished.

TURNING THE TABLES

A young man I'll call Michael Parker was one of those people who figured out a bit late that the better-paying jobs mostly go to people with college degrees. He had a chance to attend a local college on a partial scholarship plus education loans, but it meant working nights and weekends to pay his rent, food, gas, and car insurance. Michael, who always liked to find shortcuts, thought maybe there was another way, one that paid off faster and with less effort. Because he had been learning about computers from the time he got to play with one at age ten and became fascinated with finding out how they worked, he decided to see if he could "create" his own accelerated bachelor's degree in computer science.

Graduating—Without Honors

He could have broken into the computer systems of the state university, found the record of someone who had graduated with a nice B+ or A-average, copied the record, put his own name on it, and added it to the records of that year's graduating class. Thinking this through, feeling somehow uneasy about the idea, he realized there must be other records of a student having been on campus—tuition payment records, the housing office, and who knows what else. Creating just the record of courses and grades would leave too many loopholes.

Plotting further, feeling his way, it came to him that he could reach his goal by seeing if the school had a graduate with the same name as his, who had earned a computer science degree any time during an appropriate span of years. If so, he could just put down the other Michael Parker's social security number on employment application forms; any company that checked the name and social security number with the university would be told that, yes, he did have the claimed degree. (It wouldn't be obvious to most people but was obvious to him that he could put one social security number on the job application and then, if hired, put his own real number on the new-employee forms. Most companies would never think to check whether a new hire had used a different number earlier in the hiring process.)

Logging In to Trouble

How to find a Michael Parker in the university's records? He went about it like this:

Going to the main library on the university campus, he sat down at a computer terminal, got up on the Internet, and accessed the university's Web site. He then called the Registrar's office. With the person who answered, he went through one of the by-now-familiar social engineering routines: "I'm calling from the Computer Center, we're making some changes to the network configuration and we want to make sure we don't disrupt your access. Which server do you connect to?"

"What do you mean, 'server'?" he was asked.

"What computer do you connect to when you need to look up student academic information?"

The answer, admin.rnu.edu, gave him the name of the computer where student records were stored. This was the first piece of the puzzle: He now knew his target machine.

lingo

DUMB TERMINAL   A terminal that doesn't contain its own microprocessor. Dumb terminals can only accept simple commands and display text characters and numbers.

He typed that URL into the computer and got no response—as expected, there was a firewall blocking access. So he ran a program to see if he could connect to any of the services running on that computer, and found an open port with a Telnet service running, which allows one computer to connect remotely to another computer and access it as if directly connected using a *dumb terminal*. All he would need to gain access would be the standard user ID and password.

He made another call to the registrar's office, this time listening carefully to make sure he was talking to a different person. He got a lady, and again he claimed to be from the university's Computer Center. They were installing a new production system for administrative records, he told her. As a favor, he'd like her to connect to the new system, still in test mode, to see if she could access student academic records okay. He gave her the IP address to connect to, and talked her through the process.

In fact, the IP address took her to the computer Michael was sitting at in the campus library. Using the same process described in Chapter 8, he had created a login simulator—a decoy sign-in screen—looking just like the one she was accustomed to seeing when going onto the system for student records. "It's not working," she told him. "It keeps saying 'Login incorrect'."

By now the login simulator had fed the keystrokes of her account name and password to Michael's terminal; mission accomplished. He told her, "Oh, some of the accounts haven't been brought over yet to this machine. Let me set up your account, and I'll call you back." Careful about tying up loose ends, as any proficient social engineer needs to be, he would make a point of phoning later to say that the test system wasn't working right yet, and if it was okay with her, they'd call back to her or one of the other folks there when they had figured out what was causing the problem.

The Helpful Registrar

Now Michael knew what computer system he needed to access, and he had a user's ID and password. But what commands would he need in order to search the files for information on a computer science graduate with the right name and graduation date? The student database would be a proprietary one, created on campus to meet the specific requirements of the university and the Registrar's office, and would have a unique way of accessing information in the database.

First step in clearing this last hurdle: Find out who could guide him through the mysteries of searching the student database. He called the Registrar's office again, this time reaching a different person. He was from the office of the Dean of Engineering, he told the lady, and he asked, "Who are we supposed to call for help when we're having problems accessing the student academic files?"

Minutes later he was on the phone with the college's database administrator, pulling the sympathy act: "I'm Mark Sellers, in the registrar's office. You feel like taking pity on a new guy? Sorry to be calling you but they're all in a meeting this afternoon and there's no one around to help me. I need to retrieve a list of all graduates with a computer science degree, between 1990 and 2000. They need it by the end of the day and if I don't have it, I may not have this job for long. You willing to help out a guy in trouble?" Helping people out was part of what this database administrator did, so he was extra patient as he talked Michael step by step through the process.

By the time they hung up, Michael had downloaded the entire list of computer science graduates for those years. Within a few minutes he had run a search, located two Michael Parkers, chosen one of them, and obtained the guy's social security number as well as other pertinent information stored in the database.

He had just become "Michael Parker, B.S. in Computer Science, graduated with honors, 1998." In this case, the "B.S." was uniquely appropriate.

Analyzing the Con

This attack used one ruse I haven't talked about before: The attacker asking the organization's database administrator to walk him through the steps of carrying out a computer process he didn't know how to do. A powerful and effective turning of the tables, this is the equivalent of asking the owner of a store to help you carry a box containing items you've just stolen from his shelves out to your car.

Computer users are sometimes clueless about the threats and vulnerabilities associated with social engineering that exist in our world of technology. They have access to information, yet lack the detailed knowledge of what might prove to be a security threat. A social engineer will target an employee who has little understanding of how valuable the information being sought is, so the target is more likely to grant the stranger's request.

PREVENTING THE CON

Sympathy, guilt, and intimidation are three very popular psychological triggers used by the social engineer, and these stories have demonstrated the tactics in action. But what can you and your company do to avoid these types of attacks?

Protecting Data

Some stories in this chapter emphasize the danger of sending a file to someone you don't know, even when that person is (or appears to be) an employee, and the file is being sent *internally*, to an email address or fax machine within the company.

Company security policy needs to be very specific about the safeguards for surrendering valued data to anyone not personally known to the sender. Exacting procedures need to be established for transferring files with sensitive information. When the request is from someone not personally known, there must be clear steps to take for verification, with different levels of authentication depending on the sensitivity of the information.

Here are some techniques to consider:

- Establish the need to know (which may require obtaining authorization from the designated information owner).
- Keep a personal or departmental log of these transactions.
- Maintain a list of people who have been specially trained in the procedures and who are trusted to authorize sending out sensitive information. Require that only these people be allowed to send information to anyone outside the workgroup.
- If a request for the data is made in writing (email, fax, or mail) take additional security steps to verify that the request actually came from the person it appears to have come from.

About Passwords

All employees who are able to access any sensitive information—and today that means virtually every worker who uses a computer—need to understand that simple acts like changing your password, even for a few moments, can lead to a major security breach.

Security training needs to cover the topic of passwords, and that has to focus in part on when and how to change your password, what constitutes an acceptable password, and the hazards of letting anyone else become involved in the process. The training especially needs to convey to all employees that they should be suspicious of *any* request that involves their passwords.

On the surface this appears to be a simple message to get across to employees. It's not, because to appreciate this idea requires that employees grasp how a simple act like changing a password can lead to a security compromise. You can tell a child "Look both ways before crossing the street," but until the child understands why that's important, you're relying on blind obedience. And rules requiring blind obedience are typically ignored or forgotten.

> **note**
>
> Passwords are such a central focus of social engineering attacks that we devote a separate section to the topic in Chapter 16, where you will find specific recommended policies on managing passwords.

A Central Reporting Point

Your security policy should provide a person or group designated as a central point for reporting suspicious activities that appear to be attempts to infiltrate your organization. All employees need to know who to call any time they suspect an attempt at electronic or physical intrusion. The phone number of the place to make these reports should always be close at hand so employees don't have to dig for it if they become suspicious that an attack is taking place.

Protect Your Network

Employees need to understand that the name of a computer server or network is not trivial information, but rather it can give an attacker essential knowledge that helps him gain trust or find the location of the information he desires.

In particular, people such as database administrators who work with software belong to that category of those with technology expertise, and they need to operate under special and very restrictive rules about verifying the identity of people who call them for information or advice.

People who regularly provide any kind of computer help need to be well trained in what kinds of requests should be red flags, suggesting that the caller may be attempting a social engineering attack.

It's worth noting, though, that from the perspective of the database administrator in the last story in this chapter, the caller met the criteria for being legitimate: He was calling from on campus, and he was obviously on a site that required an account name and password. This just makes clear once again the importance of having standardized procedures for verifying the identity of anybody requesting information, especially in a case like this where the caller was asking for help in obtaining access to confidential records.

All of this advice goes double for colleges and universities. It's not news that computer hacking is a favorite pastime for many college students, and it should also be no surprise that student records—and sometimes faculty records, as well—are a tempting target. This abuse is so rampant that some corporations actually consider campuses a hostile environment, and create firewall rules that block access from educational institutions with addresses that end in *.edu*.

The long and short of it is that all student and personnel records of any kind should be seen as prime targets of attack, and should be well protected as sensitive information.

Training Tips

Most social engineering attacks are ridiculously easy to defend against . . . for anyone who knows what to be on the lookout for.

From the corporate perspective, there is a fundamental need for good training. But there is also a need for something else: a variety of ways to *remind* people of what they've learned.

Use splash screens that appear when the user's computer is turned on, with a different security message each day. The message should be designed so that it does not disappear automatically, but requires the user to click on some kind of acknowledgement that he/she has read it.

Another approach I recommend is to start a series of security reminders. Frequent reminder messages are important; an awareness program needs to be ongoing and never-ending. In delivering content, the reminders should not be worded the same in every instance. Studies have shown that these messages are more effectively received when they vary in wording or when used in different examples.

One excellent approach is to use short blurbs in the company newsletter. This should not be a full column on the subject, although a security column would certainly be valuable. Instead, design a two- or three-column-wide insert, something like a small display ad in your local newspaper. In each issue of the newsletter, present a new security reminder in this short, attention-catching way.

•••••••●●●●●●••••••

chapter 9

The Reverse Sting

the *Sting*, mentioned elsewhere in this book (and in my opinion probably the best movie that's ever been made about a con operation), lays out its tricky plot in fascinating detail. The sting operation in the movie is an exact depiction of how top grifters run "the wire," one of the three types of major swindles referred to as "big cons." If you want to know how a team of professionals pulls off a scam raking in a great deal of money in a single evening, there's no better textbook.

But traditional cons, whatever their particular gimmick, run according to a pattern. Sometimes a ruse is worked in the opposite direction, which is called a *reverse sting*. This is an intriguing twist in which the attacker sets up the situation so that the victim calls on the *attacker* for help, or a coworker has made a request, which the attacker is responding to.

How does this work? You're about to find out.

THE ART OF FRIENDLY PERSUASION
When the average person conjures up the picture of a computer hacker, what usually comes to mind is the uncomplimentary image of a lonely, introverted nerd whose best friend is his computer and who has difficulty carrying on a conversation, except by instant messaging. The social engineer, who often has hacker skills, also has people skills at the opposite end

lingo

REVERSE STING A con in which the person being attacked asks the attacker for help.

of the spectrum—well-developed abilities to use and manipulate people that allow him to talk his way into getting information in ways you would never have believed possible.

Angela's Caller

Place: Valley branch, Industrial Federal Bank.
Time: 11:27 A.M.

Angela Wisnowski answered a phone call from a man who said he was just about to receive a sizeable inheritance and he wanted information on the different types of savings accounts, certificates of deposit, and whatever other investments she might be able to suggest that would be safe, but earn decent interest. She explained there were quite a number of choices and asked if he'd like to come in and sit down with her to discuss them. He was leaving on a trip as soon as the money arrived, he said, and had a lot of arrangements to make. So she began suggesting some of the possibilities and giving him details of the interest rates, what happens if you sell a CD early, and so on, while trying to pin down his investment goals.

She seemed to be making progress when he said, "Oh, sorry, I've got to take this other call. What time can I finish this conversation with you so I can make some decisions? When do you leave for lunch?" She told him 12:30 and he said he'd try to call back before then or the following day.

Louis's Caller

Major banks use internal security codes that change every day. When somebody from one branch needs information from another branch, he proves he's entitled to the information by demonstrating he knows the day's code. For an added degree of security and flexibility, some major banks issue multiple codes each day. At a West Coast outfit I'll call Industrial Federal Bank, each employee finds a list of five codes for the day, identified as A through E, on his or her computer each morning.

•••••••●●●●●●•••••••

Place: Same.
Time: 12:48 P.M., same day.

Louis Halpburn didn't think anything of it when a call came in that afternoon, a call like others he handled regularly several times a week.

"Hello," the caller said. "This is Neil Webster. I'm calling from branch 3182 in Boston. Angela Wisnowski, please."

"She's at lunch. Can I help?"

"Well, she left a message asking us to fax some information on one of our customers."

The caller sounded like he had been having a bad day.

"The person who normally handles those requests is out sick," he said. "I've got a stack of these to do, it's almost 4 o'clock here and I'm supposed to be out of this place to go to a doctor's appointment in half an hour."

The manipulation—giving all the reasons why the other person should feel sorry for him—was part of softening up the mark. He went on, "Whoever took her phone message, the fax number is unreadable. It's 213-something. What's the rest?"

Louis gave the fax number, and the caller said, "Okay, thanks. Before I can fax this, I need to ask you for Code B."

"But you called me," he said with just enough chill so the man from Boston would get the message.

This is good, the caller thought. *It's so cool when people don't fall over at the first gentle shove. If they don't resist a little, the job is too easy and I could start getting lazy.*

To Louis, he said, "I've got a branch manager that's just turned paranoid about getting verification before we send anything out, is all. But listen, if you don't need us to fax the information, it's okay. No need to verify."

"Look," Louis said, "Angela will be back in half an hour or so. I can have her call you back."

"I'll just tell her I couldn't send the information today because you wouldn't identify this as a legitimate request by giving me the code. If I'm not out sick tomorrow, I'll call her back then."

"Okay."

"The message says 'Urgent.' Never mind, without verification my hands are tied. You'll tell her I tried to send it but you wouldn't give the code, okay?"

Louis gave up under the pressure. An audible sigh of annoyance came winging its way down the phone line.

"Well," he said, "wait a minute; I have to go to my computer. Which code did you want?"

"B," the caller said.

He put the call on hold and then in a bit picked up the line again. "It's 3184."

"That's not the right code."

"Yes it is—B is 3184."

"I didn't say B, I said E."

"Oh, damn. Wait a minute."

Another pause while he again looked up the codes.

"E is 9697."

"9697—right. I'll have the fax on the way. Okay?"

"Sure. Thanks."

Walter's Caller

"Industrial Federal Bank, this is Walter."

"Hey, Walter, it's Bob Grabowski in Studio City, branch 38," the caller said. "I need you to pull a sig card on a customer account and fax it to me." The sig card, or signature card, has more than just the customer's signature on it; it also has identifying information, familiar items such as the social security number, date of birth, mother's maiden name, and sometimes even a driver's license number. Very handy to a social engineer.

"Sure thing. What's Code C?"

"Another teller is using my computer right now," the caller said. "But I just used B and E, and I remember those. Ask me one of those."

"Okay, what's E?"

"E is 9697."

A few minutes later, Walter faxed the sig card as requested.

Donna Plaice's Caller

"Hi, this is Mr. Anselmo."

"How can I help you today?"

"What's that 800 number I'm supposed to call when I want to see if a deposit has been credited yet?"

"You're a customer of the bank?"

"Yes, and I haven't used the number in a while and now I don't know where I wrote it down."

"The number is 800-555-8600."

"Okay, thanks."

Vince Capelli's Tale

The son of a Spokane street cop, Vince knew from an early age that he wasn't going to spend his life slaving long hours and risking his neck for minimum wage. His two main goals in life became getting out of Spokane, and going into business for himself. The laughter of his homies all through high school only fired him up all the more—they thought it was hilarious that he was so busted on starting his own business but had no idea what business it might be.

Secretly Vince knew they were right. The only thing he was good at was playing catcher on the high school baseball team. But not good enough to capture a college scholarship, no way good enough for professional baseball. So what business was he going to be able to start?

One thing the guys in Vince's group never quite figured out: Anything one of them had—a new switchblade knife, a nifty pair of warm gloves, a sexy new girlfriend—if Vince admired it, before long the item was his. He didn't steal it, or sneak behind anybody's back; he didn't have to. The guy who had it would give it up willingly, and then wonder afterward how it had happened. Even asking Vince wouldn't have gotten you anywhere: He didn't know himself. People just seemed to let him have whatever he wanted.

Vince Capelli was a social engineer from an early age, even though he had never heard the term.

His friends stopped laughing once they all had high school diplomas in hand. While the others slogged around town looking for jobs where you didn't have to say "Do you want fries with that?" Vince's dad sent him off to talk to an old cop pal who had left the force to start his own private investigation business in San Francisco. He quickly spotted Vince's talent for the work, and took him on.

That was six years ago. He hated the part about getting the goods on unfaithful spouses, which involved achingly dull hours of sitting and watching, but felt continually challenged by assignments to dig up asset information for attorneys trying to figure out if some miserable stiff was rich enough to be worth suing. These assignments gave him plenty of chances to use his wits.

Like the time he had to look into the bank accounts of a guy named Joe Markowitz. Joe had maybe worked a shady deal on a one-time friend of his, which friend now wanted to know, if he sued, was Markowitz flush enough that the friend might get some of his money back?

Vince's first step would be to find out at least one, but preferably two, of the bank's security codes for the day. That sounds like a nearly impossible challenge: What on earth would induce a bank employee to knock a chink in his own security system? Ask yourself—if you wanted to do this, would you have any idea of how to go about it?

For people like Vince, it's too easy.

··········●●●●●●●●●●●········

People trust you if you know the inside lingo of their job and their company. It's like showing you belong to their inner circle. It's like a secret handshake.

I didn't need much of that for a job like this. Definitely not brain surgery. All's I needed to get started was a branch number. When I dialed the Beacon Street office in Buffalo, the guy that answered sounded like a teller.

"This is Tim Ackerman," I said. Any name would do, he wasn't going to write it down. "What's the branch number there?"

"The phone number or the branch number?" he wanted to know, which was pretty stupid because I had just dialed the phone number, hadn't I?

"Branch number."

"3182," he said. Just like that. No, "Whad'ya wanna know for?" or anything. 'Cause it's not sensitive information, it's written on just about every piece of paper they use.

Step Two, call the branch where my target did his banking, get the name of one of their people, and find out when the person would be out for lunch. Angela. Leaves at 12:30. So far, so good.

Step Three, call back to the same branch during Angela's lunch break, say I'm calling from branch number such-and-such in Boston, Angela needs this information faxed, gimme a code for the day. This is the tricky part; it's where the rubber meets the road. If I was making up a test to be a social engineer, I'd put something like this on it, where your victim gets suspicious—for good reason—and you still stick in there until you break him down and get the information you need. You can't do that by reciting lines from a script or learning a routine, you got to be able to read your victim, catch his mood, play him like landing a fish where you let out a little line and reel in, let out and reel in. Until you get him in the net and flop him into the boat, splat!

So I landed him and had one of the codes for the day. A big step. With most banks, one is all they use, so I would've been home free. Industrial Federal Bank uses five, so having just one out of five is long odds. With two out of five, I'd have a much better chance of getting through the next act of this little drama. I love that part about "I didn't say B, I said E." When it works, it's beautiful. And it works most of the time.

Getting a third one would have been even better. I've actually managed to get three on a single call—"B," "D," and "E" sound so much alike that you can claim they misunderstood you again. But you have to be talking to somebody who's a real pushover. This man wasn't. I'd go with two.

The day codes would be my trump to get the signature card. I call, and the guy asks for a code. C he wants, and I've only got B and E. But it's not the end of the world. You gotta stay cool at a moment like this, sound confident, keep right on going. Real smooth, I played him with the one about, "Somebody's using my computer, ask me one of these others."

We're all employees of the same company, we're all in this together, make it easy on the guy—that's what you're hoping the victim is thinking at a moment like this. And he played it right by the script. He took one of the choices I offered, I gave him the right answer, he sent the fax of the sig card.

Almost home. One more call gave me the 800 number that customers use for the automated service where an electronic voice reads you off the information you ask for. From the sig card, I had all of my target's account numbers and his PIN number, because that bank used the first five or last four digits of the social security number. Pen in hand, I called the 800 number and after a few minutes of pushing buttons, I had the latest balance in all four of the guy's accounts, and just for good measure, his most recent deposits and withdrawals in each.

Everything my client had asked for and more. I always like to give a little extra for good measure. Keep the clients happy. After all, repeat business is what keeps an operation going, right?

Analyzing the Con

The key to this entire episode was obtaining the all-important day codes, and to do that the attacker, Vince, used several different techniques.

He began with a little verbal arm-twisting when Louis proved reluctant to give him a code. Louis was right to be suspicious—the codes are designed to be used in the opposite direction. He knew that in the usual flow of things, the unknown caller would be giving *him* a security code. This was the critical moment for Vince, the hinge on which the entire success of his effort depended.

In the face of Louis's suspicion, Vince simply laid it on with manipulation, using an appeal to sympathy ("going to the doctor"), and pressure ("I've got a stack to do, it's almost 4 o'clock"), and manipulation ("Tell her you wouldn't give me the code"). Cleverly, Vince didn't actually make a threat, he just implied one: If you don't give me the security code, I won't send the customer information that your coworker needs, and I'll tell her I would have sent it but you wouldn't cooperate.

Still, let's not be too hasty in blaming Louis. After all, the person on the phone knew (or at least *appeared* to know) that coworker Angela had requested a fax. The caller knew about the security codes, and knew they were identified by letter designation. The caller said his branch manager was requiring it for greater security. There didn't really seem any reason not to give him the verification he was asking for.

Louis isn't alone. Bank employees give up security codes to social engineers every day. Incredible but true.

There's a line in the sand where a private investigator's techniques stop being legal and start being illegal. Vince stayed legal when he obtained the branch number. He even stayed legal when he conned Louis into giving him two of the day's security codes. He crossed the line when he had confidential information on a bank customer faxed to him.

But for Vince and his employer, it's a low-risk crime. When you steal money or goods, somebody will notice it's gone. When you steal information, most of the time no one will notice because the information is still in their possession.

mitnick message

> Verbal security codes are equivalent to passwords in providing a convenient and reliable means of protecting data. But employees need to be knowledgeable about the tricks that social engineers use, and trained not to give up the keys to the kingdom.

COPS AS DUPES

For a shady private investigator or social engineer, there are frequent occasions when it would be handy to know someone's driver's license number—for example, if you want to assume another person's identity in order to obtain information about her bank balances.

Short of lifting the person's wallet or peering over her shoulder at an opportune moment, finding out the driver's license number ought to be next to impossible. But for anyone with even modest social engineering skills, it's hardly a challenge.

One particular social engineer—Eric Mantini, I'll call him, needed to get driver's license and vehicle registration numbers on a regular basis. Eric figured it was unnecessarily increasing his risk to call the Department of Motor Vehicles (DMV) and go through the same ruse time after time whenever he needed that information. He wondered whether there wasn't some way to simplify the process.

Probably no one had ever thought of it before, but he figured out a way to get the information in a blink, whenever he wanted it. He did it by taking advantage of a service provided by his state's Department of Motor Vehicles. Many state DMVs (or whatever the department may be called in your state) make otherwise-privileged information about citizens available to insurance firms, private investigators, and certain other groups that the state legislature has deemed entitled to share it for the good of commerce and the society at large.

The DMV, of course, has appropriate limitations on which types of data will be given out. The insurance industry can get certain types of information from the files, but not others. A different set of limitations applies to PIs, and so on.

For law enforcement officers, a different rule generally applies: The DMV will supply any information in the records to any sworn peace officer who properly identifies himself. In the state Eric then lived in, the required identification was a Requestor Code issued by the DMV, along with the officer's driver's license number. The DMV employee would always verify by matching the officer's name against his driver's license number and one other piece of information—usually date of birth— before giving out any information.

What social engineer Eric wanted to do was nothing less than cloak himself in the identity of a law enforcement officer.

How did he manage that? By running a reverse sting on the cops!

Eric's Sting

First he called telephone information and asked for the phone number of DMV headquarters in the state capitol. He was given the number 503-555-5000; that, of course, is the number for calls from the general public. He then called a nearby sheriff's station and asked for Teletype—the office where communications are sent to and received from other law enforcement agencies, the national crime database, local warrants, and so forth. When he reached Teletype, he said he was looking for the phone number for law enforcement to use when calling the DMV state headquarters.

"Who are you?" the police officer in Teletype asked.

"This is Al. I was calling 503-555-5753," he said. This was partly an assumption, and partly a number he pulled out of thin air; certainly the special DMV office set up to take law enforcement calls would be in the same area code as the number given out for the public to call, and it was almost as certain that the next three digits, the prefix, would be the same, as well. All he really needed to find out was the last four.

A sheriff's Teletype room doesn't get calls from the public. And the caller already had most of the number. Obviously he was legitimate.

"It's 503-555-6127," the officer said.

So Eric now had the special phone number for law enforcement officers to call the DMV. But just the one number wasn't enough to satisfy him; the office would have a good many more than the single phone line, and Eric needed to know how many lines there were, and the phone number of each.

The Switch

To carry out his plan, he needed to gain access to the telephone switch that handled the law enforcement phone lines into DMV. He called the state Telecommunications Department and claimed he was from Nortel, the manufacturer of the DMS-100, one of the most widely used commercial telephone switches. He said, "Can you please transfer me to one of the switch technicians that works on the DMS-100?"

When he reached the technician, he claimed to be with the Nortel Technical Assistance Support Center in Texas, and explained that they were creating a master database to update all switches with the latest software upgrades. It would all be done remotely—no need for any switch technician to participate. But they needed the dial-in number to the switch so that they could perform the updates directly from the Support Center.

It sounded completely plausible, and the technician gave Eric the phone number. He could now dial directly into one of the state's telephone switches.

To defend against outside intruders, commercial switches of this type are password-protected, just like every corporate computer network. Any good social engineer with a phone-phreaking background knows that Nortel switches provide a default account name for software updates: NTAS (the abbreviation for Nortel Technical Assistance Support; not very subtle). But what about a password? Eric dialed in several times, each time trying one of the obvious and commonly used choices. Entering the same as the account name, NTAS, didn't work. Neither did "helper." Nor did "patch."

Then he tried "update" . . . and he was in. Typical. Using an obvious, easily guessed password is only very slightly better than having no password at all.

It helps to be up to speed in your field; Eric probably knew as much about that switch and how to program and troubleshoot it as the technician. Once he was able to access the switch as an authorized user, he would gain full control over the telephone lines that were his target. From his computer, he queried the switch for the phone number he had been given for law enforcement calls to the DMV, 555-6127. He found there were nineteen other phone lines into the same department. Obviously they handled a high volume of calls.

For each incoming call, the switch was programmed to "hunt" through the twenty lines until it found one that wasn't busy.

He picked line number eighteen in the sequence, and entered the code that added call forwarding to that line. For the call-forwarding number, he entered the phone number of his new, cheap, prepaid cell phone, the kind that drug dealers are so fond of because they're inexpensive enough to throw away after the job is over.

With call forwarding now activated on the eighteenth line, as soon as the office got busy enough to have seventeen calls in progress, the next call to come in would not ring in the DMV office but would instead be forwarded to Eric's cell phone. He sat back and waited.

A Call to DMV

Shortly before 8 o'clock that morning, the cell phone rang. This part was the best, the most delicious. Here was Eric, the social engineer, talking to a cop, someone with the authority to come and arrest him, or get a search warrant and conduct a raid to collect evidence against him.

And not just one cop would call, but a string of them, one after another. On one occasion, Eric was sitting in a restaurant having lunch with friends, fielding a call every five minutes or so, writing the information on a paper napkin using a borrowed pen. He still finds this hilarious.

But talking to police officers doesn't faze a good social engineer in the least. In fact, the thrill of deceiving these law enforcement agencies probably added to Eric's enjoyment of the act.

According to Eric, the calls went something like this:

"DMV, may I help you?"

"This is Detective Andrew Cole."

"Hi, detective. What can I do for you today?"

"I need a Soundex on driver's license 005602789," he might say, using the term familiar in law enforcement to ask for a photo—useful, for example, when officers are going out to arrest a suspect and want to know what he looks like.

"Sure, let me bring up the record," Eric would say. "And, Detective Cole, what's your agency?"

"Jefferson County." And then Eric would ask the hot questions: "Detective, what's your requestor code?" "What's your driver's license number?" "What's your date of birth?"

The caller would give his personal identifying information. Eric would go through some pretense of verifying the information, and then tell the caller that the identifying information had been confirmed, and ask for the details of what the caller wanted to find out from the DMV. He'd pretend to start looking up the name, with the caller able to hear the clicking of the keys, and then say something like, "Oh, damn, my computer just went down again. Sorry, detective, my computer has been on the blink all week. Would you mind calling back and getting another clerk to help you?"

This way he'd end the call tying up the loose ends without arousing any suspicion about why he wasn't able to assist the officer with his request. Meanwhile Eric had a stolen identity—details he could use to obtain confidential DMV information whenever he needed to.

After taking calls for a few hours and obtaining dozens of requestor codes, Eric dialed into the switch and deactivated the call forwarding.

For months after that, he'd carry on the assignments jobbed out to him by legitimate PI firms that didn't want to know how he was getting his information. Whenever he needed to, he'd dial back into the switch, turn on call forwarding, and gather another stack of police officer credentials.

Analyzing the Con

Let's run a playback on the ruses Eric pulled on a series of people to make this deceit work. In the first successful step, he got a sheriff's deputy in a Teletype room to give out a confidential DMV phone number to a complete stranger, accepting the man as a deputy without requesting any verification.

Then someone at the state Telecom Department did the same thing, accepting Eric's claim that he was with an equipment manufacturer, and providing the stranger with a phone number for dialing into the telephone switch serving the DMV.

Eric was able to get into the switch in large measure because of weak security practices on the part of the switch manufacturer in using the same account name on all their switches. That carelessness made it a walk in the park for the social engineer to guess the password, knowing once again that switch technicians, just like almost everybody else, choose passwords that will be a cinch for them to remember.

With access to the switch, he set up call forwarding from one of the DMV phone lines for law enforcement to his own cell phone.

And then, the capper and most blatant part, he conned one law enforcement officer after another into revealing not only their requestor codes but their own personal identifying information, giving Eric the ability to impersonate them.

While there was certainly technical knowledge required to pull off this stunt, it could not have worked without the help of a series of people who had no clue that they were talking to an imposter.

This story was another illustration of the phenomenon of why people don't ask "Why me?" Why would the Teletype officer give this information to some sheriff's deputy he didn't know—or, in this case, a stranger *passing himself off* as a sheriff's deputy—instead of suggesting he get the information from a fellow deputy or his own sergeant? Again, the only answer I can offer is that people rarely ask this question. It doesn't occur to them to ask? They don't want to sound challenging and unhelpful? Maybe. Any further explanation would just be guesswork. But social engineers don't care why; they only care that this little fact makes it easy to get information that otherwise might be a challenge to obtain.

mitnick
message

If you have a telephone switch at your company facilities, what would the person in charge do if he received a call from the vendor, asking for the dial-in number? And by the way, has that person ever changed the default password for the switch? Is that password an easy-to-guess word found in any dictionary?

PREVENTING THE CON

A security code, properly used, adds a valuable layer of protection. A security code improperly used can be worse than none at all because it gives the illusion of security where it doesn't really exist. What good are codes if your employees don't keep them secret?

Any company with a need for verbal security codes needs to spell out clearly for its employees when and how the codes are used. Properly trained, the character in the first story in this chapter would not have had to rely on his instincts, easily overcome, when asked to give a security code to a stranger. He sensed that he should not be asked for this information under the circumstances, but lacking a clear security policy—and good common sense—he readily gave in.

Security procedures should also set up steps to follow when an employee fields an inappropriate request for a security code. All employees should be trained to immediately report any request for authentication credentials, such as a daily code or password, made under suspicious circumstances. They should also report when an attempt to verify the identity of a requestor doesn't check out.

At the very least, the employee should record the caller's name, phone number, and office or department, and then hang up. Before calling back, he should verify that the organization really does have an employee of that name, and that the callback phone number matches the phone number in the on-line or hard-copy company directory. Most of the time, this simple tactic will be all that's needed to verify that the caller is who he says he is.

Verifying becomes a bit trickier when the company has a published phone directory instead of an on-line version. People get hired; people leave; people change departments, job positions, and phone numbers. The hard-copy directory is already out of date the day after it's published, even before being distributed. Even on-line directories can't always be relied on, because social engineers know how to modify them. If an employee can't verify the phone number from an independent source, she should be instructed to verify by some other means, such as contacting the employee's manager.

part 3

intruder
alert

chapter

10

Entering the Premises

Why is it so easy for an outsider to assume the identity of a company employee and carry off an impersonation so convincingly that even people who are highly security conscious are taken in? Why is it so easy to dupe individuals who may be fully aware of security procedures, suspicious of people they don't personally know, and protective of their company's interests?

Ponder these questions as you read the stories in this chapter.

THE EMBARRASSED SECURITY GUARD

Date/Time: Tuesday, October 17, 2:16 A.M.

Place: Skywatcher Aviation, Inc. manufacturing plant on the outskirts of Tucson, Arizona.

The Security Guard's Story

Hearing his leather heels click against the floor in the halls of the nearly deserted plant made Leroy Greene feel much better than spending the night hours of his watch in front of the video monitors in the security office. There he wasn't allowed to do anything but stare at the screens, not even read a magazine or his leather-bound Bible. You just had to sit there looking at the displays of still images where nothing ever moved.

But walking the halls, he was at least stretching his legs, and when he remembered to throw his arms and shoulders into the walk, it got him a little exercise, too. Although it didn't really count very much as exercise for a man who had played right tackle on the All-City champion high school football team. Still, he thought, a job is a job.

He turned the southwest corner and started along the gallery overlooking the half-mile-long production floor. He glanced down and saw two people walking past the line of partly built copters. The pair stopped and seemed to be pointing things out to each other. A strange sight at this time of night. "Better check," he thought.

Leroy headed for a staircase that would bring him onto the production-line floor behind the pair, and they didn't sense his approach until he stepped alongside. "Morning. Can I see your security badges, please," he said. Leroy always tried to keep his voice soft at moments like this; he knew that the sheer size of him could seem threatening.

"Hi, Leroy," one of them said, reading the name off his badge. "I'm Tom Stilton, from the Marketing office at corporate in Phoenix. I'm in town for meetings and wanted to show my friend here how the world's greatest helicopters get built."

"Yes, sir. Your badge, please," Leroy said. He couldn't help noticing how young they seemed. The Marketing guy looked barely out of high school, the other one had hair down to his shoulders and looked about fifteen.

The one with the haircut reached into his pocket for his badge, then started patting all his pockets. Leroy was suddenly beginning to have a bad feeling about this. "Damn," the guy said. "Must've left it in the car. I can get it—just take me ten minutes to go out to the parking lot and back."

Leroy had his pad out by this time. "What'd you say your name was, sir?" he asked, and carefully wrote down the response. Then he asked them to go with him to the Security Office. On the elevator to the third floor, Tom chatted about having been with the company for only six months and hoped he wasn't going to get in any trouble for this.

In the Security monitoring room, the two others on the night shift with Leroy joined him in questioning the pair. Stilton gave his telephone number, and said his boss was Judy Underwood and gave her telephone number, and the information all checked out on the computer. Leroy took the other two security people aside and they talked about what to do. Nobody wanted to get this wrong; all three agreed they better call the guy's boss even though it would mean waking her in the middle of the night.

Leroy called Mrs. Underwood himself, explained who he was and did she have a Mr. Tom Stilton working for her? She sounded like she was still half-asleep. "Yes," she said.

"Well, we found him down on the production line at 2:30 in the morning with no ID badge."

Mrs. Underwood said, "Let me talk to him."

Stilton got on the phone and said, "Judy, I'm really sorry about these guys waking you up in the middle of the night. I hope you're not going to hold this against me."

He listened and then said, "It was just that I had to be here in the morning anyway, for that meeting on the new press release. Anyway, did you get the email about the Thompson deal? We need to meet with Jim on Monday morning so we don't lose this. And I'm still having lunch with you on Tuesday, right?"

He listened a bit more and said good-bye and hung up.

That caught Leroy by surprise; he had thought he'd get the phone back so the lady could tell him everything was okay. He wondered if maybe he should call her again and ask, but thought better of it. He had already bothered her once in the middle of the night; if he called a second time, maybe she might get annoyed and complain to his boss. *"Why make waves?"* he thought.

"Okay if I show my friend the rest of the production line?" Stilton asked Leroy. "You want to come along, keep an eye on us?"

"Go on," Leroy said. "Look around. Just don't forget your badge next time. And let Security know if you need to be on the plant floor after hours—it's the rule."

"I'll remember that, Leroy," Stilton said. And they left.

Hardly ten minutes had gone by before the phone rang in the Security Office. Mrs. Underwood was on the line. "Who was that guy?!" she wanted to know. She said she kept trying to ask questions but he just kept on talking about having lunch with her and she doesn't know who the hell he is.

The security guys called the lobby and the guard at the gate to the parking lot. Both reported the two young men had left some minutes before.

Telling the story later, Leroy always finished by saying, "Lordy, did my boss chew me up one side and down the other. I'm lucky I still have a job."

Joe Harper's Story

Just to see what he could get away with, seventeen-year-old Joe Harper had been sneaking into buildings for more than a year, sometimes in the daytime, sometimes at night. The son of a musician and a cocktail waitress, both working the night shift, Joe had too much time by himself. His story of that same incident sheds instructive light on how it all happened.

●●●●●●●●●●●●

I have this friend Kenny who thinks he wants to be a helicopter pilot. He asked me, could I get him into the Skywatcher factory to see the production line where they make the choppers. He knows I've got into other places before. It's an adrenaline rush to see if you can slip into places you're not supposed to be.

But you don't just walk into a factory or office building. Got to think it through, do a lot of planning, and do a full reconnaissance on the target. Check the company's Web page for names and titles, reporting structure, and telephone numbers. Read press clippings and magazine articles. Meticulous research is my own brand of caution, so I could talk to anybody that challenged me, with as much knowledge as any employee.

So where to start? First I looked up on the Internet to see where the company had offices, and saw the corporate headquarters was in Phoenix. Perfect. I called and asked for Marketing; every company has a marketing department. A lady answered, and I said I was with Blue Pencil Graphics and we wanted to see if we could interest them in using our services and who would I talk to. She said that would be Tom Stilton. I asked for his phone number and she said they didn't give out that information but she could put me through. The call rang into voice mail, and his message said, "This is Tom Stilton in Graphics, extension 3147, please leave a message." Sure—they don't give out extensions, but this guy leaves his right on his voice mail. So that was cool. Now I had a name and extension.

Another call, back to the same office. "Hi, I was looking for Tom Stilton. He's not in. I'd like to ask his boss a quick question." The boss was out, too, but by the time I was finished, I knew the boss's name. And she had nicely left her extension number on her voice mail, too.

I could probably get us past the lobby guard with no sweat, but I've driven by that plant and I thought I remembered a fence around the parking lot. A fence means a guard who checks you when you try to drive in. And at night, they might be writing down license numbers, too, so I'd have to buy an old license plate at a flea market.

But first I'd have to get the phone number in the guard shack. I waited a little so if I got the same operator when I dialed back in, she wouldn't recognize my voice. After a bit I called and said, "We've got a complaint that the phone at the Ridge Road guard shack has reported intermittent problems—are they still having trouble?" She said she didn't know but would connect me.

The guy answered, "Ridge Road gate, this is Ryan." I said, "Hi, Ryan, this is Ben. Were you having problems with your phones there?" He's just a low-paid security guard but I guess he had some training because he right away said, "Ben who—what's your last name?" I just kept right on as if I hadn't even heard him. "Somebody reported a problem earlier."

I could hear him holding the phone away and calling out, "Hey, Bruce, Roger, was there a problem with this phone?" He came back on and said, "No, no problems we know about."

"How many phone lines do you have there?"

He had forgotten about my name. "Two," he said.

"Which one are you on now?"

"3140."

Gotcha! "And they're both working okay?"

"Seems like."

"Okay," I said. "Listen, Tom, if you have any phone problems, just call us in Telecom any time. We're here to help."

My buddy and I decided to visit the plant the very next night. Late that afternoon I called the guard booth, using the name of the Marketing guy. I said, "Hi, this is Tom Stilton in Graphics. We're on a crash deadline and I have a couple of guys driving into town to help out. Probably won't be here till one or two in the morning. Will you still be on then?"

He was happy to say that, no, he got off at midnight.

I said, "Well, just leave a note for the next guy, okay? When two guys show up and say they've come to see Tom Stilton, just wave 'em on in—okay?"

Yes, he said, that was fine. He took down my name, department, and extension number and said he'd take care of it.

We drove up to the gate a little after two, I gave Tom Stilton's name, and a sleepy guard just pointed to the door we should go in and where I should park.

When we walked into the building, there was another guard station in the lobby, with the usual book for after-hours sign-ins. I told the guard I had a report that needed to be ready in the morning, and this friend of mine wanted to see the plant. "He's crazy about helicopters," I said. "Thinks he wants to learn to pilot one." He asked me for my badge. I reached into a pocket, then patted around and said I must have left it in car; I'll go get it. I said, "It'll take about ten minutes." He said, "Never mind, it's okay, just sign in."

Walking down that production line—what a gas. Until that tree-trunk of a Leroy stopped us.

In the security office, I figured somebody who didn't really belong would look nervous and frightened. When things get tight, I just start sounding like I'm really steamed. Like I'm really who I claimed to be and it's annoying they don't believe me.

When they started talking about maybe they should call the lady I said was my boss and went to get her home phone number from the computer, I stood there thinking, "Good time to just make a break for it." But there was that parking-lot gate—even if we got out of the building, they'd close the gate and we'd never make it out.

When Leroy called the lady who was Stilton's boss and then gave me the phone, the lady started shouting at me "Who is this, who are you!" and I just kept on talking like we were having a nice conversation, and then hung up.

How long does it take to find somebody who can give you a company phone number in the middle of the night? I figured we had less than fifteen minutes to get out of there before that lady was ringing the security office and putting a bug in their ears.

We got out of there as fast as we could without looking like we were in a hurry. Sure was glad when the guy at the gate just waved us through.

Analyzing the Con

It's worth noting that in the real incident this story is based on, the intruders actually were teenagers. The intrusion was a lark, just to see if they could get away with it. But if it was so easy for a pair of teenagers, it would have been even easier for adult thieves, industrial spies, or terrorists.

How did three experienced security officers allow a pair of intruders to just walk away? And not just any intruders, but a pair so young that any reasonable person should have been very suspicious?

Leroy *was* appropriately suspicious, at first. He was correct in taking them to the Security Office, and in questioning the guy who called himself Tom Stilton and checking the names and phone numbers he gave. He was certainly correct in making the phone call to the supervisor.

But in the end he was taken in by the young man's air of confidence and indignation. It wasn't the behavior he would expect from a thief or intruder—only a real employee would have acted that way . . . or so he assumed. Leroy should have been trained to count on solid identification, not perceptions.

Why wasn't he more suspicious when the young man hung up the phone without handing it back so Leroy could hear the confirmation directly from Judy Underwood and receive her assurance that the kid had a reason for being in the plant so late at night?

Leroy was taken in by a ruse so bold that it should have been obvious. But consider the moment from his perspective: a high-school graduate, concerned for his job, uncertain whether he might get in trouble for bothering a company manager for the second time in the middle of the night. If you had been in his shoes, would you have made the follow-up call?

But of course, a second phone call wasn't the only possible action. What else could the security guard have done?

Even before placing the phone call, he could have asked both of the pair to show some kind of picture identification; they drove to the plant, so at least one of them should have a driver's license. The fact that they had originally given phony names would have been immediately obvious (a professional would have come equipped with fake ID, but these teenagers had not taken that precaution). In any case, Leroy should have examined their identification credentials and written down the information. If they both insisted they had no identification, he should then have walked them to the car to retrieve the company ID badge that "Tom Stilton" claimed he had left there.

Following the phone call, one of the security people should have stayed with the pair until they left the building. And then walked them to their

mitnick
message

Manipulative people usually have very attractive personalities. They are typically fast on their feet and quite articulate. Social engineers are also skilled at distracting people's thought processes so that they cooperate. To think that any one particular person is not vulnerable to this manipulation is to underestimate the skill and the killer instinct of the social engineer.

A good social engineer, on the other hand, never underestimates his adversary.

car and written down the license-plate number. If he had been observant enough, he would have noted that the plate (the one that the attacker had purchased at a flea market) did not have a valid registration sticker—and that should have been reason enough to detain the pair for further investigation.

DUMPSTER DIVING

Dumpster diving is a term that describes pawing through a target's garbage in search of valuable information. The amount of information you can learn about a target is astounding.

Most people don't give much thought to what they're discarding at home: phone bills, credit card statements, medical prescription bottles, bank statements, work-related materials, and so much more.

At work, employees must be made aware that people do look through trash to obtain information that may benefit them.

During my high school years, I used to go digging through the trash behind the local phone company buildings—often alone but occasionally with friends who shared an interest in learning more about the telephone company. Once you became a seasoned Dumpster diver, you learn a few tricks, such as how to make special efforts to avoid the bags from the restrooms, and the necessity of wearing gloves.

Dumpster diving isn't enjoyable, but the payoff was extraordinary—internal company telephone directories, computer manuals, employee lists, discarded printouts showing how to program switching equipment, and more—all there for the taking.

I'd schedule visits for nights when new manuals were being issued, because the trash containers would have plenty of old ones, thoughtlessly thrown away. And I'd go at other odd times as well, looking for any memos, letters, reports, and so forth, that might offer some interesting gems of information.

On arriving I'd find some cardboard boxes, pull them out and set them aside. If anyone challenged me, which happened now and then, I'd say

lingo

DUMPSTER DIVING   Going through a company's garbage (often in an outside and vulnerable Dumpster) to find discarded information that either itself has value, or provides a tool to use in a social engineering attack, such as internal phone numbers or titles.

that a friend was moving and I was just looking for boxes to help him pack. The guard never noticed all the documents I had put in the boxes to take home. In some cases, he'd tell me to get lost, so I'd just move to another phone company central office.

I don't know what it's like today, but back then it was easy to tell which bags might contain something of interest. The floor sweepings and cafeteria garbage were loose in the large bags, while the office wastebaskets were all lined with white disposable trash bags, which the cleaning crew would lift out one by one and wrap a tie around.

One time, while searching with some friends, we came up with some sheets of paper torn up by hand. And not just torn up: someone had gone to the trouble of ripping the sheets into tiny pieces, all conveniently thrown out in a single five-gallon trash bag. We took the bag to a local donut shop, dumped the pieces out on a table, and started assembling them one by one.

We were all puzzle-doers, so this offered the stimulating challenge of a giant jigsaw puzzle . . . but turned out to have more than a childish reward. When done, we had pieced together the entire account name and password list for one of the company's critical computer systems.

Were our Dumpster-diving exploits worth the risk and the effort? You bet they were. Even more than you would think, because the risk is zero. It was true then and still true today: As long as you're not trespassing, poring through someone else's trash is 100 percent legal.

Of course, phone phreaks and hackers aren't the only ones with their heads in trash cans. Police departments around the country paw through trash regularly, and a parade of people from Mafia dons to petty embezzlers have been convicted based in part on evidence gathered from their rubbish. Intelligence agencies, including our own, have resorted to this method for years.

It may be a tactic too low down for James Bond—movie-goers would much rather watch him outfoxing the villain and bedding a beauty than standing up to his knees in garbage. Real-life spies are less squeamish when something of value may be bagged among the banana peels and coffee grounds, the newspapers and grocery lists. Especially if gathering the information doesn't put them in harm's way.

Cash for Trash

Corporations play the Dumpster-diving game, too. Newspapers had a field day in June 2000, reporting that Oracle Corporation (whose CEO,

Larry Ellison, is probably the nation's most outspoken foe of Microsoft) had hired an investigative firm that had been caught with their hands in the cookie jar. It seems the investigators wanted trash from a Microsoft-supported lobbying outfit, ACT, but they didn't want to risk getting caught. According to press reports, the investigative firm sent in a woman who offered the janitors $60 to let her have the ACT trash. They turned her down. She was back the next night, upping the offer to $500 for the cleaners and $200 for the supervisor.

The janitors turned her down and then turned her in.

Leading on-line journalist Declan McCullah, taking a leaf from literature, titled his *Wired News* story on the episode, "'Twas Oracle That Spied on MS." *Time* magazine, nailing Oracle's Ellison, titled their article simply "Peeping Larry."

Analyzing the Con

Based on my own experience and the experience of Oracle, you might wonder why anybody would bother taking the risk of stealing someone's trash.

The answer, I think, is that the risk is nil and the benefits can be substantial. Okay, maybe trying to bribe the janitors increases the chance of consequences, but for anyone who's willing to get a little dirty, bribes aren't necessary.

For a social engineer, Dumpster diving has its benefits. He can get enough information to guide his assault against the target company, including memos, meeting agendas, letters and the like that reveal names, departments, titles, phone numbers, and project assignments. Trash can yield company organizational charts, information about corporate structure, travel schedules, and so on. All those details might seem trivial to insiders, yet they may be highly valuable information to an attacker.

Mark Joseph Edwards, in his book *Internet Security with Windows NT*, talks about "entire reports discarded because of typos, passwords written on scraps of paper, 'While you were out' messages with phone numbers, whole file folders with documents still in them, diskettes and tapes that weren't erased or destroyed—all of which could help a would-be intruder."

The writer goes on to ask, "And who are those people on your cleaning crew? You've decided that the cleaning crew won't [be permitted to] enter the computer room but don't forget the other trash cans. If federal agencies deem it necessary to do background checks on people who have access to their wastebaskets and shredders, you probably should as well."

Your trash may be your enemy's treasure. We don't give much consideration to the materials we discard in our personal lives, so why should we believe people have a different attitude in the workplace? It all comes down to educating the workforce about the danger (unscrupulous people digging for valuable information) and the vulnerability (sensitive information not being shredded or properly erased).

THE HUMILIATED BOSS

Nobody thought anything about it when Harlan Fortis came to work on Monday morning as usual at the County Highway Department, and said he'd left home in a hurry and forgotten his badge. The security guard had seen Harlan coming in and going out every weekday for the two years she had been working there. She had him sign for a temporary employee's badge, gave it to him, and he went on his way.

It wasn't until two days later that all hell started breaking loose. The story spread through the entire department like wildfire. Half the people who heard it said it couldn't be true. Of the rest, nobody seemed to know whether to laugh out loud or to feel sorry for the poor soul.

After all, George Adamson was a kind and compassionate person, the best head of department they'd ever had. He didn't deserve to have this happen to him. Assuming that the story was true, of course.

The trouble had begun when George called Harlan into his office late one Friday and told him, as gently as he could, that come Monday Harlan would be reporting to a new job. With the Sanitation Department. To Harlan, this wasn't like being fired. It was worse; it was humiliating. He wasn't going to take it lying down.

That same evening he seated himself on his porch to watch the homeward-bound traffic. At last he spotted the neighborhood boy named David who everyone called "The War Games Kid" going by on his moped on the way home from high school. He stopped David, gave him a Code Red Mountain Dew he had bought especially for the purpose, and offered him a deal: the latest video game player and six games in exchange for some computer help and a promise of keeping his mouth shut.

After Harlan explained the project—without giving any of the compromising specifics—David agreed. He described what he wanted Harlan to do. He was to buy a modem, go into the office, find somebody's computer where there was a spare phone jack nearby, and plug in the modem. Leave the modem under the desk where nobody would be likely to see it. Then came the risky part. Harlan had to sit down at the computer, install a remote-access software package, and get it running. Any moment the man who worked in the office might show up, or someone might walk by and see him in another person's office. He was so uptight that he could hardly read the instructions that the kid had written down for him. But he got it done, and slipped out of the building without being noticed.

Planting the Bomb

David stopped over after dinner that night. The two sat down at Harlan's computer and within in a few minutes the boy had dialed into the modem, gained access, and reached George Adamson's machine. Not very difficult, since George never had time for precautionary things like changing passwords, and was forever asking this person or that to download or email a file for him. In time, everyone in the office knew his password.

A bit of hunting turned up the file called BudgetSlides2002.ppt, which the boy downloaded onto Harlan's computer. Harlan then told the kid to go on home, and come back in a couple of hours.

When David returned, Harlan asked him to reconnect to the Highway Department computer system and put the same file back where they had found it, overwriting the earlier version. Harlan showed David the video game player, and promised that if things went well, he'd have it the next day.

Surprising George

You wouldn't think that something sounding as dull as budget hearings would be of much interest to anyone, but the meeting chamber of the County Council was packed, filled with reporters, representatives of special interest groups, members of the public, and even two television news crews.

George always felt much was at stake for him in these sessions. The County Council held the purse strings, and unless George could put on a convincing presentation, the Highways budget would be slashed. Then everyone would start complaining about potholes and stuck traffic lights and dangerous intersections, and blaming him, and life would be miserable for the whole coming year. But when he was introduced that evening, he stood up feeling confident. He had worked six weeks on this presentation and the PowerPoint visuals, which he had tried out on his wife, his top staff people, and some respected friends. Everyone agreed it was his best presentation ever.

The first three PowerPoint images played well. For a change, every Council member was paying attention. He was making his points effectively.

And then all at once everything started going wrong. The fourth image was supposed to be a beautiful photo at sunset of the new highway extension opened last year. Instead it was something else, something very embarrassing. A photograph out of a magazine like *Penthouse* or *Hustler*. He could hear the audience gasp as he hurriedly hit the button on his laptop to move to the next image.

This one was worse. Not a thing was left to the imagination.

He was still trying to click to another image when someone in the audience pulled out the power plug to the projector while the chairman banged loudly with his gavel and shouted above the din that the meeting was adjourned.

Analyzing the Con

Using a teenage hacker's expertise, a disgruntled employee managed to access the computer of the head of his department, download an important PowerPoint presentation, and replace some of the slides with images certain to cause grave embarrassment. Then he put the presentation back on the man's computer.

With the modem plugged into a jack and connected to one of the office computers, the young hacker was able to dial in from the outside. The kid had set up the remote access software in advance so that, once connected to the computer, he would have full access to every file stored on the entire system. Since the computer was connected to the organization's network and he already knew the boss's username and password, he could easily gain access to the boss's files.

Including the time to scan in the magazine images, the entire effort had taken only a few hours. The resulting damage to a good man's reputation was beyond imagining.

mitnick
message

The vast majority of employees who are transferred, fired, or let go in a down-sizing are never a problem. Yet it only takes one to make a company realize too late what steps they could have taken to prevent disaster.

Experience and statistics have clearly shown that the greatest threat to the enterprise is from *insiders*. It's the insiders who have intimate knowledge of where the valuable information resides, and where to hit the company to cause the most harm.

THE PROMOTION SEEKER

Late in the morning of a pleasant autumn day, Peter Milton walked into the lobby of the Denver regional offices of Honorable Auto Parts, a national parts wholesaler for the automobile aftermarket. He waited at the reception desk while the young lady signed in a visitor, gave driving directions to a caller, and dealt with the UPS man, all more or less at the same time.

"So how did you learn to do so many things at once?" Pete said when she had time to help him. She smiled, obviously pleased he had noticed. He was from Marketing in the Dallas office, he told her, and said that Mike Talbott from Atlanta field sales was going to be meeting him. "We have a client to visit together this afternoon," he explained. "I'll just wait here in the lobby."

"Marketing." She said the word almost wistfully, and Pete smiled at her, waiting to hear what was coming. "If I could go to college, that's what I'd take," she said. "I'd love to work in Marketing."

He smiled again. "Kaila," he said, reading her name off the sign on the counter, "We have a lady in the Dallas office who was a secretary. She got herself moved over to Marketing. That was three years ago, and now she's an assistant marketing manager, making twice what she was."

Kaila looked starry-eyed. He went on, "Can you use a computer?"

"Sure," she said.

"How would you like me to put your name in for a secretary's job in Marketing?"

She beamed. "For that I'd even move to Dallas."

"You're going to love Dallas," he said. "I can't promise an opening right away, but I'll see what I can do."

She thought that this nice man in the suit and tie and with the neatly trimmed, well-combed hair might make a big difference in her working life.

Pete sat down across the lobby, opened his laptop, and started getting some work done. After ten or fifteen minutes, he stepped back up to the counter. "Listen," he said, "it looks like Mike must've been held up. Is there a conference room where I could sit and check my emails while I'm waiting?"

Kaila called the man who coordinated the conference room scheduling and arranged for Pete to use one that wasn't booked. Following a pattern picked up from Silicon Valley companies (Apple was probably the first to do this) some of the conference rooms were named after cartoon characters, others after restaurant chains or movie stars or comic book heroes. He was told to look for the Minnie Mouse room. She had him sign in, and gave him directions to find Minnie Mouse.

He located the room, settled in, and connected his laptop to the Ethernet port.

Do you get the picture yet?

Right—the intruder had connected to the network *behind the corporate firewall.*

Anthony's Story

I guess you could call Anthony Lake a lazy businessman. Or maybe "bent" comes closer.

Instead of working for other people, he had decided he wanted to go to work for himself; he wanted to open a store, where he could be at one place all day and not have to run all over the countryside. Only he wanted to have a business that he could be as sure as possible he could make money at.

What kind of store? That didn't take long to figure out. He knew about repairing cars, so an auto parts store.

And how do you build in a guarantee of success? The answer came to him in a flash: convince auto parts wholesaler Honorable Auto Parts to sell him all the merchandise he needed at their cost.

Naturally they wouldn't do this willingly. But Anthony knew how to con people, his friend Mickey knew about breaking into other people's computers, and together they worked out a clever plan.

That autumn day he convincingly passed himself off as an employee named Peter Milton, and he had conned his way inside the Honorable Auto Parts offices and had already plugged his laptop into their network. So far, so good, but that was only the first step. What he still had to do wouldn't be easy, especially since Anthony had set himself a fifteen-minute time limit—any longer and he figured that the risk of discovery would be too high.

In an earlier phone call pretexting as a support person from their computer supplier, he had put on a song-and-dance act. "Your company has purchased a two-year support plan and we're putting you in the database so we can know when a software program you're using has come out with a patch or a new updated version. So I need to have you tell me what

> Train your people not to judge a book solely by its cover—just because someone
> is well-dressed and well-groomed he shouldn't be any more believable.

applications you're using." The response gave him a list of programs, and an accountant friend identified the one called MAS 90 as the target—the program that would hold their list of vendors and the discount and payment terms for each.

With that key knowledge, he next used a software program to identify all the working hosts on the network, and it didn't take him long to locate the correct server used by the Accounting department. From the arsenal of hacker tools on his laptop, he launched one program and used it to identify all of the authorized users on the target server. With another, he then ran a list of commonly used passwords, such as "blank," and "password" itself. "Password" worked. No surprise there. People just lose all creativity when it comes to choosing passwords.

Only six minutes gone, and the game was half over. He was in.

Another three minutes to very carefully add his new company, address, phone number, and contact name to the list of customers. And then for the crucial entry, the one that would make all the difference, the entry that said all items were to be sold to him at 1 percent over Honorable Auto Parts' cost.

In slightly under ten minutes, he was done. He stopped long enough to tell Kaila thanks, he was through checking his emails. And he had reached Mike Talbot, change of plans, he was on the way to a meeting at a client's office. And he wouldn't forget about recommending her for that job in Marketing, either.

Analyzing the Con

The intruder who called himself Peter Milton used two psychological subversion techniques—one planned, the other improvised on the spur of the moment.

He dressed like a management worker earning good money. Suit and tie, hair carefully styled—these seem like small details, but they make an impression. I discovered this myself, inadvertently. In a short time as a programmer at GTE California—a major telephone company no longer in existence—I discovered that if I came in one day without a badge, neatly dressed but casual—say, sports shirt, chinos, and Dockers—I'd be stopped and questioned. Where's your badge, who are you, where do you work? Another day I'd arrive, still without a badge but in a suit and tie, looking very corporate. I'd use a variation of the age-old piggy-backing technique, blending in with a crowd of people as they walk into a building or a secure entrance. I would latch onto some people as they approached the main entrance, and walk in chatting with the crowd as if I was one of them. I walked past, and even if the guards noticed I was badgeless, they wouldn't bother me because I looked like management and I was with people who *were* wearing badges.

From this experience, I recognized how predictable the behavior of security guards is. Like the rest of us, they were making judgments based on appearances—a serious vulnerability that social engineers learn to take advantage of.

The attacker's second psychological weapon came into play when he noticed the unusual effort that the receptionist was making. Handling several things at once, she didn't get testy but managed to make everyone feel they had her full attention. He took this as the mark of someone interested in getting ahead, in proving herself. And then when he claimed to work in the Marketing department, he watched to see her reaction, looking for clues to indicate if he was establishing a rapport with her. He was. To the attacker, this added up to someone he could manipulate through a promise of trying to help her move into a better job. (Of course, if she had said she wanted to go into the Accounting department, he would have claimed he had contacts for getting her a job there, instead.)

Intruders are also fond of another psychological weapon used in this story: building trust with a two-stage attack. He first used that chatty conversation about the job in Marketing, and he also used "name-dropping"—giving the name of another employee—a real person, incidentally, just as the name he himself used was the name of a real employee.

He could have followed up the opening conversation right away with a request to get into a conference room. But instead he sat down for a while and pretended to work, supposedly waiting for his associate, another way of allaying any possible suspicions because an intruder wouldn't hang around. He didn't hang around for very long, though; social engineers know better than to stay at the scene of the crime any longer than necessary.

Just for the record: By the laws on the books at the time of this writing, Anthony had not committed a crime when he entered the lobby. He had not committed a crime when he used the name of a real employee. He had

> Allowing a stranger into an area where he can plug a laptop into the corporate network increases the risk of a security incident. It's perfectly reasonable for an employee, especially one from offsite, to want to check his or her email from a conference room, but unless the visitor is established as a trusted employee or the network is segmented to prevent unauthorized connections, this may be the weak link that allows company files to be compromised.

not committed a crime when he talked his way into the conference room. He had not committed a crime when he plugged into the company's network and searched for the target computer.

Not until he actually broke in to the computer system did he break the law.

SNOOPING ON KEVIN

Many years ago when I was working in a small business, I began to notice that each time I walked into the office that I shared with the three other computer people who made up the IT department, this one particular guy (Joe, I'll call him here) would quickly toggle the display on his computer to a different window. I immediately recognized this as suspicious. When it happened two more times the same day, I was sure something was going on that I should know about. What was this guy up to that he didn't want me to see?

Joe's computer acted as a terminal to access the company's minicomputers, so I installed a monitoring program on the VAX minicomputer that allowed me to spy on what he was doing. The program acted as if a TV camera was looking over his shoulder, showing me exactly what he was seeing on his computer.

My desk was next to Joe's; I turned my monitor as best I could to partly mask his view, but he could have looked over at any moment and realized I was spying on him. Not a problem; he was too enthralled in what he was doing to notice.

What I saw made my jaw drop. I watched, fascinated, as the bastard called up *my* payroll data. He was looking up my salary!

I had only been there a few months at the time and I guessed Joe couldn't stand the idea that I might have been making more than he was.

A few minutes later I saw that he was downloading hacker tools used by less experienced hackers who don't know enough about programming to devise the tools for themselves. So Joe was clueless, and had no idea that one of American's most experienced hackers was sitting right next to him. I thought it was hilarious.

He already had the information about my pay; so it was too late to stop him. Besides, any employee with computer access at the IRS or the Social Security Administration can look your salary up. I sure didn't want to tip my hand by letting him know I'd found out what he was up to. My main goal at the time was maintaining a low profile, and a good social engineer doesn't advertise his abilities and knowledge. You always want people to underestimate you, not see you as a threat.

So I let it go, and laughed to myself that Joe thought he knew some secret about me, when it was the other way around: I had the upper hand by knowing what he had been up to.

In time I discovered that all three of my coworkers in the IT group amused themselves by looking up the take-home pay of this or that cute secretary or (for the one girl in the group) neat-looking guy they had spotted. And they were all finding out the salary and bonuses of anybody at the company they were curious about, including senior management.

Analyzing the Con

This story illustrates an interesting problem. The payroll files were accessible to the people who had the responsibility of maintaining the company's computer systems. So it all comes down to a personnel issue: deciding who can be trusted. In some cases, IT staff might find it irresistible to snoop around. And they have the ability to do so because they have privileges allowing them to bypass access controls on those files.

One safeguard would be to audit any access to particularly sensitive files, such as payroll. Of course, anyone with the requisite privileges could disable auditing or possibly remove any entries that would point back to them, but each additional step takes more effort to hide on the part of an unscrupulous employee.

PREVENTING THE CON

From pawing through your trash to duping a security guard or receptionist, social engineers can physically invade your corporate space. But you'll be glad to hear that there are preventive measures you can take.

Protection After Hours

All employees who arrive for work without their badges should be required to stop at the lobby desk or security office to obtain a temporary badge for the day. The incident in the first story of this chapter could have come to a much different conclusion if the company security guards had had a specific set of steps to follow when encountering anyone without the required employee badge.

For companies or areas within a company where security is not a high-level concern, it may not be important to insist that every person have a badge visible at all times. But in companies with sensitive areas, this should be a standard requirement, rigidly enforced. Employees must be trained and motivated to challenge people who do not display a badge, and higher-level employees must be taught to accept such challenges without causing embarrassment to the person who stops them.

Company policy should advise employees of the penalties for those who consistently fail to wear their badges; penalties might include sending the employee home for the day without pay, or a notation in his personnel file. Some companies institute a series of progressively more stringent penalties that may include reporting the problem to the person's manager, then issuing a formal warning.

In addition, where there is sensitive information to protect, the company should establish procedures for authorizing people who need to visit during non-business hours. One solution: require that arrangements be made through corporate security or some other designated group. This group would routinely verify the identity of any employee calling to arrange an off-hours visit by a callback to the person's supervisor or some other reasonably secure method.

Treating Trash with Respect

The Dumpster-diving story dug into the potential misuses of your corporate trash. The eight keys to wisdom regarding trash:

- Classify all sensitive information based on the degree of sensitivity.
- Establish company-wide procedures for discarding sensitive information.

- Insist that all sensitive information to be discarded first be shredded, and provide for a safe way for getting rid of important information on scraps of paper too small for shredding. Shredders must not be the low-end budget type, which turn out strips of paper that a determined attacker, given enough patience, can reassemble. Instead, they need to be the kind called cross-shredders, or those that render the output into useless pulp.

- Provide a way for rendering unusable or *completely* erasing computer media—floppy disks, Zip disks, CDs and DVDs used for storing files, removable tapes, old hard drives, and other computer media—before they are discarded. Remember that deleting files does *not* actually remove them; they can still be recovered—as Enron executives and many others have learned to their dismay. Merely dropping computer media in the trash is an invitation to your local friendly Dumpster diver. (See Chapter 16 for specific guidelines on disposal of media and devices.)

- Maintain an appropriate level of control over the selection of people on your cleaning crews, using background checks if appropriate.

- Remind employees periodically to think about the nature of the materials they are tossing into the trash.

- Lock trash Dumpsters.

- Use separate disposal containers for sensitive materials, and contract to have the materials disposed of by a bonded company that specializes in this work.

Saying Good-Bye to Employees

The point has been made earlier in these pages about the need for iron-clad procedures when a departing employee has had access to sensitive information, passwords, dial-in numbers, and the like. Your security procedures need to provide a way to keep track of who has authorization to various systems. It may be tough to keep a determined social engineer from slipping past your security barriers, but don't make it easy for an ex-employee.

Another step easily overlooked: When an employee who was authorized to retrieve backup tapes from storage leaves, a written policy must call for the storage company to be immediately notified to remove her name from its authorization list.

Chapter 16 of this book provides detailed information on this vital subject, but it will be helpful to list here some of the key security provisions that should be in place, as highlighted by this story:

- A complete and thorough checklist of steps to be taken upon the departure of an employee, with special provisions for workers who had access to sensitive data.

- A policy of terminating the employee's computer access *immediately*—preferably before the person has even left the building.

- A procedure to recover the person's ID badge, as well as any keys or electronic access devices.

- Provisions that require security guards to see photo ID before admitting any employee who does not have his or her security pass, and for checking the name against a list to verify that the person is still employed by the organization.

Some further steps will seem excessive or too expensive for some companies, but they are appropriate to others. Among these more stringent security measures are:

- Electronic ID badges combined with scanners at entrances; each employee swipes his badge through the scanner for an instantaneous electronic determination that the person is still a current employee and entitled to enter the building. (Note, however, that security guards must still be trained to be on the alert for piggybacking—an unauthorized person slipping by in the wake of a legitimate employee.)

- A requirement that all employees in the same workgroup as the person leaving (especially if the person is being fired) change their passwords. (Does this seem extreme? Many years after my short time working at General Telephone, I learned that the Pacific Bell security people, when they heard General Telephone had hired me, "rolled on the ground with laughter." But to General Telephone's credit when they realized they had a reputed hacker working for them after they laid me off, they then required that passwords be changed for *everyone in the company!*)

You don't want your facilities to feel like jails, but at the same time you need to defend against the guy who was fired yesterday but is back today intent on doing damage.

Don't Forget Anybody

Security policies tend to overlook the entry-level worker, people like receptionists who don't handle sensitive corporate information. We've seen elsewhere that receptionists are a handy target for attackers, and the story of the break-in at the auto parts company provides another example: A friendly person, dressed like a professional, who claims to be a company employee from another facility may not be what he appears. Receptionists need to be well-trained about politely asking for company ID when appropriate, and the training needs to be not just for the main reception-ist but also for everyone who sits in as relief at the reception desk during lunchtime or coffee breaks.

For visitors from outside the company, the policy should require that a photo ID be shown and the information recorded. It isn't hard to get fake ID, but at least demanding ID makes pretexting one degree harder for the would-be attacker.

In some companies, it makes sense to follow a policy requiring that vis-itors be escorted from the lobby and from meeting to meeting. Procedures should require that the escort make clear when delivering the visitor to his first appointment that this person has entered the building as an employee or nonemployee. Why is this important? Because, as we've seen in earlier stories, an attacker will often pass himself off in one guise to the first per-son encountered, and as someone else to the next. It's too easy for an attacker to show up in the lobby, convince the receptionist that he has an appointment with, say, an engineer . . . then be escorted to the engineer's office where he claims to be a rep from a company that wants to sell some product to the company . . . and then, after the meeting with the engi-neer, he has free access to roam the building.

Before admitting an off-site employee to the premises, suitable proce-dures must be followed to verify that the person is truly an employee; receptionists and guards must be aware of methods used by attackers to pretext the identity of an employee in order to gain access to company buildings.

How about protecting against the attacker who cons his way inside the building and manages to plug his laptop into a network port behind the corporate firewall? Given today's technology, this is a challenge: conference rooms, training rooms, and similar areas should not leave network ports unsecured but should protect them with firewalls or routers. But better protection would come from the use of a secure method to authenticate any users who connect to the network.

Secure IT!

A word to the wise: In your own company, every worker in IT probably knows or can find out in moments how much you are earning, how much the CEO takes home, and who's using the corporate jet to go on skiing vacations.

It's even possible in some companies for IT people or accounting people to increase their own salaries, make payments to a phony vendor, remove negative ratings from HR records, and so on. Sometimes it's only the fear of getting caught that keeps them honest . . . and then one day along comes somebody whose greed or native dishonesty makes him (or her) ignore the risk and take whatever he thinks he can get away with.

There are solutions, of course. Sensitive files can be protected by installing proper access controls so that only authorized people can open them. Some operating systems have audit controls that can be configured to maintain a log of certain events, such as each person who attempts to access a protected file, regardless of whether or not the attempt succeeds.

If your company has understood this issue and has implemented proper access controls and auditing that protects sensitive files—you're taking powerful steps in the right direction.

chapter

11

Combining Technology and Social Engineering

a social engineer lives by his ability to manipulate people into doing things that help him achieve his goal, but success often also requires a large measure of knowledge and skill with computer systems and telephone systems.

Here's a sampling of typical social engineering scams where technology played an important role.

HACKING BEHIND BARS

What are some of the most secure installations you can think of, protected against break-in, whether physical, telecommunications, or electronic in nature? Fort Knox? Sure. The White House? Absolutely. NORAD, the North American Air Defense installation buried deep under a mountain? Most definitely.

How about federal prisons and detention centers? They must be about as secure as any place in the country, right? People rarely escape, and when they do, they are normally caught in short order. You would think that a federal facility would be invulnerable to social engineering attacks. But you would be wrong—there is no such thing as foolproof security, anywhere.

A few years ago, a pair of grifters (professional swindlers) ran into a problem. It turned out they had lifted a large bundle of cash from a local judge. The pair had been in trouble with the law on and off through the years, but this time the federal authorities took an interest. They nabbed one of the grifters, Charles Gondorff, and tossed him into a correctional center near San Diego. The federal magistrate ordered him detained as a flight risk and a danger to the community.

His pal Johnny Hooker knew that Charlie was going to need a good defense attorney. But where was the money going to come from? Like most grifters, their money had always gone for good clothes, fancy cars, and the ladies as fast as it came in. Johnny barely had enough to live on.

The money for a good lawyer would have to come from running another scam. Johnny wasn't up to doing this on this own. Charlie Gondorff had always been the brains behind their cons. But Johnny didn't dare visit the detention center to ask Charlie what to do, not when the Feds knew there had been two men involved in the scam and were so eager to lay their hands on the other one. Especially since only family can visit, which meant he'd have to show fake identification and claim to be a family member. Trying to use fake ID in a federal prison didn't sound like a smart idea.

No, he'd have to get in touch with Gondorff some other way.

It wouldn't be easy. No inmate in any federal, state, or local facility is allowed to receive phone calls. A sign posted by every inmate telephone in a federal detention center says something like, "This notice is to advise the user that all conversations from this telephone are subject to monitoring, and the use of the telephone constitutes consent to the monitoring." Having government officials listen in on your phone calls while committing a crime has a way of extending your federally funded vacation plans.

Johnny knew, though, that certain phone calls were not monitored: calls between a prisoner and his attorney, protected by the Constitution as client-attorney communications, for example. In fact, the facility where Gondorff was being held had telephones connected directly to the federal Public Defender's Office. Pick up one of those phones, and a direct connection is made to the corresponding telephone in the PDO. The phone company calls this service *Direct Connect*. The unsuspecting authorities assume the service is secure and invulnerable to tampering because outgoing calls can only go to the PDO, and incoming calls are blocked. Even if someone were somehow able to find out the phone number, the phones are programmed in the telephone company switch as *deny terminate*, which is a clumsy phone company term for service where incoming calls are not permitted.

Since any halfway decent grifter is well versed in the art of deception, Johnny figured there had to be a way around this problem. From the inside, Gondorff had already tried picking up one of the PDO phones and saying, "This is Tom, at the phone company repair center. We're running

DIRECT CONNECT   Phone company term for a phone line that goes directly to a specific number when picked up.

DENY TERMINATE   A phone company service option where switching equipment is set so that incoming calls cannot be received at a phone number.

a test on this line and I need you to try dialing nine, and then zero-zero." The nine would have accessed an outside line, the zero-zero would then have reached a long-distance operator. It didn't work—the person answering the phone at the PDO was already hip to that trick.

Johnny was having better success. He readily found out that there were ten housing units in the detention center, each with a direct connect telephone line to the Public Defender's Office. Johnny encountered some obstacles, but like a social engineer, he was able to think his way around these annoying stumbling blocks. Which unit was Gondorff in? What was the telephone number to the direct connect services in that housing unit? And how would he initially get a message to Gondorff without it being intercepted by prison officials?

What may appear to be the impossible to average folks, like obtaining the secret telephone numbers located in federal institutions, is very often no more than a few phone calls away for a con artist. After a couple of tossing-and-turning nights brainstorming a plan, Johnny woke up one morning with the whole thing laid out in his mind, in five steps.

First, he'd find out the phone numbers for those ten direct-connect telephones to the PDO.

He'd have all ten changed so that the phones would allow incoming calls.

He'd find out which housing unit Gondorff was on.

Then he'd find out which phone number went to that unit.

Finally, he'd arrange with Gondorff when to expect his call, without the government suspecting a thing.

Piece a' cake, he thought.

Calling Ma Bell . . .

Johnny began by calling the phone company business office under the pretext of being from the General Services Administration, the agency responsible for purchasing goods and services for the federal government. He said he was working on an acquisition order for additional services and needed to know the billing information for any direct connect services currently in use, including the working telephone numbers and monthly cost at the San Diego detention center. The lady was happy to help.

Just to make sure, he tried dialing into one of those lines and was answered by the typical audichron recording, "This line has been disconnected or is no longer in service"—which he knew meant nothing of the kind but instead meant that the line was programmed to block incoming calls, just as he expected.

He knew from his extensive knowledge of phone company operations and procedures that he'd need to reach a department called the Recent Change Memory Authorization Center or RCMAC (I will always wonder who makes up these names!). He began by calling the phone company Business Office, said he was in Repair and needed to know the number for the RCMAC that handled the service area for the area code and prefix he gave, which was served out of the same central office for all the telephone lines in the detention center. It was a routine request, the kind provided for technicians out in the field in need of some assistance, and the clerk had no hesitation in giving him the number.

He called RCMAC, gave a phony name and again said he was in Repair. He had the lady who answered access one of the telephone numbers he had conned out of the business office a few calls earlier; when she had it up, Johnny asked, "Is the number set to deny termination?"

"Yes," she said.

"Well, that explains why the customer isn't able to receive calls!" Johnny said. "Listen, can you do me a favor. I need you to change the line class code or remove the deny terminate feature, okay?" There was a pause as she checked another computer system to verify that a service order had been placed to authorize the change. She said, "That number is *supposed* to be restricted for outgoing calls only. There's no service order for a change."

"Right, it's a mistake. We were supposed to process the order yesterday but the regular account rep that handles this customer went home sick and forgot to have someone else take care of the order for her. So now of course the customer is up in arms about it."

After a momentary pause while the lady pondered this request, which would be out of the ordinary and against standard operating procedures, she said, "Okay." He could hear her typing, entering the change. And a few seconds later, it was done.

The ice had been broken, a kind of collusion established between them. Reading the woman's attitude and willingness to help, Johnny didn't hesitate to go for it all. He said, "Do you have a few minutes more to help me?"

"Yeah," she answered. "What do you need?"

"I've got a several other lines that belong to the same customer, and all have the same problem. I'll read off the numbers, so you can make sure that they're not set for deny terminate—okay?" She said that was fine.

A few minutes later, all ten phone lines had been "fixed" to accept incoming calls.

Finding Gondorff

Next, find out what housing unit Gondorff was on. This is information that the people who run detention centers and prisons definitely don't want outsiders to know. Once again Johnny had to rely on his social engineering skills.

He placed a call to a federal prison in another city—he called Miami, but any one would have worked—and claimed he was calling from the detention center in New York. He asked to talk to somebody who worked with the Bureau's Sentry computer, the computer system that contains information on every prisoner being held in a Bureau of Prisons facility anywhere in the country.

When that person came on the phone, Johnny put on his Brooklyn accent. "Hi," he said. "This is Thomas at the FDC New York. Our connection to Sentry keeps going down, can you find the location of a prisoner for me, I think this prisoner may be at your institution," and gave Gondorff's name and his registration number.

"No, he's not here," the guy said after a couple of moments. "He's at the correctional center in San Diego."

Johnny pretended to be surprised. "San Diego! He was supposed to be transferred to Miami on the Marshal's airlift last week! Are we talking about the same guy—what's the guy's DOB?"

"12/3/60," the man read from his screen.

"Yeah, that's the same guy. What housing unit is he on?"

"He's on Ten North," the man said—blithely answering the question even though there isn't any conceivable reason why a prison employee in New York would need to know this.

Johnny now had the phones turned on for incoming calls, and knew which housing unit Gondorff was on. Next, find out which phone number connected to unit Ten North.

This one was a bit difficult. Johnny called one of the numbers. He knew the ringer of the phone would be turned off; no one would know it was ringing. So he sat there reading *Fodor's Europe's Great Cities* travel guide, while listening to the constant ringing on speakerphone until finally somebody picked up. The inmate on the other end would, of course, be trying to reach his court-appointed lawyer. Johnny was prepared with the expected response. "Public Defender's Office," he announced.

When the man asked for his attorney, Johnny said, "I'll see if he's available, what housing unit are you calling from?" He jotted down the man's answer, clicked onto hold, came back after half a minute and said, "He's in court, you'll have to call back later," and hung up.

He had spent the better part of a morning, but it could have been worse; his fourth attempt turned out to be from Ten North. So Johnny now knew the phone number to the PDO phone on Gondorff's housing unit.

Synchronize Your Watches

Now to get a message through to Gondorff on when to pick up the telephone line that connects inmates directly to the Public Defender's Office. This was easier than it might sound.

Johnny called the detention center using his official-sounding voice, identified himself as an employee, and asked to be transferred to Ten North. The call was put right through. When the correctional officer there picked up, Johnny conned him by using the insider's abbreviation for Receiving and Discharge, the unit that processes new inmates in, and departing ones out: "This is Tyson in R&D," he said. "I need to speak to inmate Gondorff. We have some property of his we have to ship and we need an address where he wants it sent. Could you call him to the phone for me?"

Johnny could hear the guard shouting across the day room. After an impatient several minutes, a familiar voice came on the line.

Johnny told him, "Don't say anything until I explain what this is." He explained the pretext so Johnny could sound like he was discussing where his property should be shipped. Johnny then said, "If you can get to the Public Defender phone at one this afternoon, don't respond. If you can't, then say a time that you can be there." Gondorff didn't reply. Johnny went on, "Good. Be there at one o'clock. I'll call you then. Pick up the phone.

If it starts to ring to the Public Defenders Office, flash the switch hook every twenty seconds. Keep trying till you hear me on the other end."

At one o'clock, Gondorff picked up the phone, and Johnny was there waiting for him. They had a chatty, enjoyable, unhurried conversation, leading to a series of similar calls to plan the scam that would raise the money to pay Gondorff's legal fees—all free from government surveillance.

Analyzing the Con

This episode offers a prime example of how a social engineer can make the seemingly impossible happen by conning several people, each one doing something that, by itself, seems inconsequential. In reality, each action provides one small piece of the puzzle until the con is complete.

The first phone company employee thought she was giving information to someone from the federal government's General Accounting Office.

The next phone company employee knew she wasn't supposed to change the class of telephone service without a service order, but helped out the friendly man anyway. This made it possible to place calls through to all ten of the public defender phone lines in the detention center.

For the man at the detention center in Miami, the request to help someone at another federal facility with a computer problem seemed perfectly reasonable. And even though there didn't seem any reason he would want to know the housing unit, why not answer the question?

And the guard on Ten North who believed that the caller was really from within the same facility, calling on official business? It was a perfectly reasonable request, so he called the inmate Gondorff to the telephone. No big deal.

A series of well-planned stories that added up to completing the sting.

THE SPEEDY DOWNLOAD

Ten years after they had finished law school, Ned Racine saw his classmates living in nice homes with front lawns, belonging to country clubs, playing golf once or twice a week, while he was still handling penny-ante cases for the kind of people who never had enough money to pay his bill. Jealousy can be a nasty companion. Finally one day, Ned had had enough.

The one good client he ever had was a small but very successful accounting firm that specialized in mergers and acquisitions. They hadn't used Ned for long, just long enough for him to realize they were involved in deals that, once they hit the newspapers, would affect the stock price of one or two publicly traded companies. Penny-ante, bulletin-board stocks, but in some ways that was even better—a small jump in price could represent a big percentage gain on an investment. If he could only tap into their files and find out what they were working on . . .

He knew a man who knew a man who was wise about things not exactly in the mainstream. The man listened to the plan, got fired up and agreed to help. For a smaller fee than he usually charged, against a percentage of Ned's stock market killing, the man gave Ned instructions on what to do. He also gave him a handy little device to use, something brand-new on the market.

For a few days in a row Ned kept watch on the parking lot of the small business park where the accounting company had its unpretentious, storefront-like offices. Most people left between 5:30 and 6. By 7, the lot was empty. The cleaning crew showed up around 7:30. Perfect.

The next night at a few minutes before 8 o'clock, Ned parked across the street from the parking lot. As he expected, the lot was empty except for the truck from the janitorial services company. Ned put his ear to the door and heard the vacuum cleaner running. He knocked at the door very loudly, and stood there waiting in his suit and tie, holding his well-worn briefcase. No answer, but he was patient. He knocked again. A man from the cleaning crew finally appeared. "Hi," Ned shouted through the glass door, showing the business card of one of the partners that he had picked up some time earlier. "I locked my keys in my car and I need to get to my desk."

The man unlocked the door, locked it again behind Ned, and then went down the corridor turning on lights so Ned could see where he was going. And why not—he was being kind to one of the people who helped put food on his table. Or so he had every reason to think.

Ned sat down at the computer of one of the partners, and turned it on. While it was starting up, he installed the small device he had been given into the USB port of the computer, a gadget small enough to carry on a

mitnick message

Industrial spies and computer intruders will sometimes make a physical entry into the targeted business. Rather than using a crowbar to break in, the social engineer uses the art of deception to influence the person on the other side of the door to open up for him.

key ring, yet able to hold more than 120 megabytes of data. He logged into the network with the username and password of the partner's secretary, which were conveniently written down on a Post-it note stuck to the display. In less than five minutes, Ned had downloaded every spreadsheet and document file stored on the workstation and from the partner's network directory and was on his way home.

EASY MONEY

When I was first introduced to computers in high school, we had to connect over a modem to one central DEC PDP 11 minicomputer in downtown Los Angeles that all the high schools in L.A. shared. The operating system on that computer was called RSTS/E, and it was the operating system I first learned to work with.

At that time, in 1981, DEC sponsored an annual conference for its product users, and one year I read that the conference was going to be held in L.A. A popular magazine for users of this operating system carried an announcement about a new security product, LOCK-11. The product was being promoted with a clever ad campaign that said something like, "It's 3:30 A.M. and Johnny down the street found your dial-in number, 555-0336, on his 336th try. He's in and you're out. Get LOCK-11." The product, the ad suggested, was hacker-proof. And it was going to be on display at the conference.

I was eager to see the product for myself. A high school buddy and friend, Vinny, my hacking partner for several years who later became a federal informant against me, shared my interest in the new DEC product, and encouraged me to go to the conference with him.

Cash on the Line

We arrived to find a big buzz already going around the crowd at the trade show about LOCK-11. It seemed that the developers were staking cash on the line in a bet that no one could break into their product. Sounded like a challenge I could not resist.

We headed straight for the LOCK-11 booth and found it manned by three guys who were the developers of the product; I recognized them and they recognized me—even as a teen, I already had a reputation as a phreaker and hacker because of a big story the *LA Times* had run about my first juvenile brush with the authorities. The article reported that I had talked my way into a Pacific Telephone building in the middle of the night and walked out with computer manuals, right under the nose of their security guard. (It appears the *Times* wanted to run a sensationalist story and it served their purposes to publish my name; because I was still a juvenile, the article violated the custom if not the law of withholding the names of minors accused of wrongdoing.)

When Vinny and I walked up, it created some interest on both sides. There was an interest on their side because they recognized me as the hacker they had read about and they were a bit shocked to see me. It created an interest on our side because each of the three developers was standing there with a $100 bill sticking out of his tradeshow badge. The prize money for anybody who could defeat their system would be the whole $300—which sounded like a lot of money to a pair of teenagers. We could hardly wait to get started.

LOCK-11 was designed on an established principle that relied on two levels of security. A user had to have a valid ID and password, as usual, but in addition that ID and password would only work when entered from authorized terminals, an approach called *terminal-based security*. To defeat the system, a hacker would need not only to have knowledge of an account ID and password, but would also have to enter that information from the correct terminal. The method was well established, and the inventors of LOCK-11 were convinced it would keep the bad guys out. We decided we were going to teach them a lesson, and earn three hundred bucks to boot.

A guy I knew who was considered an RSTS/E guru had already beaten us to the booth. Years before he had been one of the guys who had challenged me to break into the DEC internal development computer, after which his associates had turned me in. Since those days he had become a respected programmer. We found out that he had tried to defeat the LOCK-11 security program not long before we arrived, but had been unable to. The incident had given the developers greater confidence that their product really was secure.

The contest was a straightforward challenge: You break in, you win the bucks. A good publicity stunt . . . unless somebody was able to embarrass them and take the money. They were so sure of their product that they

lingo

TERMINAL-BASED SECURITY Security based in part on the identification of the particular computer terminal being used; this method of security was especially popular with IBM mainframe computers.

were even audacious enough to have a printout posted at the booth giving the account numbers and corresponding passwords to some accounts on the system. And not just regular user accounts, but all the privileged accounts.

That was actually less daring than it sounds: In this type of setup, I knew, each terminal is plugged into a port on the computer itself. It wasn't rocket science to figure out they had set up the five terminals in the conference hall so a visitor could log in only as a nonprivileged user—that is, logins were possible only to accounts without system administrator privileges. It looked as if there were only two routes: either bypass the security software altogether—exactly what the LOCK-11 was designed to prevent; or somehow get around the software in a way that the developers hadn't imagined.

Taking Up the Challenge

Vinny and I walked away and talked about the challenge, and I came up with a plan. We wandered around innocently, keeping an eye on the booth from a distance. At lunchtime, when the crowd thinned out, the three developers took advantage of the break and took off together to get something to eat, leaving behind a woman who might have been the wife or girlfriend of one of them. We sauntered back over and I distracted the woman, chatting her up about this and that, "How long have you been with the company?" "What other products does your company have on the market?" and so on.

Meanwhile Vinny, out of her sight line, had gone to work, making use of a skill he and I had both developed. Besides the fascination of breaking into computers, and my own interest in magic, we had both been intrigued by learning how to open locks. As a young kid, I had scoured the shelves of an underground bookstore in the San Fernando Valley that had volumes on picking locks, getting out of handcuffs, creating fake identities—all kinds of things a kid was not supposed to know about.

Vinny, like me, had practiced lock-picking until we were pretty good with any run-of-the-mill hardware-store lock. There had been a time when I got a kick out of pranks involving locks, like spotting somebody who was using two locks for extra protection, picking the locks, and putting them back in the opposite places, which would baffle and frustrate the owner when he tried to open each with the wrong key.

In the exhibit hall, I continued to keep the young woman distracted while Vinny, squatting down at the back of the booth so he couldn't be seen, picked the lock on the cabinet that housed their PDP-11 minicomputer and the cable terminations. To call the cabinet locked was almost a joke. It was secured with what locksmiths refer to as a wafer lock, notoriously easy to pick, even for fairly clumsy, amateur lock-pickers like us.

It took Vinny all of about a minute to open the lock. Inside the cabinet he found just what we had anticipated: the strip of ports for plugging in user terminals, and one port for what's called the console terminal. This was the terminal used by the computer operator or system administrator to control all the computers. Vinny plugged the cable leading from the console port into one of the terminals on the show floor.

That meant this one terminal was now recognized as a console terminal. I sat down at the recabled machine and logged in using a password the developers had so audaciously provided. Because the LOCK-11 software now identified that I was logging in from an authorized terminal, it granted me access, and I was connected with system administrator privileges. I patched the operating system by changing it so that from any of the terminals on the floor, I would be able to log in as a privileged user.

Once my secret patch was installed, Vinny went back to work disconnecting the terminal cable plugging it back in where it had been originally. Then he picked the lock once again, this time to fasten the cabinet door closed.

I did a directory listing to find out what files were on the computer, looking for the LOCK-11 program and associated files and stumbled on something I found shocking: a directory that should not have been on this machine. The developers had been so overconfident, so certain their software was invincible, that they hadn't bothered to remove the source code of their new product. Moving to the adjacent hard-copy terminal, I started printing out portions of the source code onto the continuous sheets of the green-striped computer paper used in those days.

Vinny had only just barely finished picking the lock closed and rejoined me when the guys returned from lunch. They found me sitting at the computer pounding the keys while the printer continued to churn away. "What'cha doing, Kevin?" one of them asked.

"Oh, just printing out your source code," I said. They assumed I was joking, of course. Until they looked at the printer and saw that it really *was* the jealously guarded source code for their product.

They didn't believe it was possible that I was logged in as a privileged user. "Type a Control-T," one of the developers commanded. I did. The display that appeared on the screen confirmed my claim. The guy smacked his forehead, as Vinny said, "Three hundred dollars, please."

They paid up. Vinny and I walked around the tradeshow floor for the rest of the day with the hundred-dollar bills stuck into our conference badges. Everyone who saw the bills knew what they represented.

Of course, Vinny and I hadn't defeated their software, and if the developer team had thought to set better rules for the contest, or had used a really secure lock, or had watched their equipment more carefully, they wouldn't have suffered the humiliation of that day—humiliation at the hands of a pair of teenagers.

I found out later that the developer team had to stop by a bank to get some cash: those hundred-dollar bills represented all the spending money they had brought with them.

THE DICTIONARY AS AN ATTACK TOOL

When someone obtains your password, he's able to invade your system. In most circumstances, you never even know that anything bad has happened.

A young attacker I'll call Ivan Peters had a target of retrieving the source code for a new electronic game. He had no trouble getting into the company's wide area network, because a hacker buddy of his had already compromised one of the company's Web servers. After finding an unpatched vulnerability in the Web server software, his buddy had just about fallen out of his chair when he realized the system had been set up as a *dual-homed host*, which meant he had an entry point into the internal network.

But once Ivan was connected, he then faced a challenge that was like being inside the Louvre and hoping to find the Mona Lisa. Without a floor plan, you could wander for weeks. The company was global, with hundreds of offices and thousands of computer servers, and they didn't exactly provide an index of development systems or the services of a tour guide to steer him to the right one.

Instead of using a technical approach to finding out what server he needed to target, Ivan used a social engineering approach. He placed phone calls based on methods similar to those described elsewhere in this book. First, calling IT technical support, he claimed to be a company employee having an interface issue on a product his group was designing, and asked for the phone number of the project leader for the gaming development team.

Then he called the name he'd been given, posing as a guy from IT. "Later tonight," he said, "we're swapping out a router and need to make sure the people on your team don't lose connectivity to your server. So we need to know which servers your team uses." The network was being upgraded all the time. And giving the name of the server wouldn't hurt anything anyway, now would it? Since it was password-protected, just having the name couldn't help anybody break in. So the guy gave the attacker the server name. Didn't even bother to call the man back to verify his story, or write down his name and phone number. He just gave the name of the servers, ATM5 and ATM6.

The Password Attack

At this point, Ivan switched to a technical approach to get the authentication information. The first step with most technical attacks on systems that provide remote access capability is to identify an account with a weak password, which provides an initial entry point into the system.

When an attacker attempts to use hacking tools for remotely identifying passwords, the effort may require him to stay connected to the company's network for hours at a time. Clearly he does this at his peril: The longer he stays connected, the greater the risk of detection and getting caught.

As a preliminary step, Ivan would do an enumeration, which reveals details about a target system. Once again the Internet conveniently provides software for the purpose (at http://ntsleuth.0catch.com; the character before "catch" is a zero). Ivan found several publicly available hacking tools on the Web that automated the enumeration process, avoiding the need to do it by hand, which would take longer and thus run a higher risk. Knowing that the organization mostly deployed Windows-based servers, he downloaded a copy of NBTEnum, a NetBIOS (basic input/output

lingo

ENUMERATION A process that reveals the services enabled on the target system, the operating system platform, and a list of account names of the users who have access to the system.

system) enumeration utility. He entered the IP (Internet protocol) address of the ATM5 server, and started running the program. The enumeration tool was able to identify several accounts that existed on the server.

Once the existing accounts had been identified, the same enumeration tool had the ability to launch a dictionary attack against the computer system. A dictionary attack is something that many computer security folks and intruders are intimately familiar with, but that most other people will probably be shocked to learn is possible. Such an attack is aimed at uncovering the password of each user on the system by using commonly used words.

We're all lazy about some things, but it never ceases to amaze me that when people choose their passwords, their creativity and imagination seem to disappear. Most of us want a password that gives us protection but that is at the same time easy to remember, which usually means something closely connected to us. Our initials, middle name, nickname, spouse's name, favorite song, movie, or brew, for example. The name of the street we live on or the town we live in, the kind of car we drive, the beachfront village we like to stay at in Hawaii, or that favorite stream with the best trout fishing around. Recognize the pattern here? These are mostly personal names, place names, or dictionary words. A dictionary attack runs through common words at a very rapid pace, trying each as a password on one or more user accounts.

Ivan ran the dictionary attack in three phases. For the first, he used a simple list of some 800 of the most common passwords; the list includes *secret, work,* and *password.* Also the program permutated the dictionary words to try each word with an appended digit, or appending the number of the current month. The program tried each attempt against all of the user accounts that had been identified. No luck.

For the next attempt, Ivan went to Google's search engine and typed, "wordlists dictionaries," and found thousands of sites with extensive wordlists and dictionaries for English and several foreign languages. He downloaded an entire electronic English dictionary. He then enhanced this by downloading a number of word lists that he found with Google. Ivan chose the site at www.outpost9.com/files/WordLists.html.

This site allowed him to download (all of this for *free)* a selection of files including family names, given names, congressional names and words, actor's names, and words and names from the Bible.

Another of the many sites offering word lists is actually provided through Oxford University, at ftp://ftp.ox.ac.uk/pub/wordlists.

Other sites offer lists with the names of cartoon characters, words used in Shakespeare, in the Odyssey, Tolkien, and the Star Trek series, as well as in science and religion, and on and on. (One on-line company sells a list containing 4.4 million words and names for only $20.) The attack program can be set to test the anagrams of the dictionary words, as well—another favorite method that many computer users think increases their safety.

Faster Than You Think

Once Ivan had decided which wordlist to use, and started the attack, the software ran on autopilot. He was able to turn his attention to other things. And here's the incredible part: You would think such an attack would allow the hacker to take a Rip van Winkle snooze and the software would still have made little progress when he awoke. In fact, depending on the platform being attacked, the security configuration of the system, and network connectivity, every word in an English dictionary can, incredibly, be attempted in less than thirty minutes!

While this attack was running, Ivan started another computer running a similar attack on the other server used by the development group, ATM6. Twenty minutes later, the attack software had done what most unsuspecting users like to think is impossible: It had broken a password, revealing that one of the users had chosen the password "Frodo," one of the Hobbits in the book *The Lord of the Rings*.

With this password in hand, Ivan was able to connect to the ATM6 server using the user's account.

There was good news and bad news for our attacker. The good news was that the account he cracked had administrator privileges, which would be essential for the next step. The bad news was that the source code for the game was not anywhere to be found. It must be, after all, on the other machine, the ATM5, which he already knew was resistant to a dictionary attack. But Ivan wasn't giving up just yet; he still had a few more tricks to try.

On some Windows and UNIX operating systems, password hashes (encrypted passwords) are openly available to anyone who has access to the computer they're stored on. The reasoning is that the encrypted passwords cannot be broken and therefore do not need to be protected. The theory is wrong. Using another tool called pwdump3, also available on the Internet, he was able to extract the password hashes from the ATM6 machine and download them.

A typical file of password hashes looks like this:

```
Administrator:500:95E4321A38AD8D6AB75E0C8D76954A50:2E48927A0
B04F3BFB341E26F6D6E9A97:::
akasper:1110:5A8D7E9E3C3954F642C5C736306CBFEF:393CE7F90A8357
F157873D72D0490821:::
digger:1111:5D15C0D58DD216C525AD3B83FA6627C7:17AD564144308B4
2B8403D01AE256558:::
ellgan:1112:2017D4A5D8D1383EFF17365FAF1FFE89:07AEC950C22CBB9
C2C734EB89320DB13:::
tabeck:1115:9F5890B3FECCAB7EAAD3B435B51404EE:1F0115A72844721
2FC05E1D2D820B35B:::
vkantar:1116:81A6A5D035596E7DAAD3B435B51404EE:B933D36DD12258
946FCC7BD153F1CD6E:::
vwallwick:1119:25904EC665BA30F4449AF42E1054F192:15B2B7953FB6
32907455D2706A432469:::
mmcdonald:1121:A4AED098D29A3217AAD3B435B51404EE:E40670F936B7
9C2ED522F5ECA9398A27:::
kworkman:1141:C5C598AF45768635AAD3B435B51404EE:DEC8E827A1212
73EF084CDBF5FD1925C:::
```

With the hashes now downloaded to his computer, Ivan used another tool that performed a different flavor of password attack known as *brute force*. This kind of attack tries every combination of alphanumeric characters and most special symbols.

Ivan used a software utility called L0phtcrack3 (pronounced loft-crack; available at www.atstake.com; another source for some excellent password recovery tools is www.elcomsoft.com). System administrators use L0phtcrack3 to audit weak passwords; attackers use it to crack passwords. The brute force feature in LC3 tries passwords with combinations of letters, numerals, and most symbols including !@#$%^&. It systematically tries every possible combination of most characters. (Note, however, that if nonprintable characters are used, LC3 will be unable to discover the password.)

The program has a nearly unbelievable speed, which can reach to as high as 2.8 million attempts a second on a machine with a 1 GHz processor. Even with this speed, and if the system administrator has configured the Windows operating system properly (disabling the use of LANMAN hashes), breaking a password can still take an excessive amount of time.

lingo

BRUTE FORCE ATTACK A password detection stategy that tries every possible combination of alphanumeric characters and special symbols.

For that reason the attacker often downloads the hashes and runs the attack on his or another machine, rather than staying on line on the target company's network and risking detection.

For Ivan, the wait was not that long. Several hours later the program presented him with passwords for every one of the development team members. But these were the passwords for users on the ATM6 machine, and he already knew the game source code he was after was not on this server.

What now? He still had not been able to get a password for an account on the ATM5 machine. Using his hacker mindset, understanding the poor security habits of typical users, he figured one of the team members might have chosen the same password for both machines.

In fact, that's exactly what he found. One of the team members was using the password "gamers" on both ATM5 and ATM6.

The door had swung wide open for Ivan to hunt around until he found the programs he was after. Once he located the source-code tree and gleefully downloaded it, he took one further step typical of system crackers: He changed the password of a dormant account that had administrator rights, just in case he wanted to get an updated version of the software at some time in the future.

Analyzing the Con

In this attack that called on both technical and people-based vulnerabilities, the attacker began with a pretext telephone call to obtain the location and host names of the development servers that held the proprietary information.

He then used a software utility to identify valid account-user names for everyone who had an account on the development server. Next he ran two successive password attacks, including a dictionary attack, which searches for commonly used passwords by trying all of the words in an English dictionary, sometimes augmented by several word lists containing names, places, and items of special interest.

Because both commercial and public-domain hacking tools can be obtained by anyone for whatever purpose they have in mind, it's all the more important that you be vigilant in protecting enterprise computer systems and your network infrastructure.

The magnitude of this threat cannot be overestimated. According to *ComputerWorld* magazine, an analysis at New York-based Oppenheimer Funds led to a startling discovery. The firm's Vice President of Network

Security and Disaster Recovery ran a password attack against the employees of his firm using one of the standard software packages. The magazine reported that within *three minutes* he managed to crack the passwords of 800 employees.

PREVENTING THE CON

Social engineering attacks may become even more destructive when the attacker adds a technology element. Preventing this kind of attack typically involves taking steps on both human and technical levels.

Just Say No

In the first story of the chapter, the telephone company RCMAC clerk should not have removed the deny terminate status from the ten phone lines when no service order existed authorizing the change. It's not enough for employees to *know* the security policies and procedures; employees must understand how important these policies are to the company in preventing damage.

Security policies should discourage deviation from procedure through a system of rewards and consequences. Naturally, the policies must be realistic, not calling on employees to carry out steps so burdensome that they are likely to be ignored. Also, a security awareness program needs to convince employees that, while it's important to complete job assignments in a timely manner, taking a shortcut that circumvents proper security procedures can be detrimental to the company and coworkers.

The same caution should be present when providing information to a stranger on the telephone. No matter how persuasively the person presents himself, regardless of the person's status or seniority in the company, absolutely *no* information should be provided that is not designated as publicly available until the caller's identity has been positively verified. If this policy had been strictly observed, the social engineering scheme in this story would have failed and federal detainee Gondorff would never have been able to plan a new scam with his pal Johnny.

This one point is so important that I reiterate it throughout this book: Verify, verify, verify. Any request not made in person should never be accepted without verifying the requestor's identity—period.

Cleaning Up

For any company that does not have security guards around the clock, the scheme wherein an attacker gains access to an office after hours presents a challenge. Cleaning people will ordinarily treat with respect anyone who appears to be with the company and appears legitimate. After all, this is someone who could get them in trouble or fired. For that reason, cleaning crews, whether internal or contracted from an outside agency, must be trained on physical security matters.

Janitorial work doesn't exactly require a college education, or even the ability to speak English, and the usual training, if any, involves nonsecurity related issues such as which kind of cleaning product to use for different tasks. Generally these people don't get an instruction like, "If someone asks you to let them in after hours, you need to see their company ID card, and then call the cleaning company office, explain the situation, and wait for authorization."

An organization needs to plan for a situation like the one in this chapter before it happens and train people accordingly. In my personal experience, I have found that most, if not all, private sector businesses are very lax in this area of physical security. You might try to approach the problem from the other end, putting the burden on your company's own employees. A company without 24-hour guard service should tell its employees that to get in after hours, they are to bring their own keys or electronic access cards, and must never put the cleaning people in the position of deciding who it is okay to admit. Then tell the janitorial company that their people must always be trained that no one is to be admitted to your premises by them at any time. This is a simple rule: Do not open the door for anyone. If appropriate, this could be put into writing as a condition of the contract with the cleaning company.

Also, cleaning crews should be trained about piggybacking techniques (unauthorized persons following an authorized person into a secure entrance). They should also be trained not to allow another person to follow them into the building just because the person looks like they might be an employee.

Follow up every now and then—say, three or four times a year—by staging a penetration test or vulnerability assessment. Have someone show up at the door when the cleaning crew is at work and try to talk her way into the building. Rather than using your own employees, you can hire a firm that specializes in this kind of penetration testing.

Pass It On: Protect Your Passwords

More and more, organizations are becoming increasingly vigilant about enforcing security policies through technical means—for example, configuring the operating system to enforce password policies and limit the number of invalid login attempts that can be made before locking out the account. In fact, Microsoft Windows business platforms generally have this feature built in. Still, recognizing how easily annoyed customers are by features that require extra effort, the products are usually delivered with security features turned off. It's really about time that software manufacturers stop delivering products with security features disabled by default when it should be the other way around. (I suspect they'll figure this out soon enough.)

Of course, corporate security policy should mandate system administrators to enforce security policy through technical means whenever possible, with the goal of not relying on fallible humans any more than necessary. It's a no-brainer that when you limit the number of successive invalid login attempts to a particular account, for example, you make an attacker's life significantly more difficult.

Every organization faces that uneasy balance between strong security and employee productivity, which leads some employees to ignore security policies, not accepting how essential these safeguards are for protecting the integrity of sensitive corporate information.

If a company's policies leave some issues unaddressed, employees may use the path of least resistance and do whatever action is most convenient and makes their job easier. Some employees may resist change and openly disregard good security habits. You may have encountered such an employee, who follows enforced rules about password length and complexity but then writes the password on a Post-it note and defiantly sticks it to his monitor.

A vital part of protecting your organization is the use of hard-to-discover passwords, combined with strong security settings in your technology.

For a detailed discussion of recommended password policies, see Chapter 16.

chapter 12

Attacks on the Entry-Level Employee

as many of the stories here demonstrate, the skilled social engineer often targets lower-level personnel in the organizational hierarchy. It can be easy to manipulate these people into revealing seemingly innocuous information that the attacker uses to advance one step closer to obtaining more sensitive company information.

An attacker targets entry-level employees because they are typically unaware of the value of specific company information or of the possible results of certain actions. Also, they tend to be easily influenced by some of the more common social engineering approaches—a caller who invokes authority; a person who seems friendly and likeable; a person who appears to know people in the company who are known to the victim; a request that the attacker claims is urgent; or the inference that the victim will gain some kind of favor or recognition.

Here are some illustrations of the attack on the lower-level employee in action.

THE HELPFUL SECURITY GUARD

Swindlers hope to find a person who's greedy because they are the ones most likely to fall for a con game. Social engineers, when targeting someone such as a member of a sanitation crew or a security guard, hope to find someone who is good-natured, friendly, and trusting of others. They are the ones most likely to be willing to help. That's just what the attacker had in mind in the following story.

Elliot's View

Date/time: 3:26 A.M. on a Tuesday morning in February 1998.

Location: Marchand Microsystems facility, Nashua, New Hampshire

Elliot Staley knew he wasn't supposed to leave his station when he wasn't on his scheduled rounds. But it was the middle of the night, for crying out loud, and he hadn't seen a single person since he had come on duty. And it was nearly time to make his rounds anyway. The poor guy on the telephone sounded like he really needed help. And it makes a person feel fine when they can do a little good for somebody.

Bill's Story

Bill Goodrock had a simple goal, one he had held on to, unaltered, since age twelve: to retire by age twenty-four, not ever touching a penny of his trust fund. To show his father, the almighty and unforgiving banker, that he could be a success on his own.

Only two years left and it's by now perfectly clear he won't make his fortune in the next twenty-four months by being a brilliant businessman and he won't do it by being a sharp investor. He once wondered about robbing banks with a gun but that's just the stuff of fiction—the risk-benefit tradeoff is so lousy. Instead he daydreams about doing a Rifkin—robbing a bank electronically.

The last time Bill was in Europe with the family, he opened a bank account in Monaco with 100 Francs. It still has only 100 francs in it, but he has a plan that could help it reach seven digits in a hurry. Maybe even eight if he's lucky.

Bill's girlfriend Annemarie worked in M&A for a large Boston bank. One day while waiting at her offices until she got out of a late meeting, he gave in to curiosity and plugged his laptop into an Ethernet port in the conference room he was using. Yes!—he was on their internal network, connected inside the bank's network . . . behind the corporate firewall. That gave him an idea.

He pooled his talent with a classmate who knew a young woman named Julia, a brilliant computer science Ph.D. candidate doing an internship at Marchand Microsystems. Julia looked like a great source for essential insider information. They told her they were writing a script for a movie and she actually believed them. She thought it was fun making up a story with them and giving them all the details about how you could actually bring off the caper they had described. She thought the idea was brilliant, actually, and kept badgering them about giving her a screen credit, too.

They warned her about how often screenplay ideas get stolen and made her swear she'd never tell anyone.

Suitably coached by Julia, Bill did the risky part himself and never doubted he could bring it off.

•••••••●●●●●●●•••••

I called in the afternoon and managed to find out that the night supervisor of the security force was a man named Isaiah Adams. At 9:30 that night I called the building and talked to the guard on the lobby security desk. My story was all based on urgency and I made myself sound a little panicky. "I'm having car trouble and I can't get to the facility," I said. "I have this emergency and I really need your help. I tried calling the guard supervisor, Isaiah, but he's not at home. Can you just do me this one-time favor, I'd really appreciate it?"

The rooms in that big facility were each labeled with a mail-stop code so I gave him the mail-stop of the computer lab and asked him if he knew where that was. He said yes, and agreed to go there for me. He said it would take him a few minutes to get to the room, and I said I'd call him in the lab, giving the excuse that I was using the only phone line available to me and I was using it to dial into the network to try to fix the problem.

He was already there and waiting by the time I called, and I told him where to find the console I was interested in, looking for one with a paper banner reading "elmer"—the host that Julia had said was used to build the release versions of the operating system that the company marketed. When he said he had found it, I knew for sure that Julia had been feeding us good information and my heart skipped a beat. I had him hit the Enter key a couple of times, and he said it printed a pound sign. Which told me the computer was logged in as root, the superuser account with all system privileges. He was a hunt-and-peck typist and got all in a sweat when I tried to talk him through entering my next command, which was more than a bit tricky:

```
echo 'fix:x:0:0::/:/bin/sh' >> /etc/passwd
```

Finally he got it right, and we had now provided an account with a name fix. And then I had him type

```
echo 'fix::10300:0:0' >> /etc/shadow
```

This established the encrypted password, which goes between the double colon. Putting nothing between those two colons meant the account would have a null password. So just those two commands was all it took to append the account fix to the password file, with a null password. Best of all, the account would have the same privileges as a superuser.

The next thing I had him do was to enter a recursive directory command that printed out a long list of file names. Then I had him feed the paper forward, tear it off, and take it with him back to his guard desk because "I may need you to read me something from it later on."

The beauty of this was that he had no idea he had created a new account. And I had him print out the directory listing of filenames because I needed to make sure the commands he typed earlier would leave the computer room with him. That way the system administrator or operator wouldn't spot anything the next morning that would alert them there had been a security breach.

I was now set up with an account, a password, and full privileges. A little before midnight I dialed in and followed the instructions Julia had carefully typed up "for the screenplay." In a blink I had access to one of the development systems that contained the master copy of the source code for the new version of the company's operating system software.

I uploaded a *patch* that Julia had written, which she said modified a routine in one of the operating system's libraries. That patch would, in effect, create a covert *backdoor* that would allow remote access into the system with a secret password.

note

> The type of backdoor used here does not change the operating system login program itself. Rather, a specific function contained within the dynamic library used by the login program is replaced to create the secret entry point. In typical attacks, computer intruders often replace or patch the login program itself, but sharp system administrators can detect the change by comparing it to the version shipped on media such as CD, or by other distribution methods.

I carefully followed the instructions she had written down for me, first installing the patch, then taking steps that removed the fix account and wiped clean all audit logs so there would be no trace of my activities, effectively erasing my tracks.

Soon the company would begin shipping the new operating system upgrade to their customers: Financial institutions all over the world. And every copy they sent out would include the backdoor I had placed into the master distribution before it was sent out, allowing me to access any computer system of every bank and brokerage house that installed the upgrade.

lingo

PATCH Traditionally a piece of code that, when placed in an executable program, fixes a problem.

Of course, I wasn't quite home free—there would still be work to do. I'd still have to gain access to the internal network of each financial institution I wanted to "visit." Then I'd have to find out which of their computers was used for money transfers, and install surveillance software to learn the details of their operations and exactly how to transfer funds.

All of that I could do long distance. From a computer located anywhere. Say, overlooking a sandy beach. Tahiti, here I come.

I called the guard back, thanked him for his help, and told him he could go ahead and toss the printout.

Analyzing the Con

The security guard had instructions about his duties, but even thorough, well-thought-out instructions can't anticipate every possible situation. Nobody had told him the harm that could be done by typing a few keystrokes on a computer for a person he thought was a company employee.

With the cooperation of the guard, it was relatively easy to gain access to a critical system that stored the distribution master, despite the fact that it was behind the locked door of a secure laboratory. The guard, of course, had keys to all locked doors.

Even a basically honest employee (or, in this case, the Ph.D. candidate and company intern, Julia) can sometimes be bribed or deceived into revealing information of crucial importance to a social engineering attack, such as where the target computer system is located and—the key to the success of this attack—when they were going to build the new release of the software for distribution. That's important, since a change of this kind made too early has a higher chance of being detected or being nullified if the operating system is rebuilt from a clean source.

Did you catch the detail of having the guard take the printout back to the lobby desk and later destroying it? This was an important step. When the computer operators came to work the next workday, the attacker didn't want them to find this damning evidence on the hard-copy terminal, or notice it in the trash. Giving the guard a plausible excuse to take the printout with him avoided that risk.

When the computer intruder cannot gain physical access to a computer system or network himself, he will try to manipulate another person to do it for him. In cases where physical access is necessary for the plan, using the victim as a proxy is even better than doing it himself, because the attacker assumes much less risk of detection and apprehension.

THE EMERGENCY PATCH

You would think a tech support guy would understand the dangers of giving access to the computer network to an outsider. But when that outsider is a clever social engineer masquerading as a helpful software vendor, the results might not be what you expect.

A Helpful Call

The caller wanted to know Who's in charge of computers there? and the telephone operator put him through to the tech support guy, Paul Ahearn.

The caller identified himself as "Edward, with SeerWare, your database vendor. Apparently a bunch of our customers didn't get the email about our emergency update, so we're calling a few for a quality control check to see whether there was a problem installing the patch. Have you installed the update yet?"

Paul said he was pretty sure he hadn't seen anything like that.

Edward said, "Well, it could cause intermittent catastrophic loss of data, so we recommend you get it installed as soon as possible." Yes, that was something he certainly wanted to do, Paul said. "Okay," the caller responded. "We can send you a tape or CD with the patch, and I want to tell you, it's really critical—two companies already lost several days of data. So you *really* should get this installed as soon as it arrives, before it happens to your company."

"Can't I download it from your Web site?" Paul wanted to know.

"It should be available soon—the tech team has been putting out all these fires. If you want, we can have our customer support center install it for you, remotely. We can either dial up or use Telnet to connect to the system, if you can support that."

"We don't allow Telnet, especially from the Internet—it's not secure," Paul answered. "If you can use SSH, that'd be okay," he said, naming a product that provides secure file transfers.

"Yeah. We have SSH. So what's the IP address?"

Paul gave him the IP address, and when Andrew asked, "and what username and password can I use," Paul gave him those, as well.

Analyzing the Con

Of course that phone call might really have come from the database manufacturer. But then the story wouldn't belong in this book.

The social engineer here influenced the victim by creating a sense of fear that critical data might be lost, and offered an immediate solution that would resolve the problem.

Also, when a social engineer targets someone who knows the value of the information, he needs to come up with very convincing and persuasive arguments for giving remote access. Sometimes he needs to add the element of urgency so the victim is distracted by the need to rush, and complies before he has had a chance to give much thought to the request.

THE NEW GIRL

What kind of information in your company's files might an attacker want to gain access to? Sometimes it can be something you didn't think you needed to protect at all.

Sarah's Call

"Human Resources, this is Sarah."

"Hi, Sarah. This is George, in the parking garage. You know the access card you use to get into the parking garage and elevators? Well, we had a problem and we need to reprogram the cards for all the new hires from the last fifteen days."

"So you need their names?"

"And their phone numbers."

"I can check our new hire list and call you back. What's your phone number?"

"I'm at 73 . . . Uh, I'm going on break, how about if I call you back in a half-hour?"

"Oh. Okay."

When he called back, she said:

"Oh, yes. Well, there's just two. Anna Myrtle, in Finance, she's a secretary. And that new VP, Mr. Underwood."

"And the phone numbers?"

"Right. . . . Okay, Mr. Underwood is 6973. Anna Myrtle is 2127."

"Hey, you've been a big help. Thanks."

Anna's Call

"Finance, Anna speaking."

"I'm glad I found somebody working late. Listen, this is Ron Vittaro, I'm publisher of the business division. I don't think we've been introduced. Welcome to the company."

"Oh, thank you."

"Anna, I'm in Los Angeles and I've got a crisis. I need to take about ten minutes of your time."

"Of course. What do you need?"

"Go up to my office. Do you know where my office is?"

"No."

"Okay, it's the corner office on the fifteenth floor—room 1502. I'll call you there in a few minutes. When you get to the office, you'll need to press the forward button on the phone so my call won't go directly to my voice mail."

"Okay, I'm on my way now."

Ten minutes later she was in his office, had cancelled his call forwarding and was waiting when the phone rang. He told her to sit down at the computer and launch Internet Explorer. When it was running he told her to type in an address: www.geocities.com/ron_insen/manuscript.doc.exe.

A dialog box appeared, and he told her to click Open. The computer appeared to start downloading the manuscript, and then the screen went blank. When she reported that something seemed to be wrong, he replied, "Oh, *no*. Not again. I've been having a problem with downloading from that Web site every so often but I thought it was fixed. Well, okay, don't worry, I'll get the file another way later." Then he asked her to restart his computer so he could be sure it would start up properly after the problem she had just had. He talked her through the steps for rebooting.

When the computer was running again properly, he thanked her warmly and hung up, and Anna went back to the Finance department to finish the job she had been working on.

Kurt Dillon's Story

Millard-Fenton Publishers was enthusiastic about the new author they were just about to sign up, the retired CEO of a Fortune 500 company who had a fascinating story to tell. Someone had steered the man to a business manager for handling his negotiations. The business manager didn't want to admit he knew zip about publishing contracts, so he hired an old friend to help him figure out what he needed to know. The old friend, unfortunately, was not a very good choice. Kurt Dillon used what we might call unusual methods in his research, methods not entirely ethical.

Kurt signed up for a free site on Geocities, in the name of Ron Vittaro, and loaded a *spyware* program onto the new site. He changed the name of the program to manuscript.doc.exe, so the name would appear to be a Word document and not raise suspicion. In fact, this worked even better than Kurt had anticipated; because the real Vittaro had never changed a default setting in his Windows operating system called "Hide file extensions for known file types." Because of that setting the file was actually displayed with the name manuscript.doc.

Then he had a lady friend call Vittaro's secretary. Following Dillon's coaching, she said, "I'm the executive assistant to Paul Spadone, president of Ultimate Bookstores, in Toronto. Mr. Vittaro met my boss at a book fair a while back, and asked him to call to discuss a project they might do together. Mr. Spadone is on the road a lot, so he said I should find out when Mr. Vittaro will be in the office."

By the time the two had finished comparing schedules, the lady friend had enough information to provide the attacker with a list of dates when Mr. Vittaro would be in the office. Which meant he also knew when Vittaro would be *out* of the office. It hadn't required much extra conversation to find out that Vittaro's secretary would be taking advantage of his absence to get in a little skiing. For a short span of time, both would be out of the office. Perfect.

lingo

SPYWARE Specialized software used to covertly monitor a target's computer activities. One form is used to track the sites visited by Internet shoppers so that on-line advertisements can be tailored to their surfing habits. The other form is analogous to a wiretap, except that the target device is a computer. The software captures the activities of the user, including passwords and keystrokes typed, email, chat conversations, instant messenger, all the Web sites visited, and screenshots of the display screen.

SILENT INSTALL   A method of installing a software application without the computer user or operator being aware that such action is taking place.

The first day they were supposed to be gone he placed a pretext urgent call just to make sure, and was told by a receptionist that "Mr. Vittaro is not in the office and neither is his secretary. Neither of them is expected any time today or tomorrow or the next day."

His very first try at conning a junior employee into taking part in his scheme was successful, and she didn't seem to blink an eye at being told to help him by downloading a "manuscript," which was actually a popular, commercially available spyware program that the attacker had modified for a *silent install*. Using this method, the installation would not be detected by any antivirus software. For some strange reason, antivirus manufacturers do not market products that will detect commercially available spyware.

Immediately after the young woman had loaded the software onto Vittaro's computer, Kurt went back up to the Geocities site and replaced the doc.exe file with a book manuscript he found on the Internet. Just in case anyone stumbled on the ruse and returned to the site to investigate what had taken place, all they'd find would be an innocuous, amateurish, unpublishable book manuscript.

Once the program had been installed and the computer rebooted, it was set to immediately become active. Ron Vittaro would return to town in a few days, start to work, and the spyware would begin forwarding all the keystrokes typed on his computer, including all outgoing emails and screen shots showing what was displayed on his screen at that moment. It would all be sent at regular intervals to a free email service provider in the Ukraine.

Within a few days after Vittaro's return, Kurt was plowing through the log files piling up in his Ukrainian mailbox and before long had located confidential emails that indicated just how far Millard-Fenton Publishing was willing to go in making a deal with the author. Armed with that knowledge, it was easy for the author's agent to negotiate much better terms than originally offered, without ever running the risk of losing the deal altogether. Which, of course, meant a bigger commission for the agent.

Analyzing the Con

In this ruse, the attacker made his success more likely by picking a new employee to act as his proxy, counting on her being more willing to cooperate and be a team player, and being less likely to have knowledge of the company, its people, and good security practices which could thwart the attempt.

Because Kurt was pretexting as a vice president in his conversation with Anna, a clerk in Finance, he knew that it would be very unlikely that she would question his authority. On the contrary, she might entertain the thought that helping a VP could gain her favor.

And the process he walked Anna through that had the effect of installing the spyware appeared innocuous on its face. Anna had no idea that her seemingly innocent actions had set an attacker up to gain valuable information that could be used against the interests of the company.

And why did he choose to forward the VP's message to an email account in the Ukraine? For several reasons a far-off destination makes tracing or taking action against an attacker much less likely. These types of crimes are generally considered low priority in countries like this, where the police tend to hold the view that committing a crime over the Internet isn't a noteworthy offense. For that reason, using email drops in countries that are unlikely to cooperate with U.S. law enforcement is an attractive strategy.

PREVENTING THE CON

A social engineer will always prefer to target an employee who is unlikely to recognize that there is something suspicious about his requests. It makes his job not only easier, but also less risky—as the stories in this chapter illustrate.

mitnick message

> Asking a coworker or subordinate to do a favor is a common practice. Social engineers know how to exploit people's natural desire to help and be a team player. An attacker exploits this positive human trait to deceive unsuspecting employees into performing actions that advance him toward his goal. It's important to understand this simple concept so you will be more likely to recognize when another person is trying to manipulate you.

Deceiving the Unwary

I've emphasized earlier the need to train employees thoroughly enough that they will never allow themselves to be talked into carrying out the instructions of a stranger. All employees also need to understand the danger of carrying out a request to take any action on another person's computer. Company policy should prohibit this except when specifically approved by a manager. Allowable situations include:

- When the request is made by a person well known to you, with the request made either face-to-face, or over the telephone when you unmistakably recognize the voice of the caller.
- When you positively verify the identity of the requestor through approved procedures.
- When the action is authorized by a supervisor or other person in authority who is personally familiar with the requestor.

Employees must be trained not to assist people they do not personally know, even if the person making the request claims to be an executive. Once security policies concerning verification have been put in place, management must support employees in adhering to these policies, even when it means that an employee challenges a member of the executive staff who is asking the employee to circumvent a security policy.

Every company also needs to have policies and procedures that guide employees in responding to requests to take any action with computers or computer-related equipment. In the story about the publishing company, the social engineer targeted a new employee who had not been trained on information security policies and procedures. To prevent this type of attack, every existing and new employee must be told to follow a simple rule: Do not use any computer system to perform an action requested by a stranger. Period.

Remember that any employee who has physical or electronic access to a computer or an item of computer-related equipment is vulnerable to being manipulated into taking some malicious action on behalf of an attacker.

Employees, and especially IT personnel, need to understand that allowing an outsider to gain access to their computer networks is like giving your bank account number to a telemarketer or giving your telephone calling card number to a stranger in jail. Employees must give thoughtful attention to whether carrying out a request can lead to disclosure of sensitive information or the compromising of the corporate computer system.

IT people must also be on their guard against unknown callers posing as vendors. In general, a company should consider having specific people designated as the contacts for each technology vendor, with a policy in place that other employees will not respond to vendor requests for information about or changes to any telephone or computer equipment. That way, the designated people become familiar with the vendor personnel who call or visit, and are less likely to be deceived by an imposter. If a vendor calls even when the company does not have a support contract, that should also raise suspicions.

Everyone in the organization needs to be made aware of information security threats and vulnerabilities. Note that security guards and the like need to be given not just security training, but training in *information* security, as well. Because security guards frequently have physical access to the entire facility, they must be able to recognize the types of social engineering attacks that may be used against them.

Beware Spyware

Commercial spyware was once used mostly by parents to monitor what their children were doing on the Internet, and by employers, supposedly to determine which employees were goofing off by surfing the Internet. A more serious use was to detect potential theft of information assets or industrial espionage. Developers market their spyware by offering it as a tool to protect the children, when in fact their true market is people who want to spy on someone. Nowadays, the sale of spyware is driven to a great extent by people's desire to know if their spouse or significant other is cheating on them.

Shortly before I began writing the spyware story in this book, the person who receives email for me (because I'm not allowed to use the Internet) found a spam email message advertising a group of spyware products. One of the items offered was described like this:

> **FAVORITE! MUST HAVE:** This powerful monitoring and spy program secretly captures all keystrokes and the time and title of all active windows to a text file, while running hidden in the background. Logs can be encrypted and automatically sent to a specified email address, or just recorded on the hard drive. Access to the program is password protected and it can be hidden from the CTRL+ALT+DEL menu.
>
> Use it to monitor typed URLs, chat sessions, emails and many other things (even passwords ;-)).
>
> **Install without detection on ANY PC and email yourself the logs!!!!!!**

Antivirus Gap?

Antivirus software doesn't detect commercial spyware, thereby treating the software as not malicious even though the intent is to spy on other people. So the computer equivalent of wiretapping goes unnoticed, creating the risk that each of us might be under illegal surveillance at any time. Of course, the antivirus software manufacturers may argue that spyware can be used for legitimate purposes, and therefore should not be treated as malicious. But the developers of certain tools once used by the hacking community, which are now being freely distributed or sold as security-related software, are nonetheless treated as malicious code. There's a double standard here, and I'm left wondering why.

Another item offered in the same email promised to capture screen shots of the user's computer, just like having a video camera looking over his shoulder. Some of these software products do not even require physical access to the victim's computer. Just install and configure the application remotely, and you have an instant computer wiretap! The FBI must love technology.

With spyware so readily available, your enterprise needs to establish two levels of protection. You should install spyware-detection software such as SpyCop (available from www.spycop.com) on all workstations, and you should require that employees initiate periodic scans. In addition, you must train employees against the danger of being deceived into downloading a program, or opening an email attachment that could install malicious software.

In addition to preventing spyware from being installed while an employee is away from his desk for a coffee break, lunch, or a meeting, a policy mandating that all employees lock their computer systems with a screen saver password or similar method will substantially mitigate the risk of an unauthorized person being able to access a worker's computer. No one slipping into the person's cubicle or office will be able to access any of their files, read their email, or install spyware or other malicious software. The resources necessary to enable the screensaver password are nil, and the benefit of protecting employee workstations is substantial. The cost-benefit analysis in this circumstance should be a no-brainer.

chapter 13

Clever Cons

by now you've figured out that when a stranger calls with a request for sensitive information or something that could be of value to an attacker, the person receiving the call must be trained to get the caller's phone number, and call back to verify that the person is really who he claims to be—a company employee, or an employee of a business partner, or a technical support representative from one of your vendors, for example.

Even when a company has an established procedure that the employees follow carefully for verifying callers, sophisticated attackers are still able to use a number of tricks to deceive their victims into believing they are who they claim to be. Even security conscious employees can be duped by methods such as the following.

THE MISLEADING CALLER ID

Anyone who has ever received a call on a cell phone has observed the feature known as caller ID—that familiar display showing the telephone number of the caller. In a business setting, it offers the advantage of allowing a worker to tell at a glance whether the call coming in is from a fellow employee or from outside the company.

Many years ago some ambitious phone phreakers introduced themselves to the wonders of caller ID before the phone company was even allowed to offer the service to the public. They had a great time freaking people out by answering the phone and greeting the caller by name before they said a word.

Just when you thought it was safe, the practice of verifying identity by trusting what you see—what appears on the caller ID display—is exactly what the attacker may be counting on.

Linda's Phone Call

Day/Time: Tuesday, July 23, 3:12 P.M.
Place: The offices of the Finance Department, Starbeat Aviation

Linda Hill's phone rang just as she was in the middle of writing a memo to her boss. She glanced at her caller ID, which showed that the call was from the corporate office in New York, but from someone named Victor Martin—not a name she recognized.

She thought of letting the call roll over to voice mail so she wouldn't break the flow of thought on the memo. But curiosity got the better of her. She picked up the phone and the caller introduced himself and said he was from PR, and working on some material for the CEO. "He's on his way to Boston for meetings with some of our bankers. He needs the top-line financials for the current quarter," he said. "And one more thing. He also needs the financial projections on the Apache project," Victor added, using the code name for a product that was to be one of the company's major releases in the spring.

She asked for his email address, but he said he was having a problem receiving email that tech support was working on, so could she fax it instead? She said that would be fine, and he gave her the internal phone extension to his fax machine.

She sent the fax a few minutes later.

But Victor did not work for the PR department. In fact, he didn't even work for the company.

Jack's Story

Jack Dawkins had started his professional career at an early age as a pickpocket working games at Yankee Stadium, on crowded subway platforms, and among the nighttime throng of Times Square tourists. He proved so nimble and artful that he could take a watch off a man's wrist without his knowing. But in his awkward teenage years he had grown clumsy and been caught. In Juvenile Hall, Jack learned a new trade with a much lower risk of getting nabbed.

His current assignment called for him to get a company's quarterly profit and loss statement and cash flow information, before the data was filed with the Securities and Exchange Commission (SEC) and made public. His client was a dentist who didn't want to explain why he wanted the information. To Jack the man's caution was laughable. He'd seen it all before—the guy probably had a gambling problem, or else an expensive girlfriend his wife hadn't found out about yet. Or maybe he had just been bragging to his wife about how smart he was in the stock market; now he had lost a bundle and wanted to make a big investment on a sure thing by knowing which way the company's stock price was going to go when they announced their quarterly results.

People are surprised to find out how little time it takes a thoughtful social engineer to figure out a way of handling a situation he's never faced before. By the time Jack got home from his meeting with the dentist, he had already formed a plan. His friend Charles Bates worked for a company, Panda Importing, that had its own telephone switch, or PBX.

In terms familiar to people knowledgeable about phone systems, the PBX was connected to a digital telephone service known as a T1, configured as Primary Rate Interface ISDN (integrated services digital network) or PRI ISDN. What this meant was that every time a call was placed from Panda, setup and other call processing information went out over a data channel to the phone company's switch; the information included the calling party number, which (unless blocked) is delivered to the caller ID device at the receiving end.

Jack's friend knew how to program the switch so the person receiving the call would see on his caller ID, not the actual phone number at the Panda office, but whatever phone number he had programmed into the switch. This trick works because local phone companies do not bother to validate the calling number received from the customer against the actual phone numbers the customer is paying for.

All Jack Dawkins needed was access to any such telephone service. Happily his friend and sometime partner in crime, Charles Bates, was always glad to lend a helping hand for a nominal fee. On this occasion, Jack and Charles temporarily reprogrammed the company's telephone switch so that calls from a particular telephone line located on the Panda premises would spoof Victor Martin's internal telephone number, making the call appear to be coming from within Starbeat Aviation.

The idea that your caller ID can be made to show any number you wish is so little known that it's seldom questioned. In this case, Linda was happy to fax the requested information to the guy she thought was from PR.

When Jack hung up, Charles reprogrammed his company's telephone switch, restoring the telephone number to the original settings.

Analyzing the Con

Some companies don't want customers or vendors to know the telephone numbers of their employees. For example, Ford may decide that calls from their Customer Support Center should show the 800-number for the Center and a name like "Ford Support," instead of the real direct-dial phone number of each support representative placing a call. Microsoft may want to give their employees the option of telling people their phone number, instead of having everyone they call be able to glance at their caller ID and know their extension. In this way the company is able to maintain the confidentiality of internal numbers.

But this same capability of reprogramming provides a handy tactic for the prankster, bill collector, telemarketer, and, of course, the social engineer.

VARIATION: THE PRESIDENT OF THE UNITED STATES IS CALLING

As co-host of a radio show in Los Angeles called "Darkside of the Internet" on KFI Talk Radio, I worked under the station's program director. David, one of the most committed and hardworking people I've ever met, is very difficult to reach by telephone because he's so busy. He's one of those people who doesn't answer a call unless he sees from the caller ID that it's someone he needs to talk to.

When I'd phone him, because I have call blocking on my cell phone, he could not tell who was calling and wouldn't pick up the call. It would roll over to voice mail, and it became very frustrating for me.

I talked over what to do about this with a long-time friend who is the cofounder of a real estate firm that provides office space for high-tech companies. Together we came up with a plan. He had access to his company's Meridian telephone switch, which gives him the ability to program the calling party number, as described in the previous story. Whenever I needed to reach the program director and couldn't get a call through, I would ask my friend to program any number of my choosing to appear on the caller ID. Sometimes I'd have him make the call look as if it was coming from David's office assistant, or sometimes from the holding company that owns the station.

But my favorite was programming the call to appear from David's own home telephone number, which he always picked up. I'll give the guy credit, though. He always had a good sense of humor about it when he'd pick up the phone and discover I had fooled him once again. The best part was that he'd then stay on the line long enough to find out what I wanted and resolve whatever the issue was.

When I demonstrated this little trick on the Art Bell Show, I spoofed my caller ID to display the name and number of the Los Angeles head-quarters of the FBI. Art was quite shocked about the whole affair and admonished me for doing something illegal. But I pointed out to him that it's perfectly legal, as long as it's not an attempt to commit fraud. After the program I received several hundred emails asking me to explain how I had done it. Now you know.

This is the perfect tool to build credibility for the social engineer. If, for example, during the research stage of the social engineering attack cycle, it was discovered that the target had caller ID, the attacker could spoof his or her own number as being from a trusted company or employee. A bill collector can make his or her calls appear to come from your place of business.

But stop and think about the implications. A computer intruder can call you at home claiming to be from the IT department at your company. The person on the line urgently needs your password to restore your files from a server crash. Or the caller ID displays the name and number of your bank or stock brokerage house, the pretty sounding girl just needs to verify your account numbers and your mother's maiden name. For good measure, she also needs to verify your ATM PIN because of some system problem. A stock market boiler-room operation can make their calls seem to come from Merrill Lynch or Citibank. Someone out to steal your iden-tity could call, apparently from Visa, and convince you to tell him your Visa card number. A guy with a grudge could call and claim to be from the IRS or the FBI.

If you have access to a telephone system connected to a PRI, plus a bit of programming knowledge that you can probably acquire from the sys-tem vendor's Web site, you can use this tactic for playing cool tricks on your friends. Know anybody with overblown political aspirations? You could program the referral number as 202 456-1414, and his caller ID will display the name "WHITE HOUSE."

He'll think he's getting a call from the president!

The moral of the story is simple: Caller ID cannot be trusted, except when being used to identify internal calls. Both at work and at home, everyone needs to become aware of the caller ID trick and recognize that the name or phone number shown in a caller ID display cannot ever be trusted for verification of identity.

THE INVISIBLE EMPLOYEE

Shirley Cutlass has found a new and exciting way to make fast money. No more putting in long hours at the salt mine. She has joined the hundreds of other scam artists involved in the crime of the decade. She is an identity thief.

Today she has set her sights on getting confidential information from the customer service department of a credit card company. After doing the usual kind of homework, she calls the target company and tells the switchboard operator who answers that she'd like to be connected to the Telecom Department. Reaching Telecom, she asks for the voice mail administrator.

Using information gathered from her research, she explains that her name is Norma Todd from the Cleveland office. Using a ruse that should by now be familiar to you, she says she'll be traveling to corporate headquarters for a week, and she'll need a voice mailbox there so she won't have to make long distance calls to check her voice mail messages. No need for a physical telephone connection, she says, just a voice mailbox. He says he'll take care of it, he'll call her back when it's set up to give her the information she'll need.

In a seductive voice, she says "I'm on my way into a meeting, can I call you back in an hour?"

When she calls back, he says it's all set up, and gives her the information— her extension number and temporary password. He asks whether she knows how to change the voice mail password, and she lets him talk her through the steps, though she knows them at least as well as he does.

"And by the way," she asks, "from my hotel, what number do I call to check my messages?" He gives her the number.

Shirley phones in, changes the password, and records her new outgoing greeting.

Shirley Attacks

So far it's all been an easy setup. She's now ready to use the art of deception.

She calls the customer service department of the company. "I'm with Collections, in the Cleveland office," she says, and then launches into a variation on the by-now familiar excuse. "My computer is being fixed by technical support and I need your help looking up this information." And she goes on to provide the name and date of birth of the person whose identity she is intent on stealing. Then she lists the information she wants: address, mother's maiden name, card number, credit limit, available credit, and payment history. "Call me back at this number," she says, giving the internal extension number that the voice mail administrator set up for her. "And if I'm not available, just leave the information on my voice mail."

She keeps busy with errands for the rest of the morning, and then checks her voice mail that afternoon. It's all there, everything she asked for. Before hanging up, Shirley clears the outgoing message; it would be careless to leave a recording of her voice behind.

And identify theft, the fastest growing crime in America, the "in" crime of the new century, is about to have another victim. Shirley uses the credit-card and identity information she just obtained, and begins running up charges on the victim's card.

Analyzing the Con

In this ruse, the attacker first duped the company's voice mail administrator into believing she was an employee, so that he would set up a temporary voice mailbox. If he bothered to check at all, he would have found that the name and telephone number she gave matched the listings in the corporate employee database.

The rest was simply a matter of giving a reasonable excuse about a computer problem, asking for the desired information, and requesting that the response be left on voice mail. And why would any employee be reluctant to share information with a coworker? Since the phone number that Shirley provided was clearly an internal extension, there was no reason for any suspicion.

mitnick
message

Try calling your own voice mail once in a while; if you hear an outgoing message that's not yours, you may have just encountered your first social engineer.

THE HELPFUL SECRETARY

Cracker Robert Jorday had been regularly breaking into the computer networks of a global company, Rudolfo Shipping, Inc. The company eventually recognized that someone was hacking into their terminal server, and that through that server the user could connect to any computer system at the company. To safeguard the corporate network, the company decided to require a dial-up password on every terminal server.

Robert called the Network Operations Center posing as an attorney with the Legal Department and said he was having trouble connecting to the network. The network administrator he reached explained that there had been some recent security issues, so all dial-up access users would need to obtain the monthly password from their manager. Robert wondered what method was being used to communicate each month's password to the managers and how he could obtain it. The answer, it turned out, was that the password for the upcoming month was sent in a memo via office mail to each company manager.

That made things easy. Robert did a little research, called the company just after the first of the month, and reached the secretary of one manager, who gave her name as Janet. He said, "Janet, hi. This is Randy Goldstein, in Research and Development. I know I probably got the memo with this month's password for logging into the terminal server from outside the company but I can't find it anywhere. Did you get your memo for this month?"

Yes, she said, she did get it.

He asked her if she would fax it to him, and she agreed. He gave her the fax number of the lobby receptionist in a different building on the company campus, where he had already made arrangements for faxes to be held for him, and would then arrange for the password fax to be forwarded. This time, though, Robert used a different fax-forwarding method. He gave the receptionist a fax number that went to an on-line fax service. When this service receives a fax, the automated system sends it to the subscriber's email address.

The new password arrived at the email dead drop that Robert set up on a free email service in China. He was sure that if the fax was ever traced, the investigator would be pulling out his hair trying to gain cooperation from Chinese officials, who, he knew, were more than a little reluctant to be helpful in matters like this. Best of all, he never had to show up physically at the location of the fax machine.

> The skilled social engineer is very clever at influencing other people to do favors for him. Receiving a fax and forwarding it to another location appears so harmless that it's all too easy to persuade a receptionist or someone else to agree to do it. When somebody asks for a favor involving information, if you don't know him or can't verify his identity, just say no.

TRAFFIC COURT

Probably everyone who has ever been given a speeding ticket has daydreamed about some way of beating it. Not by going to traffic school, or simply paying the fine, or taking a chance on trying to convince the judge about some technicality like how long it has been since the police-car speedometer or the radar gun was checked. No, the sweetest scenario would be beating the ticket by outsmarting the system.

The Con

Although I would not recommend trying this method of beating a traffic ticket (as the saying goes, don't try this at home) still, this is a good example of how the art of deception can be used to help the social engineer.

Let's call this traffic violater Paul Durea.

First Steps

"LAPD, Hollenbeck Division."

"Hi, I'd like to talk to the Subpoena Control."

"I'm the subpoena clerk."

"Fine. This is Attorney John Leland, of Meecham, Meecham, and Talbott. I need to subpoena an officer on a case."

"Okay, which officer?"

"Do you have Officer Kendall in your division?"

"What's his serial number?"

"21349."

"Yes. When do you need him?"

"Some time next month, but I need to subpoena several other witnesses on the case and then tell the court what days will work for us. Are there any days next month Officer Kendall won't be available?"

"Let's see . . . He has vacation days on the 20th through the 23rd, and he has training days on the 8th and 16th."

"Thanks. That's all I need right now. I'll call you back when the court date is set."

Municipal Court, Clerk's Counter

Paul: "I'd like to schedule a court date on this traffic ticket."

Clerk: "Okay. I can give you the 26th of next month."

"Well, I'd like to schedule an arraignment."

"You want an arraignment on a traffic ticket?"

"Yes."

"Okay. We can set the arraignment tomorrow in the morning or afternoon. What would you like?"

"Afternoon."

"Arraignment is tomorrow at 1:30 P.M. in Courtroom Six."

"Thanks. I'll be there."

Municipal Court, Courtroom Six

Date: Thursday, 1:45 P.M.

Clerk: "Mr. Durea, please approach the bench."

Judge: "Mr. Durea, do you understand the rights that have been explained to you this afternoon?"

Paul: "Yes, your honor."

Judge: "Do you want to take the opportunity to attend traffic school? Your case will be dismissed after successful completion of an eight-hour course. I've checked your record and you are presently eligible."

Paul: "No, your honor. I respectfully request that the case be set for trial. One more thing, your honor, I'll be traveling out of the country, but I'm available on the 8th or 9th. Would it be possible to set my case for trial on either of those days? I'm leaving on a business trip for Europe tomorrow, and I return in four weeks."

Judge: "Very well. Trial is set for June 8th, 8:30 A.M., Courtroom Four."

Paul: "Thank you, your honor."

Paul arrived at court early on the 8th. When the judge came in, the clerk gave him a list of the cases for which the officers had not appeared. The judge called the defendants, including Paul, and told them their cases were dismissed.

Analyzing the Con

When an officer writes a ticket, he signs it with his name and his badge number (or whatever his personal number is called in his agency). Finding his station is a piece of cake. A call to directory assistance with the name of the law enforcement agency shown on the citation (highway patrol, county sheriff, or whatever) is enough to get a foot in the door. Once the agency is contacted, they can refer the caller to the correct telephone number for the subpoena clerk serving the geographical area where the traffic stop was made.

Law enforcement officers are subpoenaed for court appearances with regularity; it comes with the territory. When a district attorney or a defense lawyer needs an officer to testify, if he knows how the system works, he first checks to make sure the officer will be available. That's easy to do; it just takes a call to the subpoena clerk for that agency.

Usually in those conversations, the attorney asks if the officer in question will be available on such-and-such a date. For this ruse, Paul needed a bit of tact; he had to offer a plausible reason why the clerk should tell him what dates the officer would *not* be available.

When he first went to the court building, why didn't Paul simply tell the court clerk what date he wanted? Easy—from what I understand, traffic-court clerks in most places don't allow members of the public to select court dates. If a date the clerk suggests doesn't work for the person, she'll offer an alternative or two, but that's as far as she will bend. On the other hand, anyone who is willing to take the extra time of showing up for an arraignment is likely to have better luck.

Paul knew he was entitled to ask for an arraignment. And he knew the judges are often willing to accommodate a request for a specific date. He carefully asked for dates that coincided with the officer's training days, knowing that in his state, officer training takes precedence over an appearance in traffic court.

And in traffic court, when the officer does not show up—case dismissed. No fines. No traffic school. No points. And, best of all, no record of a traffic offense!

My guess is that some police officials, court officers, district attorneys and the like will read this story and shake their heads because they know that this ruse does work. But shaking their heads is all they'll do. Nothing will change. I'd be willing to bet on it. As the character Cosmo says in the 1992 movie *Sneakers*, "It's all about the ones and zeros"—meaning that in the end, everything comes down to information.

As long as law enforcement agencies are willing to give information about an officer's schedule to virtually anyone who calls, the ability to get out of traffic tickets will always exist. Do you have similar gaps in your company or organization's procedures that a clever social engineer can take advantage of to get information you'd rather they didn't have?

SAMANTHA'S REVENGE

Samantha Gregson was angry.

She had worked hard for her college degree in business, and stacked up a pile of student loans to do it. It had always been drummed into her that a college degree was how you got a career instead of a job, how you earned the big bucks. And then she graduated and couldn't find a decent job anywhere.

How glad she had been to get the offer from Lambeck Manufacturing. Sure, it was humiliating to accept a secretarial position, but Mr. Cartright had said how eager they were to have her, and taking the secretarial job would put her on the spot when the next nonadministrative position opened up.

Two months later she heard that one of Cartright's junior product managers was leaving. She could hardly sleep that night, imagining herself on the fifth floor, in an office with a door, attending meetings and making decisions.

The next morning she went first thing to see Mr. Cartright. He said they felt she needed to learn more about the industry before she was ready for a professional position. And then they went and hired an amateur from outside the company who knew less about the industry than she did.

It was about then that it began to dawn on her: The company had plenty of women, but they were almost all secretaries. They weren't going to give her a management job. Ever.

Payback

It took her almost a week to figure out how she was going to pay them back. About a month earlier a guy from an industry trade magazine had tried to hit on her when he came in for the new product launch. A few weeks later he called her up at work and said if she would send him some advance information on the Cobra 273 product, he'd send her flowers, and if it was really hot information that he used in the magazine, he'd make a special trip in from Chicago just to take her out to dinner.

She had been in young Mr. Johannson's office one day shortly after that when he logged onto the corporate network. Without thinking, she had watched his fingers (*shoulder surfing*, this is sometimes called). He had entered "marty63" as his password.

Her plan was beginning to come together. There was a memo she remembered typing not long after she came to the company. She found a copy in the files and typed up a new version, using language from the original one. Her version read:

> TO: C. Pania, IT dept.
>
> FROM: L. Cartright, Development
>
> Martin Johansson will be working with a special projects team in my department.
>
> I hereby authorize him to have access to the servers used by the engineering group. Mr. Johansson's security profile is to be updated to grant him the same access rights as a product developer.
>
> Louis Cartright

lingo

SHOULDER SURFING   The act of watching a person type at his computer keyboard to detect and steal his password or other user information.

When most everybody was gone at lunch, she cut Mr. Cartright's signature from the original memo, pasted it onto her new version, and daubed Wite-Out around the edges. She made a copy of the result, and then made a copy of the copy. You could barely see the edges around the signature.

She sent the fax from the machine near Mr. Cartright's office.

Three days later, she stayed after hours and waited till everyone left. She walked into Johannson's office, and tried logging onto the network with his username and the password, marty63. It worked.

In minutes she had located the product specification files for the Cobra 273, and downloaded them to a Zip disk.

The disk was safely in her purse as she walked in the cool nighttime breeze to the parking lot. It would be on its way to the reporter that night.

Analyzing the Con

A disgruntled employee, a search through the files, a quick cut-paste-and-Wite-Out operation, a little creative copying, and a fax. And, voilà!—she has access to confidential marketing and product specifications.

And a few days later, a trade magazine journalist has a big scoop with the specs and marketing plans of a hot new product that will be in the hands of magazine subscribers throughout the industry months in advance of the product's release. Competitor companies will have several months head start on developing equivalent products and having their ad campaigns ready to undermine the Cobra 273.

Naturally the magazine will never say where they got the scoop.

PREVENTING THE CON

When asked for any valuable, sensitive, or critical information that could be of benefit to a competitor or anyone else, employees must be aware that using caller ID as a means of verifying the identity of an outside caller is not acceptable. Some other means of verification must be used, such as checking with the person's supervisor that the request was appropriate and that the user has authorization to receive the information.

The verification process requires a balancing act that each company must define for itself: Security versus productivity. What priority is going to be assigned to enforcing security measures? Will employees be resistant to following security procedures, and even circumvent them in order to complete their job responsibilities? Do employees understand why security is important to the company and themselves? These questions need to be answered to develop a security policy based on corporate culture and business needs.

Most people inevitably see anything that interferes with getting their work done as an annoyance, and may circumvent any security measures that appear to be a waste of time. Motivating employees to make security part of their everyday responsibilities through education and awareness is key.

Although caller ID service should never be used as a means of authentication for voice calls from outside the company, another method called automatic number identification (ANI) can. This service is provided when a company subscribes to toll-free services where the company pays for the incoming calls and is reliable for identification. Unlike caller ID, the telephone company switch does not use any information that is sent from a customer when providing the calling number. The number transmitted by ANI is the billing number assigned to the calling party.

Note that several modem manufacturers have added a caller ID feature into their products, protecting the corporate network by allowing remote-access calls only from a list of preauthorized telephone numbers. Caller ID modems are an acceptable means of authentication in a low-security environment but, as should be clear by now, spoofing caller ID is a relatively easy technique for computer intruders, and so should not be relied on for proving the caller's identity or location in a high-security setting.

To address the case of identity theft, as in the story about deceiving an administrator to create a voice mailbox on the corporate phone system, make it a policy that all phone service, all voice mailboxes, and all entries to the corporate directory, both in print and on line, must be requested in writing, on a form provided for the purpose. The employee's manager should sign the request, and the voice mail administrator should verify the signature.

Corporate security policy should require that new computer accounts or increases in access rights be granted only after positive verification of the person making the request, such as a callback to the system manager or administrator, or his or her designee, at the phone number listed in the print or on-line company directory. If the company uses secure email where employees can digitally sign messages, this alternative verification method may also be acceptable.

Remember that every employee, regardless of whether he has access to company computer systems, may be duped by a social engineer. Everyone must be included in security awareness training. Administrative assistants, receptionists, telephone operators, and security guards must be made familiar with the types of social engineering attack most likely to be directed against them so that they will be better prepared to defend against those attacks.

chapter 14

Industrial Espionage

the threat of information attacks against government, corporations, and university systems is well established. Almost every day, the media reports a new computer virus, denial of service attack, or theft of credit card information from an e-commerce Web site.

We read about cases of industrial espionage such as Borland accusing Symantec of stealing trade secrets, Cadence Design Systems filing a suit charging the theft of source code by a competitor. Many business people read these stories and think it could never happen at their company.

It's happening every day.

VARIATION ON A SCHEME

The ruse described in the following tale has probably been pulled off many times, even though it sounds like something taken out of a Hollywood movie like *The Insider*, or from the pages of a John Grisham novel.

Class Action

Imagine that a massive class-action lawsuit is raging against a major pharmaceutical company, Pharmomedic. The suit claims that they knew one of their very popular drugs had a devastating side effect, but one that would not be evident until a patient had been on the medication for years. The suit alleges that they had results from a number of research studies that revealed this danger, but suppressed the evidence and never turned it over to the FDA as required.

William ("Billy") Chaney, the attorney of record on the masthead of the New York law firm that filed the class-action suit, has depositions from two Pharmomedic doctors supporting the claim. But both are retired, neither has any files or documentation, and neither would make a strong, convincing witness. Billy knows he's on shaky ground. Unless he can get a copy of one of those reports, or some internal memo or communication between company executives, his whole case will fall apart.

So he hires a firm he's used before: Andreeson and Sons, private investigators. Billy doesn't know how Pete and his people get the stuff they do, and he doesn't want to know. All he knows is that Pete Andreeson is one good investigator.

To Andreeson, an assignment like this is what he calls a black bag job. The first rule is that the law firms and companies that hire him never learn how he gets his information so that they always have complete, plausible deniability. If anybody is going to have his feet shoved into boiling water, it's going to be Pete, and for what he collects in fees on the big jobs, he figures it's worth the risk. Besides, he gets such personal satisfaction from outsmarting smart people.

If the documents that Chaney wants him to find actually existed and haven't been destroyed, they'll be somewhere in the files of Pharmomedic. But finding them in the massive files of a large corporation would be a huge task. On the other hand, suppose they've turned copies over to their law firm, Jenkins and Petry? If the defense attorneys knew those documents existed and didn't turn them over as part of the discovery process, then they have violated the legal profession's canon of ethics, and violated the law, as well. In Pete's book, that makes any attack fair game.

Pete's Attack

Pete gets a couple of his people started on research and within days he knows what company Jenkins and Petry uses for storing their offsite backups. And he knows that the storage company maintains a list of the names of people whom the law firm has authorized to pick up tapes from storage. He also knows that each of these people has his or her own password. Pete sends two of his people out on a black bag job.

The men tackle the lock using a lock pick gun ordered on the Web at www.southord.com. Within several minutes they slip into the offices of the storage firm around 3 A.M. one night and boot up a PC. They smile when they see the Windows 98 logo because it means this will be a piece of cake. Windows 98 does not require any form of authentication. After a bit of searching, they locate a Microsoft Access database with the names of people authorized by each of the storage company customers to pick up tapes. They add a phony name to the authorization list for Jenkins and Petry, a name matching one on a phony driver's license one of the men has already obtained. Could they have broken into the locked storage area and tried to locate the tapes their client wanted? Sure—but then all the company's customers, including the law firm, would have certainly been notified of the breach. And the attackers would have lost an advantage: Professionals always like to leave an opening for future access, should the need arise.

Following a standard practice of industrial spies to keep something in the back pocket for future use, just in case, they also made a copy of the file containing the authorization list onto a floppy disk. None of them had any idea how it might ever prove useful, but it's just one of those "We're here, we might just as well" things that every now and then turns out to be valuable.

The next day, one of the same men called the storage company, used the name they had added to the authorization list, and gave the corresponding password. He asked for all the Jenkins and Petry tapes dated within the last month, and said that a messenger service would come by to pick up the package. By midafternoon, Andreeson had the tapes. His people restored all the data to their own computer system, ready to search at leisure. Andreeson was very pleased that the law firm, like most other businesses, didn't bother encrypting their backup data.

The tapes were delivered back to the storage company the next day and no one was the wiser.

Analyzing the Con

Because of lax physical security, the bad guys were easily able to pick the lock of the storage company, gain access to the computer, and modify the

mitnick
message

Valuable information must be protected no matter what form it takes or where it is located. An organization's customer list has the same value whether in hard-copy form or an electronic file at your office or in a storage box. Social engineers always prefer the easiest to circumvent, least defended point of attack. A company's offsite backup storage facility is seen as having less risk of detection or getting caught. Every organization that stores any valuable, sensitive, or critical data with third parties should encrypt their data to protect its confidentiality.

database containing the list of people authorized to have access to the storage unit. Adding a name to the list allowed the imposters to obtain the computer backup tapes they were after, without having to break into the firm's storage unit. Because most businesses don't encrypt backup data, the information was theirs for the taking.

This incident provides one more example of how a vendor company that does not exercise reasonable security precautions can make it easy for an attacker to compromise their customer's information assets.

THE NEW BUSINESS PARTNER

Social engineers have a big advantage over con men and grifters, and the advantage is distance. A grifter can only cheat you by being in your presence, allowing you to give a good description of him afterward or even call the cops if you catch on to the ruse early enough.

Social engineers ordinarily avoid that risk like the plague. Sometimes, though, the risk is necessary, and justified by the potential reward.

Jessica's Story

Jessica Andover was feeling very good about getting a job with a hot-shot robotics company. Sure, it was only a start-up and they couldn't pay very much, but it was small, the people were friendly, and there was the excitement of knowing her stock options just might turn out to make her rich. Okay, maybe not a millionaire like the company founders would be, but rich enough.

Which was how it happened that Rick Daggot got a glowing smile when he walked into the lobby that Tuesday morning in August. In his expensive-looking suit (Armani) and his heavy gold wrist-watch (a Rolex President), with his immaculate haircut, he had that same manly, self-confident air that had driven all the girls crazy when Jessica was in high school.

"Hi," he said. "I'm Rick Daggot and I'm here for my meeting with Larry."

Jessica's smile faded. "Larry?" she said. "Larry's on vacation all week."

"I have an appointment with him at one o'clock. I just flew in from Louisville to meet with him," Rick said, as he drew out his Palm, turned it on, and showed her.

She looked at it and gave a small shake of her head. "The 20th," she said. "That's *next* week." He took the palmtop back and stared at it. "Oh, no!" he groaned. "I can't believe what a stupid mistake I made."

"Can I book a return flight for you, at least?" she asked, feeling sorry for him.

While she made the phone call, Rick confided that he and Larry had arranged to set up a strategic marketing alliance. Rick's company was producing products for the manufacturing and assembly line, items that would perfectly complement their new product, the C2Alpha. Rick's products and the C2Alpha together would make a strong solution that would open up important industrial markets for both companies.

When Jessica had finished making his reservation on a late afternoon flight, Rick said, "Well, at least I could talk to Steve if he's available." But Steve, the company's VP and cofounder, was also out of the office.

Rick, being very friendly to Jessica and flirting just a little, then suggested that, as long as he was there and his flight home wasn't till late afternoon, he'd like to take some of the key people to lunch. And he added, "Including you, of course—is there somebody who can fill in for you at lunchtime?"

Flushed at the idea of being included, Jessica asked, "Who do you want to come?" He tapped his palmtop again and named a few people—two engineers from R&D, the new sales and marketing man, and the finance guy assigned to the project. Rick suggested she tell them about his relationship with the company, and that he'd like to introduce himself to them. He named the best restaurant in the area, a place where Jessica had always wanted to go, and said he'd book the table himself, for 12:30, and would call back later in the morning to make sure everything was all set.

When they gathered at the restaurant—the four of them plus Jessica—their table wasn't ready yet, so they settled at the bar, and Rick made it clear that drinks and lunch were on him. Rick was a man with style and class, the kind of person who makes you feel comfortable from the very first, the same way you feel with someone you've known for years. He always seemed to know just the right thing to say, had a lively remark or something funny whenever the conversation lagged, and made you feel good just being around him.

He shared just enough details about his own company's products that they could envision the joint marketing solution he seemed so animated about. He named several Fortune 500 companies that his firm was already selling to, until everyone at the table began to picture their product becoming a success from the day the first units rolled out of the factory.

Then Rick walked over to Brian, one of the engineers. While the others chatted among themselves, Rick shared some ideas privately with Brian, and drew him out about the unique features of the C2Alpha and what set it apart from anything the competition had. He found out about a couple of features the company was downplaying that Brian was proud of and thought really "neat."

Rick worked his way along the line, chatting quietly with each. The marketing guy was happy for a chance to talk about the roll-out date and marketing plans. And the bean counter pulled an envelope from his pocket and wrote down details of the material and manufacturing costs, price point and expected margin, and what kind of deal he was trying to work out with each of the vendors, which he listed by name.

By the time their table was ready, Rick had exchanged ideas with everybody and had won admirers all along the line. By the end of the meal, they each shook hands with Rick in turn and thanked him. Rick swapped business cards with each and mentioned in passing to Brian, the engineer, that he wanted to have a longer discussion as soon as Larry returned.

The following day Brian picked up his telephone to find that the caller was Rick, who said he had just finished speaking with Larry. "I'll be coming back in on Monday to work out some of the specifics with him," Rick said, "and he wants me to be up to speed on your product. He said you should email the latest designs and specs to him. He'll pick out the parts he wants me to have and forward them on to me."

The engineer said that would be fine. "Good," Rick answered. He went on, "Larry wanted you to know he's having a problem retrieving his email. Instead of sending the stuff to his regular account, he arranged with the hotel's business center to set up a Yahoo mail account for him. He says you should send the files to larryrobotics@yahoo.com."

The following Monday morning, when Larry walked into the office looking tanned and relaxed, Jessica was primed and eager to gush over Rick. "What a great guy. He took a bunch of us to lunch, even me." Larry looked confused. "Rick? Who the hell is Rick?"

"What're you talking about?—your new business partner."

"What!!!???"

"And everybody was so impressed with what good questions he asked."

"I don't know any Rick ..."

"What's the matter with you? Is this a joke, Larry—you're just fooling with me, right?"

"Get the executive team into the conference room. Like *now*. No matter what they're doing. And everybody who was at that lunch. Including you."

They sat around the table in a somber mood, hardly speaking. Larry walked in, sat down and said, "I do not know anybody named Rick. I do not have a new business partner I've been keeping secret from all of you. Which I would have thought was obvious. If there's a practical joker in our midst, I want him to speak up *now*."

Not a sound. The room seemed to be growing darker moment by moment.

Finally Brian spoke. "Why didn't you say something when I sent you that email with the product specs and source code?"

"*What* email!?"

Brian stiffened. "Oh . . . shit!"

Cliff, the other engineer, chimed in. "He gave us all business cards. We just need to call him and see what the hell's going on."

Brian pulled out his palmtop, called up an entry, and scooted the device across the table to Larry. Still hoping against hope, they all watched as if entranced while Larry dialed. After a moment, he stabbed the speakerphone button and everyone heard a busy signal. After trying the number several times over a period of twenty minutes, a frustrated Larry dialed the operator to ask for an emergency interruption.

A few moments later, the operator came back on the line. She said in a challenging tone, "Sir, where did you get this number?" Larry told her it was on the business card of a man he needed to contact urgently. The operator, said, "I'm sorry. That's a phone company test number. It always rings busy."

Larry started making a list of what information had been shared with Rick. The picture was not pretty.

Two police detectives came and took a report. After listening to the story, they pointed out that no state crime had been committed; there was nothing they could do. They advised Larry to contact the FBI because they have jurisdiction over any crimes involving interstate commerce. When Rick Daggot asked the engineer to forward the test results by misrepresenting himself, he may have committed a federal crime, but Rick would have to speak with the FBI to find out.

Three months later Larry was in his kitchen reading the morning paper over breakfast, and almost spilled his coffee. The thing he had been dreading since he had first heard about Rick had come true, his worst nightmare. There it was in black and white, on the front page of the business section: A company he'd never heard of was announcing the release of a new product that sounded exactly like the C2Alpha his company had been developing for the past two years.

Through deceit, these people had beaten him to market. His dream was destroyed. The millions of dollars invested in research and development wasted. And he probably couldn't prove a single thing against them.

Sammy Sanford's Story

Smart enough to be earning a big salary at a legitimate job, but crooked enough to prefer making a living as a con man, Sammy Sanford had done very well for himself. In time he came to the attention of a spy who had been forced into early retirement because of a drinking problem; bitter and revengeful, the man had found a way of selling the talents that the government had made him an expert in. Always on the lookout for people he could use, he had spotted Sammy the first time they met. Sammy had found it easy, and very profitable, to shift his focus from lifting people's money to lifting company secrets.

···•••●●●•••···

Most people wouldn't have the guts to do what I do. Try to cheat people over the telephone or over the Internet and nobody ever gets to see you. But any good con man, the old-fashioned, face-to-face kind (and there are plenty of them still around, more than you would think) can look you in the eye, tell you a whopper, and get you to believe it. I've known a prosecutor or two who think that's criminal. I think it's a talent.

But you can't go walking in blind, you have to size things up first. A street con, you can take a man's temperature with a little friendly conversation and couple of carefully worded suggestions. Get the right responses and Bingo!—you've bagged a pigeon.

A company job is more like what we call a big con. You've got setup to do. Find out what their buttons are, find out what they want. What they need. Plan an attack. Be patient, do your homework. Figure out the role you're going to play and learn your lines. And don't walk in the door until you're ready.

I spent better than three weeks getting up to speed for this one. The client gave me a two-day session in what I should say "my" company did and how to describe why it was going to be such a good joint marketing alliance.

Then I got lucky. I called the company and said I was from a venture capital firm and we were interested in setting up a meeting and I was juggling schedules to find a time when all of our partners would be available sometime in the next couple of months, and was there any time slot I should avoid, any period when Larry wasn't going to be in town? And she said, Yes, he hadn't had any time off in the two years since they started the company but his wife was dragging him away on a golf vacation the first week in August.

That was only two weeks away. I could wait.

Meanwhile an industry magazine gave me the name of the firm's PR company. I said I liked the amount of space they were getting for their robotics company client and I wanted to talk to whoever was handling that account about handling my company. It turned out to be an energetic young lady who liked the idea she might be able to bring in a new account. Over a pricey lunch with one more drink than she really wanted, she did her best to convince me they were oh, so good at understanding a client's problems and finding the right PR solutions. I played hard to convince. I needed some details. With a little prodding, by the time the plates were being cleared she had told me more about the new product and the company's problems than I could have hoped for.

The thing went like clockwork. The story about being so embarrassed that the meeting was *next* week but I might as well meet the team as long as I'm here, the receptionist swallowed whole. She even felt sorry for me into the bargain. The lunch set me back all of $150. With tip. And I had what I needed. Phone numbers, job titles, and one very key guy who believed I was who I said I was.

Brian had me fooled, I admit. He seemed like the kind of guy who'd just email me anything I asked for. But he sounded like he was holding back a little when I brought up the subject. It pays to expect the unexpected. That email account in Larry's name, I had it in my back pocket just in case. The Yahoo security people are probably still sitting there waiting for somebody to use the account again so they can trace him. They'll have a long wait. The fat lady has sung. I'm off on another project.

Analyzing the Con

Anyone who works a face-to-face con has to cloak himself in a look that will make him acceptable to the mark. He'll put himself together one way to appear at the race track, another to appear at a local watering hole, still another for an upscale bar at a fancy hotel.

It's the same way with industrial espionage. An attack may call for a suit and tie and an expensive briefcase if the spy is posing as an executive of an established firm, a consultant, or a sales rep. On another job, trying to pass as a software engineer, a technical person, or someone from the mail room, the clothes, the uniform—the whole look—would be different.

For infiltrating the company, the man who called himself Rick Daggot knew he had to project an image of confidence and competence, backed by a thorough knowledge of the company's product and industry.

Not much difficulty laying his hands on the information he needed in advance. He devised an easy ruse to find out when the CEO would be away. A small challenge, but still not very tough, was finding out enough details about the project that he could sound "on the inside" about what they were doing. Often this information is known to various company suppliers, as well as investors, venture capitalists they've approached about raising money, their banker, and their law firm. The attacker has to take care, though: Finding someone who will part with insider knowledge can be tricky, but trying two or three sources to turn up someone who can be squeezed for information runs the risk that people will catch on to the game. That way lies danger. The Rick Daggots of the world need to pick carefully and tread each information path only once.

The lunch was another sticky proposition. First there was the problem of arranging things so he'd have a few minutes alone with each person, out of earshot of the others. He told Jessica 12:30 but booked the table for 1 P.M., at an upscale, expense-account type of restaurant. He hoped that would mean they'd have to have drinks at the bar, which is exactly what happened. A perfect opportunity to move around and chat with each individual.

Still, there were so many ways that a misstep—a wrong answer or a careless remark—could reveal Rick to be an imposter. Only a supremely confident and wily industrial spy would dare take a chance of exposing himself that way. But years of working the streets as a confidence man had

mitnick message

While most social engineering attacks occur over the telephone or email, don't assume that a bold attacker will never appear in person at your business. In most cases, the imposter uses some form of social engineering to gain access to a building after counterfeiting an employee badge using a commonly available software program such as Photoshop.

What about the business cards with the phone company test line? The television show *The Rockford Files*, which was a series about a private investigator, illustrated a clever and somewhat humorous technique. Rockford (played by actor James Garner) had a portable business card printing machine in his car, which he used to print out a card appropriate to whatever the occasion called for. These days, a social engineer can get business cards printed in an hour at any copy store, or print them on a laser printer.

built Rick's abilities and given him the confidence that, even if he made a slip, he'd be able to cover it up well enough to quiet any suspicions. This was the most challenging, most dangerous time of the entire operation, and the elation he felt at bringing off a sting like this made him realize why he didn't have to drive fast cars or skydive or cheat on his wife—he got plenty of excitement just doing his job. How many people, he wondered, could say as much?

What leads a group of smart men and women to accept an imposter? We size up a situation by both instinct and intellect. If the story adds up—that's the intellect part—and a con man manages to project a believable image, we're usually willing to let down our guard. It's the believable image that separates a successful con man or social engineer from one who quickly lands behind bars.

Ask yourself: How sure am I that I would never fall for a story like Rick's? If you're sure you wouldn't, ask yourself whether anyone has *ever* put anything over on you. If the answer to this second question is yes, it's probably the correct answer to the first question, as well.

LEAPFROG

A challenge: The following story does not involve industrial espionage. As you read it, see if you can understand why I decided to put it in this chapter!

Harry Tardy was back living at home, and he was bitter. The Marine Corps had seemed like a great escape until he washed out of boot camp. Now he had returned to the hometown he hated, was taking computer courses at the local community college, and looking for a way to strike out at the world.

Finally he hit upon a plan. Over beers with a guy in one of his classes, he'd been complaining about their instructor, a sarcastic know-it-all, and together they cooked up a wicked scheme to burn the guy: They'd grab the source code for a popular personal digital assistant (PDA) and have it sent to the instructor's computer, and make sure to leave a trail so the company would think the instructor was the bad guy.

The new friend, Karl Alexander, said he "knew a few tricks" and would tell Harry how to bring this off. And get away with it.

Doing Their Homework

A little initial research showed Harry that the product had been engineered at the Development Center located at the PDA manufacturer's headquarters overseas. But there was also an R&D facility in the United States. That was good, Karl pointed out, because for the attempt to work there had to be some company facility in the United States that also needed access to the source code.

At that point Harry was ready to call the overseas Development Center. Here's where a plea for sympathy came in, the "Oh, dear, I'm in trouble, I need help, please, please, help me." Naturally the plea was a little more subtle than that. Karl wrote out a script, but Harry sounded completely phony trying to read it. In the end, he practiced with Karl so he could say what he needed to in a conversational tone.

What Harry finally said, with Karl sitting by his side, went something like this:

"I'm calling from R&D Minneapolis. Our server had a worm that infected the whole department. We had to install the operating system again and then when we went to restore from backup, none of the backups was any good. Guess who was supposed to be checking the integrity of the backups? Yours truly. So I'm getting yelled at by my boss, and management is up in arms that we've lost the data. Look, I need to have the latest revision of the source-code tree as quick as you can. I need you to *gzip* the source code and send it to me."

At this point Karl scribbled him a note, and Harry told the man on the other end of the phone that he just wanted him to transfer the file internally, to Minneapolis R&D. This was highly important: When the man on the other end of the phone was clear that he was just being asked to send the file to another part of the company, his mind was at ease—what could be wrong with that?

![lingo]

GZIP To archive files in a single compressed file using a Linux GNU utility.

He agreed to gzip and send it. Step by step, with Karl at his elbow, Harry talked the man there through getting started on the procedure for compressing the huge source code into a single, compact file. He also gave him a file name to use on the compressed file, "newdata," explaining that this name would avoid any confusion with their old, corrupted files.

Karl had to explain the next step twice before Harry got it, but it was central to the little game of leapfrog Karl had dreamed up. Harry was to call R&D Minneapolis and tell somebody there "I want to send a file to you, and then I want you to send it somewhere else for me"—of course all dressed up with reasons that would make it all sound plausible. What confused Harry was this: He was supposed to say "*I'm* going to send you a file," when it wasn't going to be Harry sending the file at all. He had to make the guy he was talking to at the R&D Center think the file was coming from him, when what the Center was really going to receive was the file of proprietary source code from Europe. "Why would I tell him it's coming from me when it's really coming from overseas?" Harry wanted to know.

"The guy at the R&D Center is the linchpin," Karl explained. "He's got to think he's just doing a favor for a fellow employee here in the U.S., getting a file from you and then just forwarding it for you."

Harry finally understood. He called the R&D Center, where he asked the receptionist to connect him to the Computer Center, where he asked to speak to a computer operator. A guy came on the line who sounded as young as Harry himself. Harry greeted him, explained he was calling from the Chicago fabricating division of the company and that he had this file he'd been trying to send to one of their partners working on a project with them, but, he said, "We've got this router problem and can't reach their network. I'd like to transfer the file to you, and after you receive it, I'll phone you so I can walk you through transferring it to the partner's computer."

So far, so good. Harry then asked the young man whether his computer center had an *anonymous FTP* account, a setup that allows anyone to transfer files in and out of a directory where no password is required. Yes,

lingo

ANONYMOUS FTP   A program that provides access to a remote computer even though you don't have an account by using the File Transfer protocol (FTP). Although anonymous FTP can be accessed without a password, generally user-access rights to certain folders are restricted.

an anonymous FTP was available, and he gave Harry the internal Internet Protocol (IP) address for reaching it.

With that information in hand, Harry called back the Development Center overseas. By now the compressed file was ready, and Harry gave the instructions for transferring the file to the anonymous FTP site. In less than five minutes, the compressed source-code file was sent to the kid at the R&D Center.

Setting Up the Victim

Halfway to the goal. Now Harry and Karl had to wait to make sure the file had arrived before proceeding. During the wait, they walked across the room to the instructor's desk and took care of two other necessary steps. They first set up an anonymous FTP server on his machine, which would serve as a destination for the file in the last leg of their scheme.

The second step provided a solution for an otherwise tricky problem. Clearly they couldn't tell their man at the R&D Center to send the file to an address such as, say, warren@rms.ca.edu. The ".edu" domain would be a dead giveaway, since any half-awake computer guy would recognize it as the address of a school, immediately blowing the whole operation. To avoid this, they went into Windows on the instructor's computer and looked up the machine's IP address, which they would give as the address for sending the file.

By then it was time to call back the computer operator at the R&D Center. Harry got him on the phone and said, "I just transferred the file that I talked to you about. Can you check that you received it?" Yes, it had arrived. Harry then asked him to try forwarding it, and gave him the IP address. He stayed on the phone while the young man made the connection and started transmitting the file, and they watched with big grins from across the room as the light on the hard drive of the instructor's computer blinked and blinked—busy receiving the download.

Harry exchanged a couple of remarks with the guy about how maybe one day computers and peripherals would be more reliable, thanked him and said good-bye.

The two copied the file from the instructor's machine onto a pair of Zip disks, one for each of them, just so they could look at it later, like stealing a painting from a museum that you can enjoy yourself but don't dare show to your friends. Except, in this case, it was more like they had taken a duplicate original of the painting, and the museum still had their own original.

Karl then talked Harry through the steps of removing the FTP server from the instructor's machine, and erasing the audit trail so there would be no evidence of what they had done—only the stolen file, left where it could be located easily.

As a final step, they posted a section of the source code on Usenet directly from the instructor's computer. Only a section, so they wouldn't do any great damage to the company, but leaving clear tracks directly back to the instructor. He would have some difficult explaining to do.

Analyzing the Con

Although it took the combination of a number of elements to make this escapade work, it could not have succeeded without some skillful play-acting of an appeal for sympathy and help: I'm getting yelled at by my boss, and management is up in arms, and so on. That, combined with a pointed explanation of how the man on the other end of the phone could help solve the problem, proved to be a powerfully convincing con. It worked here, and has worked many other times.

The second crucial element: The man who understood the value of the file was asked to send it to an address *within* the company.

And the third piece of the puzzle: The computer operator could see that the file had been transferred to him from within the company. That could only mean—or so it seemed—that the man who sent it to him could himself have sent it on to the final destination if only his external network connection had been working. What could possibly be wrong with helping him out by sending it for him?

But what about having the compressed file assigned a different name? Seemingly a small item, but an important one. The attacker couldn't afford taking a chance of the file arriving with a name identifying it as source code, or a name related to the product. A request to send a file with a name like that outside the company might have set off alarm bells. Having the file relabeled with an innocuous name was crucial. As worked out by the attackers, the second young man had no qualms about sending the file outside the company; a file with a name like newdata, giving no clue as to the true nature of the information, would hardly make him suspicious.

Finally, did you figure out what this story is doing in a chapter on industrial espionage? If not, here's the answer: What these two students did as a malicious prank could just as easily have been done by a professional industrial spy, perhaps in the pay of a competitor, or perhaps in the pay of

a foreign government. Either way, the damage could have been devastating to the company, severely eroding the sales of their new product once the competitive product reached the market.

How easily could the same type of attack be carried out against your company?

PREVENTING THE CON

Industrial espionage, which has long been a challenge to businesses, has now become the bread and butter of traditional spies who have focused their efforts on obtaining company secrets for a price, now that the Cold War has ended. Foreign governments and corporations are now using freelance industrial spies to steal information. Domestic companies also hire information brokers who cross the line in their efforts to obtain competitive intelligence. In many cases these are former military spies turned industrial information brokers who have the prerequisite knowledge and experience to easily exploit organizations, especially those that have failed to deploy safeguards to protect their information and educate their people.

Safety Off-Site

What could have helped the company that ran into problems with their off-site storage facility? The danger here could have been avoided if the company had been encrypting their data. Yes, encryption requires extra time and expense, but it's well worth the effort. Encrypted files need to be spot-checked regularly to be sure that the encryption/decryption is working smoothly.

There's always the danger that the encryption keys will be lost or that the only person who knows the keys will be hit by a bus. But the nuisance level can be minimized, and anyone who stores sensitive information off-site with a commercial firm and does not use encryption is, excuse me for being blunt, an idiot. It's like walking down the street in a bad neighborhood with twenty-dollar bills sticking out of your pockets, essentially asking to be robbed.

Leaving backup media where someone could walk off with it is a common flaw in security. Several years ago, I was employed at a firm that could have made better efforts to protect client information. The operation's staff left the firm's backup tapes *outside* the locked computer room door for a messenger to pick up each day. Anyone could have walked off with the backup tapes, which contained all of the firm's word-processed documents in unencrypted text. If backup data is encrypted, loss of the material is a nuisance; if it's not encrypted—well, you can envision the impact on your company better than I can.

The need in larger companies for reliable offsite storage is pretty much a given. But your company's security procedures need to include an investigation of your storage company to see how conscientious they are about their own security policies and practices. If they're not as dedicated as your own company, all your security efforts could be undermined.

Smaller companies have a good alternate choice for backup: Send the new and changed files each night to one of the companies offering on-line storage. Again, it's essential that the data be encrypted. Otherwise, the information is available not just to a bent employee at the storage company but to every computer intruder who can breach the on-line storage company's computer systems or network.

And of course, when you set up an encryption system to protect the security of your backup files, you must also set up a highly secure procedure for storing the encryption keys or the pass phrases that unlock them. Secret keys used to encrypt data should be stored in a safe or vault. Standard company practice needs to provide for the possibility that the employee handling this data could suddenly leave, die, or take another job. There must always be at least two people who know the storage place and the encryption/decryption procedures, as well as the policies for how and when keys are to be changed. The policies must also require that encryption keys be changed immediately upon the departure of any employee who had access to them.

Who Is That?

The example in this chapter of a slick con artist who uses charm to get employees to share information reinforces the importance of verification of identity. The request to have source code forwarded to an FTP site also points to the importance of knowing your requester.

In Chapter 16 you will find specific policies for verifying the identity of any stranger who makes a request for information or a request that some action be taken. We've talked about the need for verification throughout the book; in Chapter 16 you'll get specifics of how this should be done.

•••••••●●●•••••••

part4

raising the bar

chapter 15

Information Security Awareness and Training

a social engineer has been given the assignment of obtaining the plans to your hot new product due for release in two months. What's going to stop him?

Your firewall? No.

Strong authentication devices? No.

Intrusion detection systems? No.

Encryption? No.

Limited access to phone numbers for dial-up modems? No.

Code names for servers that make it difficult for an outsider to determine which server might contain the product plans? No.

The truth is that there is no technology in the world that can prevent a social engineering attack.

SECURITY THROUGH TECHNOLOGY, TRAINING, AND PROCEDURES

Companies that conduct security penetration tests report that their attempts to break into client company computer systems by social engineering methods are nearly *100 percent* successful. Security technologies can make these types of attacks more difficult by removing people from the decision-making process. However the only truly effective way to mitigate the threat of social engineering is through the use of security awareness *combined with* security policies that set ground rules for employee behavior, and appropriate education and training for employees.

There is only one way to keep your product plans safe and that is by having a trained, aware, and a conscientious workforce. This involves training on the policies and procedures, but also—and probably even more important—an ongoing awareness program. Some authorities recommend that 40 percent of a company's overall security budget be targeted to awareness training.

The first step is to make everyone in the enterprise aware that unscrupulous people exist who will use deception to psychologically manipulate them. Employees must be educated about what information needs to be protected, and how to protect it. Once people have a better understanding of how they can be manipulated, they are in a far better position to recognize that an attack is underway.

Security awareness also means educating everyone in the enterprise on the company's security policies and procedures. As discussed in Chapter 17, policies are necessary rules to guide employee behavior to protect corporate information systems and sensitive information.

This chapter and the next one provide a security blueprint that could save you from costly attacks. If you don't have trained and alert employees following well-thought-out procedures, it's not a matter of *if*, but *when* you will lose valuable information to a social engineer. Don't wait for an attack to happen to you before instituting these policies: It could be devastating to your business and to your employees' welfare.

UNDERSTANDING HOW ATTACKERS TAKE ADVANTAGE OF HUMAN NATURE

To develop a successful training program, you have to understand why people are vulnerable to attacks in the first place. By identifying these tendencies in your training—for example, by drawing attention to them in role-playing discussions—you can help your employees to understand why we can all be manipulated by social engineers.

Manipulation has been studied by social scientists for at least fifty years. Robert B. Cialdini, writing in *Scientific American* (February 2001), summarized this research, presenting six "basic tendencies of human nature" that are involved in an attempt to obtain compliance to a request.

These six tendencies are those that social engineers rely on (consciously or, most often, unconsciously) in their attempts to manipulate.

Authority

People have a tendency to comply when a request is made by a person in authority. As discussed elsewhere in these pages, a person can be convinced to comply with a request if he or she believes the requestor is a person in authority or a person who is authorized to make such a request.

In his book *Influence,* Dr. Cialdini writes of a study at three Midwestern hospitals in which twenty-two separate nurses' stations were contacted by a caller who claimed to be a hospital physician, and given instructions for administering a prescription drug to a patient on the ward. The nurses who received these instructions did not know the caller. They did not even know whether he was really a doctor (he was not). They received the instructions for the prescription by telephone, which was a violation of hospital policy. The drug they were told to administer was not authorized for use on the wards, and the dosage they were told to administer was twice the maximum daily dosage, and thus could have endangered the life of the patient. Yet in 95 percent of the cases, Cialdini reported, "the nurse proceeded to obtain the necessary dosage from the ward medicine cabinet and was on her way to administer it to the patient" before being intercepted by an observer and told of the experiment.

> **Examples of attacks:** A social engineer attempts to cloak himself in the mantle of authority by claiming that he is with the IT department, or that he is an executive or works for an executive in the company.

Liking

People have the tendency to comply when the person making a request has been able to establish himself as likable, or as having similar interests, beliefs, and attitudes as the victim.

> **Examples of attacks**: Through conversation, the attacker manages to learn a hobby or interest of the victim, and claims an interest and enthusiasm for the same hobby or interest. Or he may claim to be from the same state or school, or to have similar goals. The social engineer will also attempt to mimic the behaviors of his target to create the appearance of similarity.

Reciprocation

We may automatically comply with a request when we have been given or promised something of value. The gift may be a material item, or advice, or help. When someone has done something for you, you feel an inclination to reciprocate. This strong tendency to reciprocate exists even in situations where the person receiving the gift hasn't asked for it. One of the most effective ways to influence people to do us a "favor" (comply with a request) is by giving some gift or assistance that forms an underlying obligation.

Members of the Hare Krishna religious cult were very effective at influencing people to donate to their cause by first giving them a book or flower as a gift. If the recipient tried to return the gift, the giver would refuse remarking, "It's our gift to you." This behavioral principle of reciprocation was used by the Krishnas to substantially increase donations.

> **Examples of attacks:** An employee receives a call from a person who identifies himself as being from the IT department. The caller explains that some company computers have been infected with a new virus not recognized by the antivirus software that can destroy all files on a computer, and offers to talk the person through some steps to prevent problems. Following this, the caller asks the person to test a software utility that has just been recently upgraded for allowing users to change passwords. The employee is reluctant to refuse, because the caller has just provided help that will supposedly protect the user from a virus. He reciprocates by complying with the caller's request.

Consistency

People have the tendency to comply after having made a public commitment or endorsement for a cause. Once we have promised we will do something, we don't want to appear untrustworthy or undesirable and will tend to follow through in order to be consistent with our statement or promise.

> **Example of attack:** The attacker contacts a relatively new employee and advises her of the agreement to abide by certain security policies and procedures as a condition of being allowed to use company information systems. After discussing a few security practices, the caller asks the user for her password "to verify compliance" with policy on choosing a difficult-to-guess password. Once the user reveals her password, the caller makes a recommendation to construct future passwords in such a way that the attacker will be able to guess it. The victim complies because of her prior agreement to abide by company policies and her assumption that the caller is merely verifying her compliance.

Social Validation

People have the tendency to comply when doing so appears to be in line with what others are doing. The action of others is accepted as validation that the behavior in question is the correct and appropriate action.

> **Examples of attacks:** The caller says he is conducting a survey and names other people in the department who he claims have already cooperated with him. The victim, believing that cooperation by others validates the authenticity of the request, agrees to take part. The caller then asks a series of questions, among which are questions that draw the victim into revealing his computer username and password.

Scarcity

People have the tendency to comply when it is believed that the object sought is in short supply and others are competing for it, or that it is available only for a short period of time.

> **Example of attack:** The attacker sends emails claiming that the first 500 people to register at the company's new Web site will win free tickets to a hot new movie. When an unsuspecting employee registers at the site, he is asked to provide his company email address and to choose a password. Many people, motivated by convenience, have the propensity to use the same or a similar password on every computer system they use. Taking advantage of this, the attacker then attempts to compromise the target's work and home computer systems with the username and password that have been entered during the Web site registration process.

CREATING TRAINING AND AWARENESS PROGRAMS

Issuing an information security policy pamphlet or directing employees to an intranet page that details security policies will not, by itself, mitigate your risk. Every business must not only define the rules with written policies, but must make the extra effort to direct *everyone* who works with corporate information or computer systems to learn and follow the rules. Furthermore, you must ensure that everyone understands the reason behind each policy so that people don't circumvent the rule as a matter of convenience. Otherwise, ignorance will always be the worker's excuse, and the precise vulnerability that social engineers will exploit.

The central goal of any security awareness program is to influence people to change their behavior and attitudes by motivating every employee to *want* to chip in and do his part to protect the organization's information assets. A great motivator in this instance is to explain how their participation will benefit not just the company, but the individual employees as well. Since the company retains certain private information about every worker, when employees do their part to protect information or information systems, they are actually protecting their own information, too.

A security training program requires substantial support. The training effort needs to reach every person who has access to sensitive information or corporate computer systems, must be on-going, and must be continuously revised to update personnel on new threats and vulnerabilities. Employees must see that senior management is fully committed to the program. That commitment must be real, not just a rubber-stamped "We give our blessings" memo. And the program must be backed up with sufficient resources to develop, communicate, test it, and to measure success.

Goals

The basic guideline that should be kept in mind during development of an information security training and awareness program is that the program needs to focus on creating in all employees an awareness that their company might be under attack at any time. They must learn that each employee plays a role in defending against any attempt to gain entry to computer systems or to steal sensitive data.

Because many aspects of information security involve technology, it's too easy for employees to think that the problem is being handled by firewalls and other security technologies. A primary goal of training should be to create awareness in each employee that they are the front line needed to protect the overall security of the organization.

Security training must have a significantly greater aim than simply imparting rules. The training program designer must recognize the strong temptation on the part of employees, under pressure of getting their jobs done, to overlook or ignore their security responsibilities. Knowledge about the tactics of social engineering and how to defend against the attacks is important, but it will only be of value if the training is designed to focus heavily on *motivating* employees to use the knowledge.

The company can count the program as meeting its bottom-line goal if everyone completing the training is thoroughly convinced and motivated by one basic notion: that information security is part of his or her job.

Employees must come to appreciate and accept that the threat of social engineering attacks is real, and that a serious loss of sensitive corporate information could endanger the company as well as their own personal information and jobs. In a sense, being careless about information security at work is equivalent to being careless with one's ATM PIN or credit card number. This can be a compelling analogy for building enthusiasm for security practices.

Establishing the Training and Awareness Program

The person responsible for designing the information security program needs to recognize that this is not a one-size-fits-all project. Rather, the training needs to be developed to suit the specific requirements of several different groups within the enterprise. While many of the security policies outlined in Chapter 16 apply to all employees across the board, many others are unique. At a minimum, most companies will need training programs tailored to these distinct groups: managers; IT personnel; computer users; nontechnical personnel; administrative assistants; receptionists; and security guards. (See the breakdown of policies by job assignment in Chapter 16.)

Since the personnel of a company's industrial security force are not ordinarily expected to be computer proficient, and, except perhaps in a very limited way, do not come into contact with company computers, they are not usually considered when designing training of this kind. However, social engineers can deceive security guards or others into allowing them into a building or office, or into performing an action that results in a computer intrusion. While members of the guard force certainly don't need the full training of personnel who operate or use computers, nonetheless they must not be overlooked in the security awareness program.

Within the corporate world there are probably few subjects about which all employees need to be educated that are simultaneously as important and as inherently dull as security. The best designed information security training programs must both inform and capture the attention and enthusiasm of the learners.

The aim should be to make security information awareness and training an engaging and interactive experience. Techniques could include demonstrating social engineering methods through role-playing; reviewing media reports of recent attacks on other less fortunate businesses and discussing the ways the companies could have prevented the loss; or showing a security video that's entertaining and educational at the same time. There are several security awareness companies that market videos and related materials.

For those businesses that do not have the resources to develop a program in-house, there are several training companies that offer security awareness training services. Trade shows such as Secure World Expo (www.secure worldexpo.com) are gathering places for these companies.

The stories in this book provide plenty of material to explain the methods and tactics of social engineering, to raise awareness of the threat, and to demonstrate the vulnerabilities in human behavior. Consider using their scenarios as a basis for role-playing activities. The stories also offer colorful opportunities for lively discussion on how the victims could have responded differently to prevent the attacks from being successful.

A skillful course developer and skillful trainers will find plenty of challenges, but also plenty of opportunities, for keeping the classroom time lively, and, in the process, motivate people to become part of the solution.

Structure of the Training

A basic security awareness training program should be developed that all employees are required to attend. New employees should be required to attend the training as part of their initial indoctrination. I recommend that no employee be provided computer access until he has attended a basic security awareness session.

For this initial awareness and training, I suggest a session focused enough to hold attention, and short enough that the important messages will be remembered. While the amount of material to be covered certainly justifies longer training, the importance of providing awareness and motivation along with a reasonable number of essential messages in my view outweighs any notion of half-day or full-day sessions that leave people numb with too much information.

The emphasis of these sessions should be on conveying an appreciation of the harm that can be done to the company, and to employees individually, unless all employees follow good security work habits. More important than learning about specific security practices is the motivation that leads employees to accept personal responsibility for security.

In situations where some employees cannot readily attend classroom sessions, the company should consider developing awareness training using other forms of instruction, such as videos, computer-based training, online courses, or written materials.

After the initial short training session, longer sessions should be designed to educate employees about specific vulnerabilities and attack techniques relative to their position in the company. Refresher training should be required at least once a year. The nature of the threat and the methods used to exploit people are ever-changing, so the content of the program should be kept up to date. Moreover, people's awareness and alertness diminish over time, so training must be repeated at reasonable intervals to reinforce security principles. Here again the emphasis needs to be as much on keeping employees convinced of the importance of security policies and motivated to adhere to them, as on exposing specific threats and social engineering methods.

Managers must allow reasonable time for their subordinates to become familiar with security policies and procedures, and to participate in the security awareness program. Employees should not be expected to study security policies or attend security classes on their own time. New employees should be given ample time to review security policies and published security practices prior to beginning their job responsibilities.

Employees who change positions within the organization to a job that involves access to sensitive information or computer systems should, of course, be required to complete a security training program tailored to their new responsibilities. For example, when a computer operator becomes a systems administrator, or a receptionist becomes an administrative assistant, new training is required.

Training Course Contents

When reduced to their fundamentals, all social engineering attacks have the same common element: deception. The victim is led to believe that the attacker is a fellow employee or some other person who is authorized to access sensitive information, or authorized to give the victim instructions that involve taking actions with a computer or computer-related equipment. Almost all of these attacks could be foiled if the targeted employee simply follows two steps:

- Verify the identity of the person making the request: Is the person making the request really who he claims to be?
- Verify whether the person is authorized: Does the person have the need to know, or is he otherwise authorized to make this request?

Because security awareness and training are never perfect, use security technologies whenever possible to create a system of defense in depth. This means that the security measure is provided by the technology rather than by individual employees, for example, when the operating system is configured to prevent employees from downloading software from the Internet, or choosing a short, easily guessed password.

If awareness training sessions could change behavior so that each employee would always be consistent about testing any request against these criteria, the risk associated with social engineering attacks would be dramatically reduced.

A practical information security awareness and training program that addresses human behavior and social engineering aspects should include the following:

- A description of how attackers use social engineering skills to deceive people.
- The methods used by social engineers to accomplish their objectives.
- How to recognize a possible social engineering attack.
- The procedure for handling a suspicious request.
- Where to report social engineering attempts or successful attacks.
- The importance of challenging anyone who makes a suspicious request, regardless of the person's claimed position or importance.
- The fact that they should not implicitly trust others without proper verification, even though their impulse is to give others the benefit of the doubt.
- The importance of verifying the identity and authority of any person making a request for information or action. (See "Verification and Authorization Procedures," Chapter 16, for ways to verify identity.)
- Procedures for protecting sensitive information, including familiarity with any data classification system.

- The location of the company's security policies and procedures, and their importance to the protection of information and corporate information systems.

- A summary of key security policies and an explanation of their meaning. For example, every employee should be instructed in how to devise a difficult-to-guess password.

- The obligation of every employee to comply with the policies, and the consequences for noncompliance.

Social engineering by definition involves some kind of human interaction. An attacker will very frequently use a variety of communication methods and technologies in attempting to achieve his or her goal. For this reason, a well-rounded awareness program should attempt to cover some or all of the following:

- Security policies related to computer and voice mail passwords.

- The procedure for disclosing sensitive information or materials.

- Email usage policy, including the safeguards to prevent malicious code attacks including viruses, worms, and Trojan Horses.

- Physical security requirements such as wearing a badge.

- The responsibility to challenge people on the premises who aren't wearing a badge.

- Best security practices of voice mail usage.

- How to determine the classification of information, and the proper safeguards for protecting sensitive information.

- Proper disposal of sensitive documents and computer media that contain, or have at any time in the past contained, confidential materials.

Also, if the company plans to use penetration testing to determine the effectiveness of defenses against social engineering attacks, a warning should be given putting employees on notice of this practice. Let employees know that at some time they may receive a phone call or other communication using an attacker's techniques as part of such a test. Use the results of those tests not to punish, but to define the need for additional training in some areas.

Details concerning all of the above items will be found in Chapter 16.

TESTING

Your company may want to test employees on their mastery of the information presented in the security awareness training, before allowing computer system access. If you design tests to be given on line, many assessment design software programs allow you to readily analyze test results to determine areas of the training that need to be strengthened.

Your company may also consider providing a certificate testifying to the completion of the security training as a reward and employee motivator.

As a routine part of completing the program, it is recommended that each employee be asked to sign an agreement to abide by the security policies and principles taught in the program. Research suggests that a person who makes the commitment of signing such an agreement is more likely to make an effort to abide by the procedures.

ONGOING AWARENESS

Most people are aware that learning, even about important matters, tends to fade unless reinforced periodically. Because of the importance of keeping employees up to speed on the subject of defending against social engineering attacks, an ongoing awareness program is vital.

One method to keep security at the forefront of employee thinking is to make information security a specific job responsibility for *every* person in the enterprise. This encourages employees to recognize their crucial role in the overall security of the company. Otherwise there is a strong tendency to feel that security "is not my job."

While overall responsibility for an information security program is normally assigned to a person in the security department or the information technology department, development of an information security awareness program is probably best structured as a joint project with the training department.

The ongoing awareness program needs to be creative and use every available channel for communicating security messages in ways that are memorable so that employees are constantly reminded about good security habits. Methods should use all of the traditional channels, plus as many nontraditional ones as the people assigned to develop and implement the program can imagine. As with traditional advertising, humor and cleverness help. Varying the wording of messages keeps them from becoming so familiar that they are ignored.

The list of possibilities for an ongoing awareness program might include:

- Providing copies of this book to all employees.
- Including informational items in the company newsletter: articles, boxed reminders (preferably short, attention-getting items), or cartoons, for example.
- Posting a picture of the Security Employee of the Month.
- Hanging posters in employee areas.
- Posting bulletin-board notices.
- Providing printed enclosures in paycheck envelopes.
- Sending email reminders.
- Using security-related screen savers.
- Broadcasting security reminder announcements through the voice mail system.
- Printing phone stickers with messages such as "Is your caller who he says he is?"
- Setting up reminder messages to appear on the computer when logging in, such as "If you are sending confidential information in an email, encrypt it."
- Including security awareness as a standard item on employee performance reports and annual reviews.
- Providing security awareness reminders on the intranet, perhaps using cartoons or humor, or in some other way enticing employees to read them.
- Using an electronic message display board in the cafeteria, with a frequently changing security reminder.
- Distributing flyers or brochures.
- And think gimmicks, such as free fortune cookies in the cafeteria, each containing a security reminder instead of a fortune.

The threat is constant; the reminders must be constant as well.

WHAT'S IN IT FOR ME?

In addition to security awareness and training programs, I strongly recommend an active and well-publicized reward program. You must acknowledge employees who have detected and prevented an attempted social engineering attack, or in some other way significantly contributed to the success of the information security program. The existence of the reward program should be made known to employees at all security awareness sessions, and security violations should be widely publicized throughout the organization.

On the other side of the coin, people must be made aware of the consequences of failing to abide by information security policies, whether through carelessness or resistance. Though we all make mistakes, repeated violations of security procedures must not be tolerated.

•••••••●●●••••••

chapter 16

Recommended Corporate Information Security Policies

nine out of every ten large corporations and government agencies have been attacked by computer intruders, to judge from the results of a survey conducted by the FBI and reported by the Associated Press in April 2002. Interestingly, the study found that only about one company in three reported or publicly acknowledged any attacks. That reticence to reveal their victimization makes sense. To avoid loss of customer confidence and to prevent further attacks by intruders who learn that a company may be vulnerable, most businesses do not publicly report computer security incidents.

It appears that there are no statistics on social engineering attacks, and if there were, the numbers would be highly unreliable; in most cases a company never knows when a social engineer has "stolen" information, so many attacks go unnoticed and unreported.

Effective countermeasures can be put into place against most types of social engineering attacks. But let's face reality here—unless everyone in the enterprise understands that security is important and makes it his or her business to know and adhere to a company's security policies, social engineering attacks will always present a grave risk to the enterprise.

In fact, as improvements are made in the technological weapons against security breaches, the social engineering approach to using people to access proprietary company information or penetrate the corporate network will almost certainly become significantly more frequent and attractive to information thieves. An industrial spy will naturally attempt to accomplish his or her objective using the easiest method and the one involving the least risk of detection. As a matter of fact, a company that has protected its computer systems and network by deploying state-of-the-art security technologies may thereafter be at more risk from attackers who use social engineering strategies, methods, and tactics to accomplish their objectives.

This chapter presents specific policies designed to minimize a company's risk with respect to social engineering attacks. The policies address attacks that are based not strictly on exploiting technical vulnerabilities. They involve using some kind of pretext or ruse to deceive a trusted employee into providing information or performing an action that gives the perpetrator access to sensitive business information or to enterprise computer systems and networks.

WHAT IS A SECURITY POLICY?

Security policies are clear instructions that provide the guidelines for employee behavior for safeguarding information, and are a fundamental building block in developing effective controls to counter potential security threats. These policies are even more significant when it comes to preventing and detecting social engineering attacks.

Effective security controls are implemented by training employees with well-documented policies and procedures. However, it is important to note that security policies, even if religiously followed by all employees, are not guaranteed to prevent every social engineering attack. Rather, the reasonable goal is always to mitigate the risk to an acceptable level.

The policies presented here include measures that, while not strictly focused on social engineering issues, nonetheless belong here because they deal with techniques commonly used in social engineering attacks. For example, policies about opening email attachments—which could install malicious Trojan Horse software allowing the attacker to take over the victim's computer—address a method frequently used by computer intruders.

Steps to Developing a Program

A comprehensive information security program usually starts with a risk assessment aimed at determining:

- What enterprise information assets need to be protected?
- What specific threats exist against these assets?

- What damage would be caused to the enterprise if these potential threats were to materialize?

The primary goal of risk assessment is to prioritize which information assets are in need of immediate safeguards, and whether instituting safeguards will be cost-effective based on a cost-benefit analysis. Simply put, what assets are going to be protected first, and how much money should be spent to protect these assets?

It's essential that senior management buy into and strongly support the necessity of developing security policies and an information security program. As with any other corporate program, if a security program is to succeed, management must do more than merely provide an endorsement, it must demonstrate a commitment by personal example. Employees need to be aware that management strongly subscribes to the belief that information security is vital to the company's operation, that protection of company business information is essential for the company to remain in business, and that every employee's job may depend on the success of the program.

The person assigned to draft information security policies needs to understand that the policies should be written in a style free of technical jargon and readily understood by the nontechnical employee. It's also important that the document make clear why each policy is important; otherwise employees may disregard some policies as a waste of time. The policy writer should create a document that presents the policies, and a separate document for procedures, because policies will probably change much less frequently than the specific procedures used to implement them.

In addition, the policy writer should be aware of ways in which security *technologies* can be used to enforce good information security practices. For example, most operating systems make it possible to require that user passwords conform to certain specifications such as length. In some companies, a policy prohibiting users from downloading programs can be controlled via local or global policy settings within the operating system. The policies should require use of security technology whenever cost-effective to remove human-based decision-making.

Employees must be advised of the consequences for failing to comply with security policies and procedures. A set of appropriate consequences for violating the policies should be developed and widely publicized. Also, a reward program should be created for employees who demonstrate good security practices or who recognize and report a security incident. Whenever an employee is rewarded for foiling a security breach, it should be widely publicized throughout the company, for example in an article in the company newsletter.

One goal of a security awareness program is to communicate the importance of security policies and the harm that can result from failure to follow such rules. Given human nature, employees will, at times, ignore or circumvent policies that appear unjustified or too time-consuming. It is a management responsibility to insure that employees understand the importance of the policies and are motivated to comply, rather than treating them as obstacles to be circumvented.

It's important to note that information security policies cannot be written in stone. As business needs change, as new security technologies come to market, and as security vulnerabilities evolve, the policies need to be modified or supplemented. A process for regular review and updating should be put into place. Make the corporate security policies and procedures available via the corporate intranet or maintain such policies in a publicly available folder. This increases the likelihood that such policies and procedures will be reviewed more frequently, and provides a convenient method for employees to quickly find the answer to any information-security related question.

Finally, periodic penetration tests and vulnerability assessments using social engineering methods and tactics should be conducted to expose any weakness in training or lack of adherence to company policies and procedures. Prior to using any deceptive penetration-testing tactics, employees should be put on notice that such testing may occur from time to time.

How to Use These Policies

The detailed policies presented in this chapter represent only a subset of the information security policies I believe are necessary to mitigate all security risks. Accordingly, the policies included here should not be considered as a comprehensive list of information security policies. Rather, they are the basis for building a comprehensive body of security policies appropriate to the specific needs of your company.

Policy writers for an organization will have to choose the policies that are appropriate based on their company's unique environment and business goals. Each organization, having different security requirements based on business needs, legal requirements, organizational culture, and the information systems used by the company, will take what it needs from the policies presented, and omit the rest.

There are also choices to be made about how stringent policies will be in each category. A smaller company located in a single facility where most employees know one another does not need to be much concerned about an attacker calling on the phone and pretending to be an employee (although of course an imposter may masquerade as a vendor). Also, despite the increased risks, a company framed around a casual, relaxed corporate culture may wish to adopt only a limited subset of recommended policies to meet its security objectives.

DATA CLASSIFICATION

A data classification policy is fundamental to protecting an organization's information assets, and sets up categories for governing the release of sensitive information. This policy provides a framework for protecting corporate information by making all employees aware of the level of sensitivity of each piece of information.

Operating without a data classification policy—the status quo in almost all companies today—leaves most of these decisions in the hands of individual workers. Naturally, employee decisions are largely based on subjective factors, rather than on the sensitivity, criticality, and value of information. Information is also released because employees are ignorant of the possibility that in responding to a request for the information, they may be putting it into the hands of an attacker.

The data classification policy sets forth guidelines for classifying valuable information into one of several levels. With each item assigned a classification, employees can follow a set of data-handling procedures that protect the company from inadvertent or careless release of sensitive information. These procedures mitigate the possibility that employees will be duped into revealing sensitive information to unauthorized persons.

Every employee must be trained on the corporate data classification policy, including those who do not typically use computers or corporate communications systems. Because every member of the corporate workforce—including the cleaning crew, building guards, and copy-room staff, as well as consultants, contractors, and even interns—may have access to sensitive information, anyone could be the target of an attack.

Management must assign an *Information Owner* to be responsible for any information that is currently in use at the company. Among other things, the Information Owner is responsible for the protection of the information assets. Ordinarily, the Owner decides what level of classification to assign based on the need to protect the information, periodically reassesses the classification level assigned, and decides if any changes are needed. The Information Owner may also delegate the responsibility of protecting the data to a *Custodian* or *Designee*.

Classification Categories and Definitions

Information should be separated into varying levels of classification based on its sensitivity. Once a particular classification system is set up, it's an expensive and time-consuming process to reclassify information into new categories. In our example policy I chose four classification levels, which is appropriate for most medium-to-large businesses. Depending on the number and types of sensitive information, business may choose to add more categories to further control specific types of information. In smaller businesses, a three-level classification scheme may be sufficient. Remember—the more complex the classification scheme, the more expense to the organization in training employees and enforcing the system.

Confidential. This category of information is the most sensitive. Confidential information is intended for use only within the organization. In most cases, it should only be shared with a very limited number of people with an absolute need to know. The nature of Confidential information is such that any unauthorized disclosure could seriously impact the company, its shareholders, its business partners, and/or its customers. Items of Confidential information generally fall into one of these categories:

- Information concerning trade secrets, proprietary source code, technical or functional specifications, or product information that could be of advantage to a competitor.
- Marketing and financial information not available to the public.
- Any other information that is vital to the operation of the company such as future business strategies.

Private. This category covers information of a personal nature that is intended for use only within the organization. Any unauthorized disclosure of Private information could seriously impact employees, or the company if obtained by any unauthorized persons (especially social engineers). Items of Private information would include employee medical history, health benefits, bank account information, salary history, or any other personal identifying information that is not of public record.

The Internal category of information is often termed Sensitive by security personnel. I have chosen to use Internal because the term itself explains the intended audience. I have used the term Sensitive not as a security classification but as a convenient method of referring to Confidential, Private, and Internal information; put another way, Sensitive refers to any company information that is not specifically designated as Public.

Internal. This category of information can be freely provided to any persons employed by the organization. Ordinarily, unauthorized disclosure of Internal information is not expected to cause serious harm to the company, its shareholders, its business partners, its customers, or its employees. However, persons adept in social engineering skills can use this information to masquerade as an authorized employee, contractor, or vendor to deceive unsuspecting personnel into providing more sensitive information that would result in unauthorized access to corporate computer systems.

A confidentiality agreement must be signed before Internal information may be disclosed to third parties, such as employees of vendor firms, contractor labor, partner firms, and so on. Internal information generally includes anything used in the course of daily business activity that should not be released to outsiders, such as corporate organizational charts, network dial-up numbers, internal system names, remote access procedures, cost center codes, and so on.

Public. Information that is specifically designated for release to the public. This type of information can be freely distributed to anyone, such as press releases, customer-support contact information, or product brochures. Note that any information not specifically designated as Public should be treated as Sensitive information.

Classified Data Terminology

Based on its classification, data should be distributed to certain categories of people. A number of policies in this chapter refer to information being given to an *Unverified Person.* For the purposes of these policies, an Unverified Person is someone whom the employee does not personally know to be an active employee or to be an employee with the proper rank to have access to information, or who has not been vouched for by a trusted third party.

For the purposes of these policies, a *Trusted Person* is a person you have met face-to-face who is known to you as a company employee, customer, or consultant to the company with the proper rank to have access to information. A Trusted Person might also be an employee of a company having an established relationship with your company (for example, a customer, vendor, or strategic business partner that has signed a non-disclosure agreement).

In *third party vouching,* a Trusted Person provides verification of a person's employment or status, and the person's authority to request information or an action. Note that in some instances, these policies require you to verify that the Trusted Person is still employed by the company before responding to a request for information or action by someone for whom they have vouched.

A *privileged account* is a computer or other account requiring access permission beyond the basic user account, such as a systems administrator account. Employees with privileged accounts typically have the ability to modify user privileges or perform system functions.

A *general departmental mailbox* is a voice mailbox answered with a generic message for the department. Such a mailbox is used in order to protect names and phone extensions of employees who work in a particular department.

VERIFICATION AND AUTHORIZATION PROCEDURES

Information thieves commonly use deceptive tactics to access or obtain confidential business information by masquerading as legitimate employees, contractors, vendors, or business partners. To maintain effective information security, an employee receiving a request to perform an action or provide sensitive information must positively identify the caller and verify his authority prior to granting a request.

The recommended procedures given in this chapter are designed to help an employee who receives a request via any communication method such as telephone, email, or fax to determine whether the request and the person making it are legitimate.

Requests from a Trusted Person

A request for information or action from a Trusted Person may require:

- Verification that the company actively employs or has a relationship with the person where such a relationship is a condition of access to this category of information. This is to prevent terminated employees, vendors, contractors, and others who no longer are associated with the company from masquerading as active personnel.

- Verification that the person has a need to know, and is authorized to have access to the information or to request the action.

Requests from an Unverified Person

When a request is made by an Unverified Person, a reasonable verification process must be deployed to positively identify the person making the request as authorized to receive the requested information, especially when the request in any way involves computers or computer-related equipment. This process is the fundamental control to prevent successful social engineering attacks: If these verification procedures are followed, they will dramatically reduce successful social engineering attacks.

It is important that you not make the process so cumbersome that it is cost-prohibitive, or that employees ignore it.

As detailed below, the verification process involves three steps:

- Verifying that the person is who he or she claims to be.
- Determining that the requester is currently employed or shares a need-to-know relationship with the company.
- Determining that the person is authorized to receive the specific information or to call for the requested action.

Step One: Verification of Identity

The recommended steps for verification are listed below in order of effectiveness—the higher the number, the more effective the method. Also included with each item is a statement about the weakness of that particular method, and the way in which a social engineer can defeat or circumvent the method to deceive an employee.

1. **Caller ID** (assuming this feature is included in the company telephone system). From the caller ID display, ascertain whether the call is from inside or outside the company, and that the name or telephone number displayed matches the identity provided by the caller.

   Weakness: External caller ID information can be falsified by anyone with access to a PBX or telephone switch connected to digital phone service.

2. **Callback.** Look up the requester in the company directory, and call back to the listed extension to verify that the requester is an employee.

   Weakness: An attacker with sufficient knowledge can call-forward a company extension so that, when the employee places the verification call to the listed phone number, the call is transferred to the attacker's outside phone number.

3. **Vouching.** A Trusted Person who vouches for the requester's identity verifies the requester.

   Weakness: Attackers using a pretext are frequently able to convince another employee of their identity, and get that employee to vouch for them.

4. **Shared Secret.** Use an enterprise-wide shared secret, such as a password or daily code.

   Weakness: If many people know the shared secret, it may be easy for an attacker to learn it.

5. **Employee's Supervisor/Manager.** Telephone the employee's immediate supervisor and request verification.

   Weakness: If the requester has provided the telephone number for reaching his or her manager, the person the employee reaches when calling the number may not be the real manager but may, in fact, be an accomplice of the attacker.

6. **Secure Email**. Request a digitally signed message.

   Weakness: If an attacker has already compromised an employee's computer and installed a keystroke logger to obtain the employee's pass phrase, he can send digitally signed email that appears to be from the employee.

7. **Personal Voice Recognition.** The person receiving the request has dealt with the requester (preferably face-to-face), knows for certain that the person actually is a Trusted Person, and is familiar enough with the person to recognize his or her voice on the telephone.

   Weakness: This is a fairly secure method, not easily circumvented by an attacker, but is of no use if the person receiving the request has never met or spoken with the requester.

8. **Dynamic Password Solution.** The requester authenticates himself or herself through the use of a dynamic password solution such as a Secure ID.

   Weakness: To defeat this method, an attacker would have to obtain one of the dynamic password devices, as well the accompanying PIN of the employee to whom the device rightfully belongs, or would have to deceive an employee into reading the information on the display of the device and providing the PIN.

9. **In Person with ID.** The requester appears in person and presents an employee badge or other suitable identification, preferably a picture ID.

   Weakness: Attackers are often able to steal an employee badge, or create a phony badge that appears authentic; however, attackers generally shun this approach because appearing in person puts the attacker at significant risk of being identified and apprehended.

Step Two: Verification of Employment Status

The greatest information security threat is not from the professional social engineer, nor from the skilled computer intruder, but from someone much closer: the just-fired employee seeking revenge or hoping to set himself up in business using information stolen from the company. (Note that a version of this procedure can also be used to verify that someone still enjoys another kind of business relationship with your company, such as a vendor, consultant, or contract worker.)

Before providing Sensitive information to another person or accepting instructions for actions involving the computer or computer-related equipment, verify that the requester is still a current employee by using one of these methods:

Employee Directory Check. If the company maintains an on-line employee directory that accurately reflects active employees, verify that the requester is still listed.

Requester's Manager Verification. Call the requester's manager using a phone number listed in the company directory, not a number provided by the requester.

Requester's Department or Workgroup Verification. Call the requester's department or workgroup and determine from anyone in that department or workgroup that the requester is still employed by the company.

Step Three: Verification of Need to Know

Beyond verifying that the requester is a current employee or has a relationship with your company, there still remains the issue of whether the requester is authorized to have access to the information being requested, or is authorized to request that specific actions affecting computers or computer-related equipment be taken.

This determination may be made by using one of these methods:

Consult job title/workgroup/responsibilities lists. A company can provide ready access to authorization information by publishing lists of which employees are entitled to what information. These lists may be organized in terms of employee job title, employee departments and workgroups, employee responsibilities, or by some combination of these. Such lists would need to be maintained on line to be kept current and provide quick access to authorization information. Ordinarily, Information Owners would be responsible for overseeing the creation and maintenance of the lists for access to information under the Owner's control.

It is important to note that maintaining such lists is an invitation to the social engineer. Consider: If an attacker targeting a company becomes aware that the company maintains such lists, there is a strong motivation to obtain one. Once in hand, such a list opens many doors to the attacker and puts the company at serious risk.

Obtain Authority from a Manager.   An employee contacts his or her own manager, or the manager of the requester, for authority to comply with the request.

Obtain Authority from the Information Owner or a Designee.   The information Owner is the ultimate judge of whether a particular person should be granted access. The process for computer-based access control is for the employee to contact his or her immediate manager to approve a request for access to information based on existing job profiles. If such a profile does not exist, it is the manager's responsibility to contact the relevant data Owner for permission. This chain of command should be followed so that Information Owners are not barraged with requests when there is a frequent need to know.

Obtain Authority by Means of a Proprietary Software Package.   For a large company in a highly competitive industry, it may be practical to develop a proprietary software package that provides need-to-know authorization. Such a database stores employee names and access privileges to classified information. Users would not be able to look up each individual's access rights, but instead would enter the requester's name, and the identifier associated with the information being sought. The software then provides a response indicating whether or not the employee is authorized to access such information. This alternative avoids the danger of creating a list of personnel with respective access rights to valuable, critical, or sensitive information that could be stolen.

MANAGEMENT POLICIES

The following policies pertain to management-level employees. These are divided into the areas of Data Classification, Information Disclosure, Phone Administration, and Miscellaneous Policies. Note that each category of policies uses a unique numbering structure for easy identification of individual policies.

Data Classification Policies

Data Classification refers to how your company classifies the sensitivity of information and who should have access to that information.

1-1 Assign data classification

Policy: All valuable, sensitive, or critical business information must be assigned to a classification category by the designated Information Owner or delegate.

Explanation/Notes: The designated Owner or delegate will assign the appropriate data classification to any information routinely used to accomplish business goals. The Owner also controls who can access such information and what use can be made of it. The Owner of the information may reassign the classification and may designate a time period for automatic declassification.

Any item not otherwise marked should be classified as Sensitive.

1-2 Publish classified handling procedures

Policy: The company must establish procedures governing the release of information in each category.

Explanation/Notes: Once classifications are established, procedures for release of information to employees and to outsiders must be set up, as detailed in the Verification and Authorization Procedures outlined earlier in this chapter.

1-3 Label all items

Policy: Clearly mark both printed materials and media storage containing Confidential, Private, or Internal information to show the appropriate data classification.

Explanation/Notes: Hard copy documents must have a cover sheet, with a classification label prominently displayed, and a classification label on every page that is visible when the document is open.

All electronic files that cannot easily be labeled with appropriate data classifications (database or raw data files) must be protected via access controls to insure that such information is not improperly disclosed, and that it cannot be changed, destroyed, or made inaccessible.

All computer media such as floppy disks, tapes, and CD-ROMs must be labeled with the highest classification of any information contained therein.

Information Disclosure

Information disclosure involves the release of information to various parties based on their identity and need to know.

2-1 Employee verification procedure

Policy: The company should establish comprehensive procedures to be used by employees for verifying the identity, employment status, and authorization of an individual before releasing Confidential or Sensitive information or performing any task that involves use of any computer hardware or software.

Explanation/Notes: Where justified by size of company and security needs, advanced security technologies should be used to authenticate identity. The best security practice would be to deploy authentication tokens in combination with a shared secret to positively identify persons making requests. While this practice would substantially minimize risk, the cost may be prohibitive for some businesses. In those circumstances, the company should use a company-wide shared secret, such as a daily password or code.

2-2 Release of information to third parties

Policy: A set of recommended information disclosure procedures must be made available and all employees should be trained to follow them.

Explanation/Notes: Generally, distribution procedures need to be established for:

- Information made available within the company.
- Distribution of information to individuals and employees of organizations having an established relationship with the company, such as consultants, temporary workers, interns, employees of organizations that have a vendor relationship or strategic partnership arrangement with the company, and so on.
- Information made available outside the company.
- Information at each classification level, when the information is being delivered in person, by telephone, by email, by facsimile, by voice mail, by postal service, by signature delivery service, and by electronic transfer.

2-3 Distribution of Confidential information

Policy: Confidential information, which is company information that could cause substantial harm if obtained by unauthorized persons, may be delivered only to a Trusted Person who is authorized to receive it.

Explanation/Notes: Confidential information in a physical form (that is, printed copy or on a removable storage medium) may be delivered:

- In person.
- By internal mail, sealed and marked with the Confidential classification.
- Outside the company by a reputable delivery service (that is, FedEx, UPS, and so on) with signature of recipient required, or by a postal service using a certified or registered class of mail.

Confidential information in electronic form (computer files, database files, email) may be delivered:

- Within the body of encrypted email.
- By email attachment, as an encrypted file.
- By electronic transfer to a server within the company internal network.
- By a fax program from a computer, provided that only the intended recipient uses the destination machine, or that the intended recipient is waiting at the destination machine while the fax is being sent. As an alternative, facsimiles can be sent without the recipient present if sent over an encrypted telephone link to a password-protected fax server.

Confidential information may be discussed in person; by telephone within the company; by telephone outside the company if encrypted; by encrypted satellite transmission; by encrypted videoconferencing link; and by encrypted Voice Over Internet Protocol (VoIP).

For transmission by fax machine, the recommended method calls for the sender to transmit a cover page; the recipient, on receiving the page, transmits a page in response, demonstrating that he/she is at the fax machine. The sender then transmits the fax.

The following means of communication are not acceptable for discussing or distributing Confidential information: unencrypted email, voice mail message, regular mail, or any wireless communication method (cellular, Short Message Service, or cordless).

2-4 Distribution of Private information

Policy: Private information, which is personal information about an employee or employees that, if disclosed, could be used to harm employees or the company, may be delivered only to a Trusted Person who is authorized to receive it.

Explanation/Notes: Private information in a physical form (that is, hard-copy or data on a removable storage medium) may be delivered:

- In person
- By internal mail, sealed and marked with the Private classification
- By regular mail

Private information in electronic form (computer files, database files, email) may be delivered:

- By internal email.
- By electronic transfer to a server within the company internal network.
- By facsimile, provided that only the intended recipient uses the destination machine, or that the intended recipient is waiting at the destination machine while the fax is being sent. Facsimiles can also be sent to password-protected fax servers. As an alternative, facsimiles can be sent without the recipient present if sent over an encrypted telephone link to a password-protected fax server.

Private information may be discussed in person; by telephone; by satellite transmission; by videoconferencing link; and by encrypted VoIP.

The following means of communication are not acceptable for discussing or distributing Private information: unencrypted email, voice mail message, regular mail, and by any wireless communication method (cellular, SMS, or cordless).

2-5 Distribution of Internal information

Policy: Internal information is information to be shared only within the company or with other Trusted persons who have signed a nondisclosure agreement. You must establish guidelines for the distribution of Internal information.

Explanation/Notes: Internal information may be distributed in any form, including internal email, but may not be distributed outside the company in email form unless encrypted.

2-6 Discussing Sensitive information over the telephone

Policy: Prior to releasing any information that is not designated as Public over the telephone, the person releasing such information must personally recognize the requester's voice through prior business contact, or the company phone system must identify the call as being from an internal telephone number that has been assigned to the requester.

Explanation/Notes: If the requester's voice is not known, call the requester's internal phone number to verify the requester voice through a recorded voice mail message, or have the requester's manager verify the requester's identity and need to know.

2-7 Lobby or reception personnel procedures

Policy: Lobby personnel must obtain photo identification prior to releasing any package to any person who is not known to be an active employee. A log should be kept for recording the person's name, driver's license number, birth date, the item picked up, and the date and time of such pickup.

Explanation/Notes: This policy also applies to handing over outgoing packages to any messenger or courier service such as FedEx, UPS, or Airborne Express. These companies issue identification cards that can be used to verify employee identity.

2-8 Transfer of software to third parties

Policy: Prior to the transfer or disclosure of any software, program, or computer instructions, the requester's identity must be positively verified, and it must be established whether such release is consistent with the data classification assigned to such information. Ordinarily, software developed in-house in source-code format is considered highly proprietary, and classified Confidential.

Explanation/Notes: Determination of authorization is usually based on whether the requester needs access to the software to do his or her job.

2-9 Sales and marketing qualification of customer leads

Policy: Sales and marketing personnel must qualify leads before releasing internal callback numbers, product plans, product group contacts, or other Sensitive information to any potential customer.

Explanation/Notes: It is a common tactic for industrial spies to contact a sales and marketing representative and make him believe that a big purchase may be in the offing. In an effort to take advantage of the sales opportunity, sales and marketing reps often release information that can be used by the attacker as a poker chip to obtain access to Sensitive information.

2-10 Transfer of files or data

Policy: Files or other electronic data should not be transferred to any removable media unless the requester is a Trusted Person whose identity has been verified and who has a need to have such data in that format.

Explanation/Notes: A social engineer can easily dupe an employee by providing a plausible request for having Sensitive information copied to a tape, Zip disc, or other removable media, and sent to him or held in the lobby for pickup.

Phone Administration

Phone administration policies ensure that employees can verify caller identity, and protect their own contact information from those calling into the company.

3-1 Call forwarding on dial-up or fax numbers

Policy: Call forwarding services that permit forwarding calls to external telephone numbers will not be placed on any dial-up modem or fax telephone numbers within the company.

Explanation/Notes: Sophisticated attackers may attempt to dupe telephone company personnel or internal telecom workers into forwarding internal numbers to an external phone line under control of an attacker. This attack allows the intruder to intercept faxes, request Confidential information to be faxed within the company (personnel assume that faxing within the organization must be safe) or dupe dial-in users into providing their account passwords by forwarding the dial-up lines to a decoy computer that simulates the login process.

Depending on the telephone service used within the company, the call forwarding feature may be under control of the communications provider, rather than the telecommunications department. In such circumstances, a request will be made to the communications provider to insure the call forwarding feature is not present on the telephone numbers assigned to dial-up and fax lines.

3-2 Caller ID

Policy: The corporate telephone system must provide caller line identification (caller ID) on all internal telephone sets, and, if possible, enable distinctive ringing to indicate when a call is from outside the company.

Explanation/Notes: If employees can verify the identity of telephone calls from outside the company it may help them prevent an attack, or identify the attacker to appropriate security personnel.

3-3 Courtesy phones

Policy: To prevent visitors from masquerading as company workers, every courtesy telephone will clearly indicate the location of the caller (for example, "Lobby") on the recipient's caller ID.

Explanation/Notes: If the caller ID for internal calls shows extension number only, appropriate provision must be made for calls placed from company phones in the reception area and any other public areas. It must not be possible for an attacker to place a call from one of these phones and deceive an employee into believing that the call has been placed internally from an employee telephone.

3-4 Manufacturer default passwords shipped with phone systems

Policy: The voice mail administrator should change all default passwords that were shipped with the phone system prior to use by company personnel.

Explanation/Notes: Social engineers can obtain lists of default passwords from manufacturers and use these to access administrator accounts.

3-5 Department voice mailboxes

Policy: Set up a generic voice mailbox for every department that ordinarily has contact with the public.

Explanation/Notes: The first step of social engineering involves gathering information about the target company and its personnel. By limiting the accessibility of the names and telephone numbers of employees, a company makes it more difficult for the social engineer to identify targets in the company, or names of legitimate employees for use in deceiving other personnel.

3-6 Verification of telephone system vendor

Policy: No vendor-support technicians will be permitted to remotely access the company telephone system without positive identification of vendor and authorization to perform such work.

Explanation/Notes: Computer intruders who gain access to corporate telephone systems gain the ability to create voice mailboxes, intercept messages intended for other users, or make free phone calls at the corporation's expense.

3-7 Configuration of phone system

Policy: The voice mail administrator will enforce security requirements by configuring the appropriate security parameters in the telephone system.

Explanation/Notes: Phone systems can be set up with greater or lesser degrees of security for voice mail messages. The administrator should be aware of company security concerns, and work with security personnel to configure the phone system to protect Sensitive data.

3-8 Call trace feature

Policy: Depending on limitations of the communications provider, the call trace feature will be enabled globally to allow employees to activate the trap-and-trace feature when the caller is suspected of being an attacker.

Explanation/Notes: Employees must be trained on call trace usage and the appropriate circumstances when it should be used. A call trace should be initiated when the caller is clearly attempting to gain unauthorized access to corporate computer systems or requesting Sensitive information. Whenever an employee activates the call trace feature, immediate notification must be sent to the Incident Reporting Group.

3-9 Automated phone systems

Policy: If the company uses an automated phone answering system, the system must be programmed so that telephone extensions are not announced when transferring a call to an employee or department.

Explanation/Notes: Attackers can use a company's automated telephone system to map employee names to telephone extensions. Attackers can then use knowledge of those extensions to convince call recipients that they are employees with a right to insider information.

3-10 Voice mailboxes to become disabled after successive invalid access attempts

Policy: Program the corporate telephone system to lock out any voice mail account whenever a specified number of successive invalid access attempts have been made.

Explanation/Notes: The Telecommunications administrator must lock out a voice mailbox after five successive invalid attempts to log in. The administrator must then reset any voice mail lockouts manually.

3-11 Restricted telephone extensions

Policy: All internal telephone extensions to departments or workgroups that ordinarily do not receive calls from external callers (help desk, computer room, employee technical support, and so on) should be programmed so that these telephones can be reached only from internal extensions. Alternately, they can be password-protected so that employees and other authorized persons calling from the outside must enter the correct password.

Explanation/Notes: While use of this policy will block most attempts by amateur social engineers to reach their likely targets, it should be noted that a determined attacker will sometimes be able to talk an employee into calling the restricted extension and asking the person who answers the phone to call the attacker, or simply conference in the restricted extension. During security training, this method of tricking employees into assisting the intruder should be discussed to raise employee awareness about these tactics.

Miscellaneous
4-1 Employee badge design

Policy: Employee badges must be designed to include a large photo that can be recognized from a distance.

Explanation/Notes: The photograph on corporate ID badges of standard design is, for security purposes, only slightly better than worthless. The distance between a person entering the building and the guard or receptionist who has the responsibility to check identification is usually great enough that the picture is too small to recognize when the person walks by. For the photo to be of value in this situation, a redesign of the badge is necessary.

4-2 Access rights review when changing position or responsibilities

Policy: Whenever a company employee changes positions or is given increased or decreased job responsibilities, the employee's manager will notify IT of the change in the employee's responsibilities so that the appropriate security profile can be assigned.

Explanation/Notes: Managing the access rights of personnel is necessary to limit disclosure of protected information. The rule of *least privilege* will apply: The access rights assigned to users will be the minimum necessary to perform their jobs. Any requests for changes that result in elevated access rights must be in accordance with a policy on granting elevated access rights.

The worker's manager or the human resources department will have the responsibility of notifying the information technology department to properly adjust the account holder's access rights as needed.

4-3 Special identification for nonemployees

Policy: Your company should issue a special photo company badge to trusted delivery people and nonemployees who have a business need to enter company premises on a regular basis.

Explanation/Notes: Nonemployees who need to enter the building regularly (for example, to make food or beverage deliveries to the cafeteria, or to repair copying machines or make telephone installations) can pose a threat to your company. In addition to issuing identification to these visitors, make sure your employees are trained to spot a visitor without a badge and know how to act in that situation.

4-4 Disabling computer accounts for contractors

Policy: Whenever a contractor who has been issued a computer account has completed his or her assignment, or when the contract expires, the responsible manager will immediately notify the information technology department to disable the contractor's computer accounts, including any accounts used for database access, dial-up, or Internet access from remote locations.

Explanation/Notes: When a worker's employment is terminated, there is a danger that he or she will use knowledge of your company's systems and procedures to gain access to data. All computer accounts used by or known to the worker must be promptly disabled. This includes accounts that provide access to production databases, remote dial-in accounts, and any accounts used to access computer-related devices.

4-5 Incident reporting organization

Policy: An incident reporting organization must be established or, in smaller companies, an incident reporting individual and backup person designated, for receiving and distributing alerts concerning possible security incidents in progress.

Explanation/Notes: By centralizing the reporting of suspected security incidents, an attack that may otherwise have gone unnoticed can be detected. In the event that systematic attacks across the organization are detected and reported, the incident reporting organization may be able to determine what the attacker is targeting so that special efforts can be made to protect those assets.

Employees assigned to receive incident reports must become familiar with social engineering methods and tactics, enabling them to evaluate reports and recognize when an attack may be in progress.

4-6 Incident reporting hotline

Policy: A hotline to the incident reporting organization or person, which may consist of an easy-to-remember phone extension, must be established.

Explanation/Notes: When employees suspect that they are the target of a social engineering attack, they must be able to immediately notify the incident reporting organization. In order for the notification to be timely, all company telephone operators and receptionists must have the number posted or otherwise immediately available to them.

A company-wide early warning system can substantially aid the organization in detecting and responding to an ongoing attack. Employees must be sufficiently well trained that one who suspects he or she has been the target of a social engineering attack will immediately call the incident reporting hotline. In accordance with published procedures, the incident reporting personnel will immediately notify the targeted groups that an intrusion may be in progress so personnel will be on alert. In order for the notification to be timely, the reporting hotline number must be widely distributed throughout the company.

4-7 Sensitive areas must be secured

Policy: A security guard will screen access to sensitive or secure areas and should require two forms of authentication.

Explanation/Notes: One acceptable form of authentication uses a digital electronic lock that requires an employee to swipe his employee badge and enter an access code. The best method to secure sensitive areas is to post a security guard who observes any access-controlled entry. In organizations where this is not cost-effective, two forms of authentication should be used to validate identity. Depending on risk and cost, a biometric-enabled access card is recommended.

4-8 Network and phone cabinets

Policy: Cabinets, closets, or rooms containing network cabling, phone wiring, or network access points must be secured at all times.

Explanation/Notes: Only authorized personnel will be permitted access to telephone and network closets, rooms, or cabinets. Any outside maintenance people or vendor personnel must be positively identified using the procedures published by the department responsible for information security. Access to phone lines, network hubs, switches, bridges, or other related equipment could be used by an attacker to compromise computer and network security.

4-9 Intracompany mail bins

Policy: Intracompany mail bins must not be located in publicly accessible areas.

Explanation/Notes: Industrial spies or computer intruders who have access to any intracompany mail pickup points can easily send forged authorization letters or internal forms that authorize personnel to release Confidential information or to perform an action that assists the attacker. Additionally, the attacker can mail a floppy disk or electronic media with instructions to install a software update, or open a file that has embedded macro commands that serve the intruder's objectives. Naturally, any request received by intracompany mail is assumed to be authentic by the party who receives it.

4-10 The company bulletin board

Policy: Bulletin boards for the benefit of company workers should not be posted in locations where the public has access.

Explanation/Notes: Many businesses have bulletin boards where private company or personnel information is posted for anyone to read. Employer notices, employee lists, internal memorandums, employee home contact numbers listed in advertisements, and other, similar information are frequently posted on the board.

Bulletin boards may be located near company cafeterias, or in close proximity to smoking or break areas where visitors have free access. This type of information should not be made available to visitors or the public.

4-11 Computer center entrance

Policy: The computer room or data center should be locked at all times and personnel must authenticate their identity prior to entering.

Explanation/Notes: Corporate security ought to consider deploying an electronic badge or access card reader so all entries can be electronically logged and audited.

4-12 Customer accounts with service providers

Policy: Company personnel who place service orders with vendors that supply critical services to the company must set up an account password to prevent unauthorized persons from placing orders on behalf of the company.

Explanation/Notes: Utility companies and many other vendors allow customers to set up a password on request; the company should establish passwords with all vendors that provide mission-critical services. This policy is especially critical to telecommunication and Internet services. Any time critical services can be affected, a shared secret is necessary to verify that the caller is authorized to place such orders. Note, too, identifiers such as social security number, corporate taxpayer identification number, mother's maiden name, or similar identifiers must not be used.

A social engineer might, for example, call the telephone company and give orders to add features such as call forwarding to dial-in modem lines, or make a request to the Internet Service Provider to change translation information to provide a bogus IP address when users perform a hostname lookup.

4-13 Departmental contact person

Policy: Your company may institute a program under which each department or workgroup assigns an employee the responsibility of acting as a point contact so that any personnel can easily verify the identity of unknown persons claiming to be from that department. For example, the help desk may contact the departmental point person to verify the identity of an employee who is requesting support.

Explanation/Notes: This method of verifying identity reduces the pool of employees who are authorized to vouch for employees within their department when such employees request support such as resetting passwords or other computer account-related issues.

Social engineering attacks are successful in part because technical support personnel are pressed for time and do not properly verify the identity of requesters. Typically support staff cannot personally recognize all authorized personnel because of the number of employees in larger organizations. The point-person method of vouching limits the number of employees that technical support staff need to be personally familiar with for verification purposes.

4-14 Customer passwords

Policy: Customer service representatives shall not have the ability to retrieve customer account passwords.

Explanation/Notes: Social engineers frequently call customer service departments and, under a pretext, attempt to obtain a customer's authentication information, such as the password or social security number. With this information, the social engineer can then call another service representative, pretend to be the customer, and obtain information or place fraudulent orders.

To prevent these attempts from succeeding, customer service software must be designed so that representatives can only type in the authentication information provided by the caller, and receive a response from the system indicating whether the password is correct or not.

4-15 Vulnerability testing

Policy: Notification of company use of social engineering tactics to test security vulnerabilities is required during security awareness training and employee orientation.

Explanation/Notes: Without notification of social engineering-penetration testing, company personnel may suffer embarrassment, anger, or other emotional trauma from the use of deceptive tactics used against them by other employees or contractors. By placing new hires on notice during the orientation process that they may be subject to this testing, you prevent such conflict.

4-16 Display of company Confidential information

Policy: Company information not designated for public release shall not be displayed in any publicly accessible areas.

Explanation/Notes: In addition to Confidential product or procedure information, internal contact information such as internal telephone or employee lists, or building rosters that contain a list of management personnel for each department within the company must also be kept out of view.

4-17 Security awareness training

Policy: All persons employed by the company must complete a security awareness training course during employee orientation. Furthermore, each employee must take a security awareness refresher course at periodic intervals, not to exceed twelve months, as required by the department assigned with security-training responsibility.

Explanation/Notes: Many organizations disregard end-user awareness training altogether. According to the 2001 Global Information Security Survey, only 30 percent of the surveyed organizations spend money on awareness training for their user-community. Awareness training is an essential requirement to mitigate successful security breaches utilizing social engineering techniques.

4-18 Security training course for computer access

Policy: Personnel must attend and successfully complete a security information course before being given access to any corporate computer systems.

Explanation/Notes: Social engineers frequently target new employees, knowing that as a group they are generally the people least likely to be aware of the company's security policies and the proper procedures to determine classification and handling of sensitive information.

Training should include an opportunity for employees to ask questions about security policies. After training, the account holder should be required to sign a document acknowledging their understanding of the security policies, and their agreement to abide by the policies.

4-19 Employee badge must be color-coded

Policy: Identification badges must be color-coded to indicate whether the badge holder is an employee, contractor, temporary, vendor, consultant, visitor, or intern.

Explanation/Notes: The color of the badge is an excellent way to determine the status of a person from a distance. An alternative would be to use large lettering to indicate the badgeholder's status, but using a color-coded scheme is unmistakable and easier to see.

A common social engineering tactic to gain access to a physical building is to dress up as a delivery person or repair technician. Once inside the facility, the attacker will masquerade as another employee or lie about his status to obtain cooperation from unsuspecting employees. The purpose of this policy is to prevent people from entering the building legitimately and then entering areas they should not have access to. For example, a person entering the facility as a telephone repair technician would not be able to masquerade as an employee: The color of the badge would give him away.

INFORMATION TECHNOLOGY POLICIES

The information technology department of any company has a special need for policies that help it protect the organization's information assets. To reflect the typical structure of IT operations in an organization, I have divided the IT policies into General, Help Desk, Computer Administration, and Computer Operations.

General
5-1 IT department employee contact information

Policy: Phone numbers and email addresses of individual IT department employees should not be disclosed to any person without a need to know.

Explanation/Notes: The purpose of this policy is to prevent contact information from being abused by social engineers. By only disclosing a general contact number or email address for IT, outsiders will be blocked from contacting IT department personnel directly. The email address for site administrative and technical contacts should only consist of generic names such as admin@companyname.com; published telephone numbers should connect to a departmental voice mailbox, not to individual workers.

When direct contact information is available, it becomes easy for a computer intruder to reach specific IT employees and trick them into providing information that can be used in an attack, or to impersonate IT employees by using their names and contact information.

5-2 Technical support requests

Policy: All technical support requests must be referred to the group that handles such requests.

Explanation/Notes: Social engineers may attempt to target IT personnel who do not ordinarily handle technical support issues, and who may not be aware of the proper security procedures when handling such requests. Accordingly, IT staff must be trained to deny these requests and refer the caller to the group that has the responsibility of providing support.

Help Desk
6-1 Remote access procedures

Policy: Help desk personnel must not divulge details or instructions regarding remote access, including external network access points or dial-up numbers, unless the requester has been:

- Verified as authorized to receive Internal information; and,
- Verified as authorized to connect to the corporate network as an external user. Unless known on a person-to-person basis, the requester must be positively identified in accordance with the Verification and Authorization Procedures outlined at the beginning of this chapter.

Explanation/Notes: The corporate help desk is often a primary target for the social engineer, both because the nature of their work is to assist users with computer-related issues, and because they usually have elevated system privileges. All help desk personnel must be trained to act as a human firewall to prevent unauthorized disclosure of information that will assist any unauthorized persons from gaining access to company resources. The simple rule is to never disclose remote access procedures to anyone until positive verification of identity has been made.

6-2 Resetting passwords

Policy: The password to a user account may be reset only at the request of the account holder.

Explanation/Notes: The most common ploy used by social engineers is to have another person's account password reset or changed. The attacker poses as the employee using the pretext that their password was lost or forgotten. In an effort to reduce the success of this type of attack, an IT employee receiving a request for a password reset must call the employee back prior to taking any action; the callback must not be made to a phone number provided by the requester, but to a number obtained from the employee telephone directory. See Verification and Authorization Procedures for more about this procedure.

6-3 Changing access privileges

Policy: All requests to increase a user's privileges or access rights must be approved in writing by the account holder's manager. When the change is made a confirmation must be sent to the requesting manager via intracompany mail. Furthermore, such requests must be verified as authentic in accordance with the Verification and Authorization Procedures.

Explanation/Notes: Once a computer intruder has compromised a standard user account, the next step is to elevate his or her privileges so that the attacker has complete control over the compromised system. An attacker who has knowledge of the authorization process can spoof an authorized request when email, fax, or telephone are used to transmit it. For example, the attacker may phone technical support or the help desk and attempt to persuade a technician to grant additional access rights to the compromised account.

6-4 New account authorization

Policy: A request to create a new account for an employee, contractor, or other authorized person must be made either in writing and signed by the employee's manager, or sent by digitally signed electronic mail. These requests must also be verified by sending a confirmation of the request through intracompany mail.

Explanation/Notes: Because passwords and other information useful in breaking into computer systems are the highest priority targets of information thieves for gaining access, special precautions are necessary. The intention of this policy is to prevent computer intruders from impersonating authorized personnel or forging requests for new accounts. Therefore, all such requests must be positively verified using the Verification and Authorization Procedures.

6-5 Delivery of new passwords

Policy: New passwords must be handled as company Confidential information, delivered by secure methods including in person; by a signature-required delivery service such as registered mail; or by UPS or FedEx. See policies concerning distribution of Confidential information.

Explanation/Notes: Intracompany mail may also be used, but it is recommended that passwords be sent in secure envelopes that obscure the content. A suggested method is to establish a computer point person in each department who has the responsibility of handling distribution of new account details and vouching for the identity of personnel who lose or forget their passwords. In these circumstances, support personnel would always be working with a smaller group of employees that would be personally recognized.

6-6 Disabling an account

Policy: Prior to disabling a user's account you must require positive verification that the request was made by authorized personnel.

Explanation/Notes: The intention of this policy is to prevent an attacker from spoofing a request to disable an account, and then calling to troubleshoot the user's inability to access the computer system. When the social engineer calls posing as a technician with preexisting knowledge of the user's inability to log in, the victim often complies with a request to reveal his or her password during the troubleshooting process.

6-7 Disabling network ports or devices

Policy: No employee should disable any network device or port for any unverified technical support personnel.

Explanation/Notes: The intention of this policy is to prevent an attacker from spoofing a request to disable a network port, and then calling the worker to troubleshoot his or her inability to access the network.

When the social engineer, posing as a helpful technician, calls with preexisting knowledge of the user's network problem, the victim often complies with a request to reveal his or her password during the troubleshooting process.

6-8 Disclosure of procedures for wireless access

Policy: No personnel should disclose procedures for accessing company systems over wireless networks to any parties not authorized to connect to the wireless network.

Explanation/Notes: Always obtain prior verification of a requester as a person authorized to connect to the corporate network as an external user before releasing wireless access information. See Verification and Authorization Procedures.

6-9 User trouble tickets

Policy: The names of any employees who have reported computer-related problems should not be revealed outside the information technology department.

Explanation/Notes: In a typical attack, a social engineer will call the help desk and request the names of any personnel who have reported recent computer problems. The caller may pretend to be an employee, vendor, or an employee of the telephone company. Once he obtains the names of persons reporting trouble, the social engineer, posing as a help desk or technical support person, contacts the employee and says he/she is calling to troubleshoot the problem. During the call, the attacker deceives the victim into providing the desired information or into performing an action that facilitates the attacker's objective.

6-10 Initiating execute commands or running programs

Policy: Personnel employed in the IT department who have privileged accounts should not execute any commands or run any application programs at the request of any person not personally known to them.

Explanation/Notes: A common method attackers use to install a Trojan Horse program or other malicious software is to change the name of an existing program, and then call the help desk complaining that an error message is displayed whenever an attempt is made to run the program. The attacker persuades the help desk technician to run the program himself. When the technician complies, the malicious software inherits the privileges of the user executing the program and performs a task, which gives the attacker the same computer privileges as the help desk employee. This may allow the attacker to take control of the company system.

This policy establishes a countermeasure to this tactic by requiring that support personnel verify employment status prior to running any program at the request of a caller.

Computer Administration
7-1 Changing global access rights

Policy: A request to change the global access rights associated with an electronic job profile must be approved by the group assigned the responsibility of managing access rights on the corporate network.

Explanation/Notes: Authorized personnel will analyze each such request to determine whether the change might entail a threat to information security. If so, the responsible employee will address the pertinent issues with the requester and jointly arrive at a decision about the changes to be made.

7-2 Remote access requests

Policy: Remote computer access will only be provided to personnel who have a demonstrated need to access corporate computer systems from off-site locations. The request must be made by an employee's manager and verified as described in the Verification and Authorization Procedures section.

Explanation/Notes: Recognizing the need for off-site access into the corporate network by authorized personnel, limiting such access only to people with a need may dramatically reduce risk and management of remote access users. The smaller the number of people with external dial-up privileges, the smaller the pool of potential targets for an attacker. Never forget that the attacker also may target remote users with the intent of hijacking their connection into the corporate network, or by masquerading as them during a pretext call.

7-3 Resetting privileged account passwords

Policy: A request to reset a password to a privileged account must be approved by the system manager or administrator responsible for the computer on which the account exists. The new password must be sent through intracompany mail or delivered in person.

Explanation/Notes: Privileged accounts have access to all system resources and files stored on the computer system. Naturally, these accounts deserve the greatest protection possible.

7-4 Outside support personnel remote access

Policy: No outside support person (such as software or hardware vendor personnel) may be given any remote access information or be allowed to access any company computer system or related devices without positive verification of identity and authorization to perform such services. If the vendor requires privileged access to provide support services, the password to the account used by the vendor shall be changed immediately after the vendor services have been completed.

Explanation/Notes: Computer attackers may pose as vendors to gain access to corporate computer or telecommunication networks. Therefore, it is essential that the identity of the vendor be verified in addition to their authorization to perform any work on the system. Moreover, the doors into the system must be slammed shut once their job is done by changing the account password used by the vendor.

No vendor should be allowed to pick his or her own password for any account, even temporarily. Some vendors have been known to use the same or similar passwords across multiple customer systems. For example, one network service company set up privileged accounts on all their customers' systems with the same password, and, to add insult to injury, with outside Telnet access enabled.

7-5 Strong authentication for remote access to corporate systems

Policy: All connection points into the corporate network from remote locations must be protected through the use of strong authentication devices, such as dynamic passwords or biometrics.

Explanation/Notes: Many businesses rely on static passwords as the sole means of authentication for remote users. This practice is dangerous because it is insecure: computer intruders target any remote access point that might be the weak link in the victim's network. Remember that you never know when someone else knows your password.

Accordingly, any remote access points must be protected with strong authentication such as time-based tokens, smart cards, or biometric devices, so that intercepted passwords are of no value to an attacker.

When authentication based on dynamic passwords is impractical, computer users must religiously adhere to the policy for choosing hard-to-guess passwords.

7-6 Operating system configuration

Policy: Systems administrators shall ensure that, wherever possible, operating systems are configured so that they are consistent with all pertinent security policies and procedures.

Explanation/Notes: Drafting and distributing security policies is a fundamental step toward reducing risk, but in most cases, compliance is necessarily left up to the individual employee. There are, however, any number of computer-related policies that can be made mandatory through operating-system settings, such as the required length of passwords. Automating security policies by configuration of operating system parameters effectively takes the decision out of the human element's hands, increasing the overall security of the organization.

7-7 Mandatory expiration

Policy: All computer accounts must be set to expire after one year.

Explanation/Notes: The intention of this policy is to eliminate the existence of computer accounts that are no longer being used, since computer intruders commonly target dormant accounts. The process insures that any computer accounts belonging to former employees or contractors that have been inadvertently left in place are automatically disabled.

At management discretion, you may require that employees must take a security refresher training course at renewal time, or must review information security policies and sign an acknowledgment of their agreement to adhere to them.

7-8 Generic email addresses

Policy: The information technology department shall set up a generic email address for each department within the organization that ordinarily communicates with the public.

Explanation/Notes: The generic email address can be released to the public by the telephone receptionist or published on the company Web site. Otherwise, each employee shall only disclose his or her personal email address to people who have genuine need to know.

During the first phase of a social engineering attack, the attacker often tries to obtain telephone numbers, names, and titles of employees. In most cases, this information is publicly available on the company Web site or just for the asking. Creation of generic voice mailboxes and/or email addresses makes it difficult to associate employee names with particular departments or responsibilities.

7-9 Contact information for domain registrations

Policy: When registering for acquisition of Internet address space or host names, the contact information for administrative, technical, or other personnel should not identify any individual personnel by name. Instead, you should list a generic email address and the main corporate telephone number.

Explanation/Notes: The purpose of this policy is to prevent contact information from being abused by a computer intruder. When the names and phone numbers of individuals are provided, an intruder can use this information to contact the individuals and attempt to deceive them into revealing system information, or to perform an action item that facilitates an attacker's objective. Or the social engineer can impersonate a listed person in an effort to deceive other company personnel.

Instead of an email address to a particular employee, contact information must be in the form of administrator@company.com. Telecommunications department personnel can establish a generic voice mailbox for administrative or technical contacts so as to limit information disclosure that would be useful in a social engineering attack.

7-10 Installation of security and operating system updates

Policy: All security patches for operating system and application software shall be installed as soon as they become available. If this policy conflicts with the operation of mission-critical productions systems, such updates should be performed as soon as practicable.

Explanation/Notes: Once a vulnerability has been identified, the software manufacturer should be contacted immediately to determine whether a patch or a temporary fix has been made available to close the vulnerability. An unpatched computer system represents one of the greatest security threats to the enterprise. When system administrators procrastinate about applying the necessary fixes, the window of exposure is open wide so that any attacker can climb through.

Dozens of security vulnerabilities are identified and published weekly on the Internet. Until information technology staff are vigilant in their efforts to apply all security patches and fixes as soon as practical, despite these systems being behind the company firewall, the corporate network will always be at risk of suffering a security incident. It is extremely important to keep apprised of published security vulnerabilities identified in the operating system or any application programs used during the course of business.

7-11 Contact information on Web sites

Policy: The company's external Web site shall not reveal any details of corporate structure or identify any employees by name.

Explanation/Notes: Corporate structure information such as organization charts, hierarchy charts, employee or departmental lists, reporting structure, names, positions, internal contact numbers, employee numbers, or similar information that is used for internal processes should not be made available on publicly accessible Web sites.

Computer intruders often obtain very useful information on a target's Web site. The attacker uses this information to appear as a knowledgeable employee when using a pretext or ruse. The social engineer is more likely to establish credibility by having this information at his or her disposal. Moreover, the attacker can analyze this information to find out the likely targets who have access to valuable, sensitive, or critical information.

7-12 Creation of privileged accounts

Policy: No privileged account should be created or system privileges granted to any account unless authorized by the system administrator or system manager.

Explanation/Notes: Computer intruders frequently pose as hardware or software vendors in an attempt to dupe information technology personnel into creating unauthorized accounts. The intention of this policy is to block these attacks by establishing greater control over the creation of privileged accounts. The system manager or administrator of the computer system must approve any request to create an account with elevated privileges.

7-13 Guest accounts

Policy: Guest accounts on any computer systems or related networked devices shall be disabled or removed, except for an FTP (file transfer protocol) server approved by management with anonymous access enabled.

Explanation/Notes: The intention of the guest account is to provide temporary access for persons who do not need to have their own account. Several operating systems are installed by default with a guest account enabled. Guest accounts should always be disabled because their existence violates the principle of user accountability. IT should be able to audit any computer-related activity and relate it to a specific user.

Social engineers are easily able to take advantage of these guest accounts for gaining unauthorized access, either directly or by duping authorized personnel into using a guest account.

7-14 Encryption of off-site backup data

Policy: Any company data that is stored off site should be encrypted to prevent unauthorized access.

Explanation/Notes: Operations staff must insure that all data is recoverable in the event that any information needs to be restored. This requires regular test decryption of a random sampling of encrypted files to make sure the data can be recovered. Furthermore, keys used to encrypt data shall be escrowed with a trusted manager in the event the encryption keys are lost or unavailable.

7-15 Visitor access to network connections

Policy: All publicly accessible Ethernet access points must be on a segmented network to prevent unauthorized access to the internal network.

Explanation/Notes: The intention of this policy is to prevent any outsiders from connecting to the internal network when on company premises. Ethernet jacks installed in conference rooms, the cafeteria, training centers, or other areas accessible to visitors shall be filtered to prevent unauthorized access by visitors to the corporate computer systems.

The network or security administrator may choose to set up a virtual LAN in a switch, if available, to control access from these locations.

7-16 Dial-in modems

Policy: Modems used for dial-in calls shall be set to answer no earlier than the fourth ring.

Explanation/Notes: As depicted in the movie *War Games*, hackers use a technique known as war-dialing to locate telephone lines that have modems connected to them. The process begins with the attacker identifying the telephone prefixes used in the area where the target company is located. A scanning program is then used to try every telephone number in those prefixes, to locate those that answer with a modem. To speed up the process, these programs are configured to wait for one or two rings for a modem response before going on to try the next number. When a company sets the auto answer on modem lines to at least four rings, scanning programs will fail to recognize the line as a modem line.

7-17 Antivirus software

Policy: Every computer system shall have current versions of antivirus software installed and activated.

Explanation/Notes: For those businesses that do not automatically push down antivirus software and pattern files (programs that recognize patterns common to virus software to recognize new viruses) to user desktops or workstations, individual users must take the responsibility for installing and maintaining the software on their own systems, including any computer systems used for accessing the corporate network remotely.

If feasible, this software must be set for automatic update of virus signatures nightly. When pattern or signature files are not pushed down to user desktops, computer users shall have the responsibility to update pattern files at least on a weekly basis.

These provisions apply to all desktop machines and laptops used to access company computer systems, and apply whether the computer is company property or personally owned.

7-18 Incoming email attachments (high security requirements)

Policy: In an organization with high security requirements, the corporate firewall shall be configured to filter out all email attachments.

Explanation/Notes: This policy applies only to businesses with high security requirements, or to those that have no business need to receive attachments through electronic mail.

7-19 Authentication of software

Policy: All new software or software fixes or upgrades, whether on physical media or obtained over the Internet, must be verified as authentic prior to installation. This policy is especially relevant to the information technology department when installing any software that requires system privileges.

Explanation/Notes: Computer software referred to in this policy includes operating system components, application software, hot fixes, patches, or any software updates. Many software manufacturers have implemented methods whereby customers can check the integrity of any distribution, usually by a digital signature. In any case where the integrity cannot be verified, the manufacturer must be consulted to verify that the software is authentic.

Computer attackers have been known to send software to a victim, packaged to appear as if the software manufacturer had produced it and shipped it to the company. It is essential that you verify any software you receive as authentic, especially if unsolicited, before installing it on company systems.

Note that a sophisticated attacker might find out that your organization has ordered software from a manufacturer. With that information in hand, the attacker can cancel the order with the real manufacturer, and order the software himself. The software is then modified to perform some malicious function, and is shipped or delivered to your company, in the original packaging, with shrink-wrapping if necessary. Once the product is installed, the attacker is in control.

7-20 Default passwords

Policy: All operating system software and hardware devices that initially have a password set to a default value must have their passwords reset in accordance with the company password policy.

Explanation/Notes: Several operating systems and computer-related devices are shipped with default passwords—that is, with the same password enabled on every unit sold. Failure to change default passwords is a grave mistake that places the company at risk.

Default passwords are widely known and are available on Internet Web sites. In an attack, the first password an intruder tries is the manufacturer's default password.

7-21 Invalid access attempts lockout (low to medium security)

Policy: Especially in an organization with low to medium security requirements, whenever a specified number of successive invalid login attempts to a particular account have been made, the account should be locked out for a period of time.

Explanation/Notes: All company workstations and servers must be set to limit the number of successive invalid attempts to sign in. This policy is necessary to prevent password guessing by trial and error, dictionary attacks, or brute force attempts to gain unauthorized access.

The system administrator must configure the security settings to lock out an account whenever the desired threshold of successive invalid attempts has been reached. It is recommended that an account be locked out for at least thirty minutes after seven successive login attempts.

7-22 Invalid access attempts account disabled (high security)

Policy: In an organization with high security requirements, whenever a specified number of successive invalid login attempts to a particular account has been made, the account should be disabled until reset by the group responsible for providing account support.

Explanation/Notes: All company workstations and servers must be set to limit the number of successive invalid attempts to sign in. This policy is a necessary control to prevent password guessing by trial and error, dictionary attacks, or brute force attempts to gain unauthorized access.

The system administrator must configure the security settings to disable the account after five invalid login attempts. Following such an attack, the account holder will need to call technical support or the group responsible for account support to enable the account. Prior to resetting the account, the department responsible must positively identify the account holder, following the Verification and Authorization Procedures.

7-23 Periodic change of privileged account passwords

Policy: All privileged account holders shall be required to change their passwords at least every thirty days.

Explanation/Notes: Depending on operating system limitations, the systems administrator must enforce this policy by configuration of security parameters in system software.

7-24 Periodic change of user passwords

Policy: All account holders must change their passwords at least every sixty days.

Explanation/Notes: With operating systems that provide this feature, the systems administrator must enforce this policy by configuration of security parameters in the software.

7-25 New account password set up

Policy: New computer accounts must be established with an initial password that is preexpired, requiring the account holder to select a new password upon initial use.

Explanation/Notes: This requirement ensures that only the account holder will have knowledge of his or her password.

7-26 Boot-up passwords

Policy: All computer systems must be configured to require a boot-up password.

Explanation/Notes: Computers must be configured so that when the computer is turned on, a password is required before the operating system will boot. This prevents any unauthorized person from turning on and using another person's computer. This policy applies to all computers on company premises.

7-27 Password requirements for privileged accounts

Policy: All privileged accounts must have a strong password: The password must:

- Not be a word found in a dictionary in any language
- Be mixed upper and lower case with at least one letter, one symbol, and one numeral
- Be at least 12 characters in length
- Not be related to the company or individual in any way.

Explanation/Notes: In most cases computer intruders will target specific accounts that have system privileges. Occasionally the attacker will exploit other vulnerabilities to gain full control over the system.

The first passwords an intruder will try are the simple, commonly used words found in a dictionary. Selecting strong passwords enhances the security by reducing the chance an attacker will find the password by trial and error, dictionary attack, or brute force attack.

7-28 Wireless access points

Policy: All users who access a wireless network must use VPN (Virtual Private Network) technology to protect the corporate network.

Explanation/Notes: Wireless networks are being attacked by a new technique called *war driving*. This technique involves simply driving or walking around with a laptop equipped with an 802.11B NIC card until a wireless network is detected.

Many companies have deployed wireless networks without even enabling WEP (wireless equivalency protocol), which is used to secure the wireless connection through use of encryption. But even when activated, the current version of WEP (mid-2002) is ineffective: It has been cracked wide open, and several Web sites are devoted to providing the means for locating open wireless systems and cracking WEP-enabled wireless access points.

Accordingly, it is essential to add a layer of protection around the 802.11B protocol by deploying VPN technology.

7-29 Updating antivirus pattern files

Policy: Every computer system must be programmed to automatically update antivirus/anti-Trojan pattern files.

Explanation/Notes: At a minimum, such updates shall occur at least weekly. In businesses where employees leave their computers turned on, it is highly recommended that pattern files be updated on a nightly basis.

Antivirus software is ineffective if it is not updated to detect all new forms of malicious code. Since the threat of virus, worm, and Trojan Horse infections is substantially increased if pattern files are not updated, it is essential that antivirus or malicious code products be kept up to date.

Computer Operations
8-1 Entering commands or running programs

Policy: Computer operations personnel must not enter commands or run programs at the request of any person not known to them. If a situation arises where an Unverified Person seems to have reason to make such a request, it should not be complied with without first getting manager approval.

Explanation/Notes: Computer operations employees are popular targets of social engineers, since their positions usually require privileged account access, and the attacker expects that they will be less experienced and less knowledgeable about company procedures than other IT workers. The intention of this policy is to add an appropriate check and balance to prevent social engineers from duping computer operations personnel.

8-2 Workers with privileged accounts

Policy: Employees with privileged accounts must not provide assistance or information to any Unverified Person. In particular this refers to not providing computer help (such as training on application use), accessing any company database, downloading software, or revealing names of personnel who have remote access capabilities,

Explanation/Notes: Social engineers often target employees with privileged accounts. The intent of this policy is to direct IT staff with privileged accounts to successfully handle calls that might represent social engineering attacks.

8-3 Internal systems information

Policy: Computer Operations staff must never disclose any information related to enterprise computer systems or related devices without positively verifying the identity of the requester.

Explanation/Notes: Computer intruders often contact computer operations employees to obtain valuable information such as system access procedures, external points for remote access, and dial-in telephone numbers that are of substantial value to the attacker.

In companies that have technical support staff or a help desk, requests to the computer operations staff for information about computer systems or related devices should be considered unusual. Any information request should be scrutinized under the corporate data classification policy to determine whether the requester is authorized to have such information. When the class of information cannot be determined, the information should be considered to be Internal.

In some cases, outside vendor technical support will need to communicate with persons who have access to enterprise computer systems. Vendors must have specific contacts in the IT department so that those individuals can recognize each other for verification purposes.

8-4 Disclosure of passwords

Policy: Computer operations staff must never reveal their password, or any other passwords entrusted to them, without prior approval of an information technology manager.

Explanation/Notes: In general terms, revealing any password to another is strictly prohibited. This policy recognizes that operations personnel may need to disclose a password to a third party when exigent situations arise. This exception to the general policy prohibiting disclosure of any password requires specific approval of an information technology manager. For extra precaution, this responsibility of disclosing authentication information should be limited to a small group of individuals who have received special training on verification procedures.

8-5 Electronic media

Policy: All electronic media that contains information not designated for public release shall be locked in a physically secure location.

Explanation/Notes: The intention of this policy is to prevent physical theft of Sensitive information stored on electronic media.

8-6 Backup media

Policy: Operations personnel should store backup media in a company safe or other secure location.

Explanation/Notes: Backup media is another prime target of computer intruders. An attacker is not going to spend time attempting to compromise a computer system or network when the weakest link in the chain might be physically unprotected backup media. Once backup media is stolen, the attacker can compromise the confidentiality of any data stored on it, unless the data is encrypted. Therefore, physically securing backup media is an essential process to protect the confidentiality of corporate information.

POLICIES FOR ALL EMPLOYEES

Whether in IT or human resources, the accounting department, or the maintenance staff, there are certain security policies that every employee of your company must know. These policies fall into the categories of General, Computer Use, Email Use, policies for Telecommuters, Phone Use, Fax Use, Voice Mail Use, and Passwords.

General
9-1 Reporting suspicious calls

Policy: Employees who suspect that they may be the subject of a security violation, including any suspicious requests to disclose information or to perform action items on a computer, must immediately report the event to the company's incident reporting group.

Explanation/Notes: When a social engineer fails to convince his or her target to comply with a demand, the attacker will always try someone else. By reporting a suspicious call or event, an employee takes the first step in alerting the company that an attack may be under way. Thus, individual employees are the first line of defense against social engineering attacks.

9-2 Documenting suspicious calls

Policy: In the event of a suspicious phone call that appears to be a social engineering attack, the employee shall, to the extent practical, draw out the caller to learn details that might reveal what the attacker is attempting to accomplish, and make notes of these details for reporting purposes.

Explanation/Notes: When reported to the incident reporting group, such details can help them spot the object or pattern of an attack.

9-3 Disclosure of dial-up numbers

Policy: Company personnel must not disclose company modem telephone numbers, but should always refer such requests to the help desk or to technical support personnel.

Explanation/Notes: Dial-up telephone numbers must be treated as Internal information, to be provided only to employees who have a need to know such information to carry out their job responsibilities.

Social engineers routinely target employees or departments that are likely to be less protective of the requested information. For example, the attacker may call the accounts payable department masquerading as a telephone company employee who is trying to resolve a billing problem. The attacker then asks for any known fax or dial-in numbers in order to resolve the problem. The intruder often targets an employee who is unlikely to realize the danger of releasing such information, or who lacks training with respect to company disclosure policy and procedures.

9-4 Corporate ID badges

Policy: Except when in their immediate office area, all company personnel, including management and executive staff, must wear their employee badges at all times.

Explanation/Notes: All workers, including corporate executives, should be trained and motivated to understand that wearing an ID badge is mandatory everywhere on company premises other than public areas and the person's own office or workgroup area.

9-5 Challenging ID badge violations

Policy: All employees must immediately challenge any unfamiliar person who is not wearing an employee badge or visitor's badge.

Explanation/Notes: While no company wants to create a culture where eagle-eyed employees look for a way to ensnare coworkers for venturing into the hallway without their badges, nonetheless any company concerned with protecting its information needs to take seriously the threat of a social engineer wandering its facilities unchallenged. Motivation for employees who prove diligent in helping enforce the badges-always policy may be acknowledged in familiar ways, such as recognition in the company newspaper or on bulletin boards; a few hours off with pay; or a letter of commendation in their personnel records.

9-6 Piggybacking (passing through secure entrances)

Policy: Employees entering a building must not allow anyone not personally known to them to follow behind them when they have used a secure means, such as a card key, to gain entrance *(piggybacking)*.

Explanation/Notes: Employees must understand that it is not rude to require unknown persons to authenticate themselves before helping them enter a facility or access a secure area.

Social engineers frequently use a technique known as piggybacking, in which they lie in wait for another person who is entering a facility or Sensitive area, and then simply enter with them. Most people feel uncomfortable challenging others, assuming that they are probably legitimate employees. Another piggybacking technique is to carry several boxes so that an unsuspecting worker opens or holds the door to help.

9-7 Shredding Sensitive documents

Policy: Sensitive documents to be discarded must be cross-shredded; media including hard drives that have ever contained Sensitive information or materials must be destroyed in accordance with the procedures set forth by the group responsible for information security.

Explanation/Notes: Standard shredders do not adequately destroy documents; cross-shredders turn documents into pulp. The best security practice is to presume that the organization's chief competitors will be rifling through discarded materials looking for any intelligence that could be beneficial to them.

Industrial spies and computer attackers regularly obtain Sensitive information from materials tossed in the trash. In some cases, business competitors have been known to attempt bribery of cleaning crews to turn over company trash. In one recent example, an employee at Goldman Sachs discovered items that were used in an insider-trading scheme from the trash.

9-8 Personal identifiers

Policy: Personal identifiers such as employee number, social security number, driver's license number, date and place of birth, and mother's maiden name should never be used as a means of verifying identity. These identifiers are not secret and can be obtained by numerous means.

Explanation/Notes: A social engineer can obtain other people's personal identifiers for a price. And in fact, contrary to popular belief, anyone with a credit card and access to the Internet can obtain these pieces of personal identification. Yet despite the obvious danger, banks, utility companies, and credit card companies commonly use these identifiers. This is one reason that identity theft is the fastest growing crime of the decade.

9-9 Organization charts

Policy: Details shown on the company's organization chart must not be disclosed to anyone other than company employees.

Explanation/Notes: Corporate structure information includes organization charts, hierarchy charts, departmental employee lists, reporting structure, employee names, employee positions, internal contact numbers, employee numbers, or similar information.

In the first phase of a social engineering attack, the goal is to gather information about the internal structure of the company. This information is then used to strategize an attack plan. The attacker can also analyze this information to determine which employees are likely to have access to the data that he seeks. During the attack, the information makes the attacker appear as a knowledgeable employee; making it more likely he'll dupe his victim into compliance.

9-10 Private information about employees

Policy: Any requests for private employee information must be referred to human resources.

Explanation/Notes: An exception to this policy may be the telephone number for an employee who needs to be contacted regarding a work-related issue or who is acting in an on-call role. However, it is always preferable to get the requester's phone number, and have the employee call him or her back.

Computer Use
10-1 Entering commands into a computer

Policy: Company personnel should never enter commands into a computer or computer-related equipment at the request of another person unless the requester has been verified as an employee of the information technology department.

Explanation/Notes: One common ploy of social engineers is to request that an employee enter a command that makes a change to the system's configuration, allows the attacker to access the victim's computer without providing authentication, or allows the attacker to retrieve information that can be used to facilitate a technical attack.

10-2 Internal naming conventions

Policy: Employees must not disclose the internal names of computer systems or databases without prior verification that the requester is employed by the company.

Explanation/Notes: Social engineers will sometimes attempt to obtain the names of company computer systems; once the names are known, the attacker places a call to the company and masquerades as a legitimate employee having trouble accessing or using one of the systems. By knowing the internal name assigned to the particular system, the social engineer gains credibility.

10-3 Requests to run programs

Policy: Company personnel should never run any computer applications or programs at the request of another person unless the requester has been verified as an employee of the information technology department.

Explanation/Notes: Any request to run programs, applications, or perform any activity on a computer must be refused unless the requester is positively identified as an employee in the information technology department. If the request involves revealing Confidential information from any file or electronic message, responding to the request must be in accordance with the procedures for releasing Confidential information. See Information Disclosure Policy.

Computer attackers deceive people into executing programs that enable the intruder to gain control of the system. When an unsuspecting user runs a program planted by an attacker, the result may give the intruder access to the victim's computer system. Other programs record the activities of the computer user and return that information to the attacker. While a social engineer can trick a person into executing computer instructions that may do damage, a technically based attack tricks the computer's operating system into executing computer instructions that may cause the same sort of damage.

10-4 Downloading or installing software

Policy: Company personnel must never download or install software at the request of another person, unless the requester has been verified as an employee with the information technology department.

Explanation/Notes: Employees should be on the alert for any unusual request that involves any sort of transaction with computer-related equipment.

A common tactic used by social engineers is to deceive unsuspecting victims into downloading and installing a program that helps the attacker accomplish his or her goal of compromising computer or network security. In some instances, the program may covertly spy on the user or allow the attacker to take control of the computer system through use of a covert remote control application.

10-5 Plain text passwords and email

Policy: Passwords shall not be sent through email unless encrypted.

Explanation/Notes: While it's discouraged, this policy may be waived by e-commerce sites in certain limited circumstances, such as:

- Sending passwords to customers who have registered on the site.
- Sending passwords to customers who have lost or forgotten their passwords.

10-6 Security-related software

Policy: Company personnel must never remove or disable antivirus/ Trojan Horse, firewall, or other security-related software without prior approval from the information technology department.

Explanation/Notes: Computer users sometimes disable security-related software without provocation, thinking it will increase the speed of their computer.

A social engineer may attempt to deceive an employee into disabling or removing software that is needed to protect the company against security-related threats.

10-7 Installation of modems

Policy: No modems may be connected to any computer until prior approval has been obtained from the IT department.

Explanation/Notes: It is important to recognize that modems on desktops or workstations in the workplace pose a substantial security threat, especially if connected to the corporate network. Accordingly, this policy controls modem connection procedures.

Hackers use a technique called war dialing to identify any active modem lines within a range of telephone numbers. The same technique may be used to locate telephone numbers connected to modems within the enterprise. An attacker can easily compromise the corporate network if he or she identifies a computer system connected to a modem running vulnerable remote access software, which is configured with an easily guessed password or no password at all.

10-8 Modems and auto-answer settings

Policy: All desktops or workstations with IT-approved modems shall have the modem auto-answer feature disabled to prevent anyone from dialing into the computer system.

Explanation/Notes: Whenever feasible, the information technology department should deploy a dial-out modem pool for those employees who need to dial out to external computer systems via modem.

10-9 Cracking tools

Policy: Employees will not download or use any software tools designed to defeat software protection mechanisms.

Explanation/Notes: The Internet has dozens of sites devoted to software designed to crack shareware and commercial software products. The use of these tools not only violates a software owner's copyright, but also is extremely dangerous. Because these programs originate from unknown sources, they may contain hidden malicious code that may cause damage to the user's computer or plant a Trojan Horse that gives the author of the program access to the user's computer.

10-10 Posting company information on line

Policy: Employees shall not disclose any details regarding company hardware or software in any public newsgroup, forum, or bulletin board, and shall not disclose contact information other than in accordance with policy.

Explanation/Notes: Any message posted to the Usenet, on-line forums, bulletin boards, or mailing lists can be searched to gather intelligence on a target company or a target individual. During the research phase of a social engineering attack, the attacker may search the Internet for any posts that contain useful information about the company, its products or its people.

Some posts contain very useful tidbits of information that the attacker can use to further an attack. For example, a network administrator may post a question about configuring firewall filters on a particular brand and model of firewall. An attacker who discovers this message will learn valuable information about the type and configuration of the company's firewall that enables him to circumvent it to gain access to the enterprise network.

This problem can be reduced or avoided by implementing a policy that allows employees to post to newsgroups from anonymous accounts that do not identify the company from which they originated. Naturally, the policy must require employees not to include any contact information that may identify the company.

10-11 Floppy disks and other electronic media

Policy: If media used to store computer information, such as floppy disks or CD-ROMS have been left in a work area or on an employee's desk, and that media is from an unknown source, it must not be inserted into any computer system.

Explanation/Notes: One method used by attackers to install malicious code is to place programs onto a floppy or CD-ROM and label it with something very enticing (for example, "Personnel Payroll Data—Confidential"). They then drop several copies in areas used by employees. If a single copy is inserted into a computer and the files on it opened, the attacker's malicious code is executed. This may create a backdoor, which is used to compromise the system, or may cause other damage to the network.

10-12 Discarding removable media

Policy: Before discarding any electronic media that ever contained Sensitive company information, even if that information has been deleted, the item shall be thoroughly degaussed or damaged beyond recovery.

Explanation/Notes: While shredding hard-copy documents is commonplace these days, company workers may overlook the threat of discarding electronic media that contained Sensitive data at any time. Computer attackers attempt to recover any data stored on discarded electronic media. Workers may presume that by just deleting files, they ensure that those files cannot be recovered. This presumption is absolutely incorrect and can cause confidential business information to fall into the wrong hands. Accordingly, all electronic media that contains or previously contained information not designated as Public must be wiped clean or destroyed using the procedures approved by the responsible group.

10-13 Password-protected screen savers

Policy: All computer users must set a screen saver password and the inactivity time-out limit to lock the computer after a certain period of inactivity.

Explanation/Notes: All employees are responsible for setting a screen saver password, and setting the inactivity timeout for no more than ten minutes. The intention of this policy is to prevent any unauthorized person from using another person's computer. Additionally, this policy protects company computer systems from being easily accessed by outsiders who have gained access to the building.

10-14 Disclosure or sharing of passwords statement

Policy: Prior to creation of a new computer account, the employee or contractor must sign a written statement acknowledging that he or she understands that passwords must never be disclosed or shared with anyone, and that he or she agrees to abide by this policy.

Explanation/Notes: The agreement should also include a notice that violation of such agreement may lead to disciplinary action up to and including termination.

Email Use
11-1 Email attachments

Policy: Email attachments must not be opened unless the attachment was expected in the course of business or was sent by a Trusted Person.

Explanation/Notes: All email attachments must be scrutinized closely. You may require that prior notice be given by a Trusted Person that an email attachment is being sent before the recipient opens any attachment. This will reduce the risk of attackers using social engineering tactics to deceive people into opening attachments.

One method of compromising a computer system is to trick an employee into running a malicious program that creates a vulnerability, providing the attacker with access to the system. By sending an email attachment that has executable code or macros, the attacker may be able to gain control of the user's computer.

A social engineer may send a malicious email attachment, then call and attempt to persuade the recipient to open the attachment.

11-2 Automatic forwarding to external addresses

Policy: Automatic forwarding of incoming email to an external email address is prohibited.

Explanation/Notes: The intention of this policy is to prevent an outsider from receiving email sent to an internal email address.

Employees occasionally set up email forwarding of their incoming mail to an email address outside the company when they will be away from the office. Or an attacker may be able to deceive an employee into setting up an internal email address that forwards to an address outside the company. The attacker can then pose as a legitimate insider by having an internal company email address and get people to email Sensitive information to the internal email address.

11-3 Forwarding emails

Policy: Any request from an Unverified Person to relay an electronic mail message to another Unverified Person requires verification of the requester's identity.

11-4 Verifying email

Policy: An email message that appears to be from a Trusted Person that contains a request to provide information not designated as Public, or to perform an action with any computer-related equipment, requires an additional form of authentication. See Verification and Authorization Procedures.

Explanation/Notes: An attacker can easily forge an email message and its header, making it appear as if the message originated from another email address. An attacker can also send an email message from a compromised computer system, providing phony authorization to disclose information or perform an action. Even by examining the header of an email message you cannot detect email messages sent from a compromised internal computer system.

Phone Use

12-1 Participating in telephone surveys

Policy: Employees may not participate in surveys by answering any questions from any outside organization or person. Such requests must be referred to the public relations department or other designated person.

Explanation/Notes: A method used by social engineers to obtain valuable information that may be used against the enterprise is to call an employee and claim to be doing a survey. It's surprising how many people are happy to provide information about the company and themselves to strangers when they believe they're taking part in legitimate research. Among the innocuous questions, the caller will insert a few questions that the attacker wants to know. Eventually, such information may be used to compromise the corporate network.

12-2 Disclosure of internal telephone numbers

Policy: If an Unverified Person asks an employee for his phone number the employee may make a reasonable determination of whether disclosure is necessary to conduct company business.

Explanation/Notes: The intention of this policy is to require employees to make a considered decision on whether disclosure of their telephone extension is necessary. When dealing with people who have not demonstrated a genuine need to know the extension, the safest course is to require them to call the main company phone number and be transferred.

12-3 Passwords in voice mail messages

Policy: Leaving messages containing password information on anyone's voice mailbox is prohibited.

Explanation/Notes: A social engineer can often gain access to an employee's voice mailbox because it is inadequately protected with an easy-to-guess access code. In one type of attack, a sophisticated computer intruder is able to create his own phony voice mailbox and persuade another employee to leave a message relaying password information. This policy defeats such a ruse.

Fax Use
13-1 Relaying faxes

Policy: No fax may be received and forwarded to another party without verification of the requester's identity.

Explanation/Notes: Information thieves may trick trusted employees into faxing sensitive information to a fax machine located on the company's premises. Prior to the attacker giving the fax number to the victim, the imposter telephones an unsuspecting employee, such as a secretary or administrative assistant, and asks if a document can be faxed to them for later pickup. Subsequently, after the unsuspecting employee receives the fax, the attacker telephones the employee and requests that the fax be sent to another location, perhaps claiming that it is needed for an urgent meeting. Since the person asked to relay the fax usually has no understanding of the value of the information, he or she complies with the request.

13-2 Verification of faxed authorizations

Policy: Prior to carrying out any instructions received by facsimile, the sender must be verified as an employee or other Trusted Person. Placing a telephone call to the sender to verify the request is usually sufficient.

Explanation/Notes: Employees must exercise caution when unusual requests are sent by fax, such as a request to enter commands into a computer or disclose information. The data in the header of a faxed document can be falsified by changing the settings of the sending fax machine. Therefore the header on a fax must not be accepted as a means of establishing identity or authorization.

13-3 Sending sensitive information by fax

Policy: Before sending Sensitive information by fax to a machine that is located in an area accessible to other personnel, the sender shall transmit a cover page. The recipient, on receiving the page, transmits a page in response, demonstrating that he/she is physically present at the fax machine. The sender then transmits the fax.

Explanation/Notes: This handshake process assures the sender that the recipient is physically present at the receiving end. Moreover, this process verifies that the receiving fax telephone number has not been forwarded to another location.

13-4 Faxing passwords prohibited

Policy: Passwords must not be sent via facsimile under any circumstances.

Explanation/Notes: Sending authentication information by facsimile is not secure. Most fax machines are accessible to a number of employees. Furthermore, they rely on the public telephone switched network, which can be manipulated by call forwarding the phone number for the receiving fax machine so that the fax is actually sent to the attacker at another number.

Voice Mail Use
14-1 Voice mail passwords

Policy: Voice mail passwords must never be disclosed to anyone for any purpose. In addition, voice mail passwords must be changed every ninety days or sooner.

Explanation/Notes: Confidential company information may be left in voice mail messages. To protect this information, employees should change their voice mail passwords frequently, and never disclose them. In addition, voice mail users should not use the same or similar voice mail passwords within a twelve-month period.

14-2 Passwords on multiple systems

Policy: Voice mail users must not use the same password on any other phone or computer system, whether internal or external to the company.

Explanation/Notes: Use of a similar or identical password for multiple devices, such as voice mail and computer, makes it easier for social engineers to guess all the passwords of a user after identifying only one.

14-3 Setting voice mail passwords

Policy: Voice mail users and administrators must create voice mail passwords that are difficult to guess. They must not be related in any way to the person using it, or the company, and should not contain a predictable pattern that is likely to be guessed.

Explanation/Notes: Passwords must not contain sequential or repeating digits (i.e. 1111, 1234, 1010), must not be the same as or based on the telephone extension number, and must not be related to address, zip code, birth date, license plate, phone number, weight, I.Q., or other predictable personal information.

14-4 Mail messages marked as "old"

Policy: When previously unheard voice mail messages are not marked as new messages, the voice mail administrator must be notified of a possible security violation and the voice mail password must immediately be changed.

Explanation/Notes: Social engineers may gain access to a voice mailbox in a variety of ways. An employee who becomes aware that messages they have never listened to are not being announced as new messages must assume that another person has obtained unauthorized access to the voice mailbox and listened to the messages themselves.

14-5 External voice mail greetings

Policy: Company workers shall limit their disclosure of information on their external outgoing greeting on their voice mail. Ordinarily information related to a worker's daily routine or travel schedule should not be disclosed.

Explanation/Notes: An external greeting (played to outside callers) should not include last name, extension, or reason for absence (such as travel, vacation schedule, or daily itinerary). An attacker can use this information to develop a plausible story in his attempt to dupe other personnel.

14-6 Voice mail password patterns

Policy: Voice mail users shall not select a password where one part of the password remains fixed, while another part changes in a predictable pattern.

Explanation/Notes: For example, do not use a password such as 743501, 743502, 743503, and so on, where the last two digits correspond to the current month.

14-7 Confidential or Private information

Policy: Confidential or Private information shall not be disclosed in a voice mail message.

Explanation/Notes: The corporate telephone system is typically more vulnerable than corporate computer systems. The passwords are usually a string of digits, which substantially limits the number of possibilities for an attacker to guess. Further, in some organizations, voice mail passwords may be shared with secretaries or another administrative staff who have the responsibility of taking messages for their managers. In light of the above, no Sensitive information should ever be left on anyone's voice mail.

Passwords
15-1 Telephone security

Policy: Passwords shall not be disclosed over the telephone at any time.

Explanation/Notes: Attackers may find ways to listen in to phone conversations, either in person or through a technological device.

15-2 Revealing computer passwords

Policy: Under no circumstances shall any computer user reveal his or her password to anyone for any purpose without prior written consent of the responsible information technology manager.

Explanation/Notes: The goal of many social engineering attacks involves deceiving unsuspecting persons into revealing their account names and passwords. This policy is a crucial step in reducing the risk of successful social engineering attacks against the enterprise. Accordingly, this policy needs to be followed religiously throughout the company.

15-3 Internet passwords

Policy: Personnel must never use a password that is the same as or similar to one they are using on any corporate system on an Internet site.

Explanation/Notes: Malicious Web site operators may set up a site that purports to offer something of value or the possibility of winning a prize. To register, a visitor to the site must enter an email address, username, and password. Since many people use the same or similar sign-on information repeatedly, the malicious Web site operator will attempt to use the chosen password and variations of it for attacking the target's work- or home-computer system. The visitor's work computer can sometimes be identified by the email address entered during the registration process.

15-4 Passwords on multiple systems

Policy: Company personnel must never use the same or a similar password in more than one system. This policy pertains to various types of devices (computer or voice mail); various locations of devices (home or work); and various types of systems, devices (router or firewall), or programs (database or application).

Explanation/Notes: Attackers rely on human nature to break into computer systems and networks. They know that, to avoid the hassle of keeping track of several passwords, many people use the same or a similar password on every system they access. As such, the intruder will attempt to learn the password of one system where the target has an account. Once obtained, it's highly likely that this password or a variation thereof will give access to other systems and devices used by the employee.

15-5 Reusing passwords

Policy: No computer user shall use the same or a similar password within the same eighteen-month period.

Explanation/Note: If an attacker does discover a user's password, frequent changing of the password minimizes the damage that can be done. Making the new password unique from previous passwords makes it harder for the attacker to guess it.

15-6 Password patterns

Policy: Employees must not select a password where one part remains fixed, and another element changes in a predictable pattern.

Explanation/Notes: For example, do not use a password such as Kevin01, Kevin02, Kevin03, and so on, where the last two digits correspond to the current month.

15-7 Choosing passwords

Policy: Computer users should create or choose a password that adheres to the following requirements. The password must:

- Be at least eight characters long for standard user accounts and at least twelve characters long for privileged accounts.
- Contain at least one number, at least one symbol (such as $, _, !, &), at least one lowercase letter, and at least one uppercase letter (to the extent that such variables are supported by the operating system).

- Not be any of the following items: words in a dictionary in any language; any word that is related to an employee's family, hobbies, vehicle, work, license plate, social security number, address, telephone, pet's name, birthday, or phrases containing those words.

- Not be a variation of a previously used password, with one element remaining the same and another element changing, such as kevin, kevin1, kevin2; or kevinjan, kevinfeb.

Explanation/Notes: The parameters listed above will produce a password that is difficult for the social engineer to guess. Another option is the consonant-vowel method, which provides an easy-to-remember and pronounceable password. To construct this kind of password substitute consonants for each letter C and vowels for the letter V, using the mask of "CVCVCVCV." Examples would be MIXOCASO; CUSOJENA.

15-8 Writing passwords down

Policy: Employees should write passwords down only when they store them in a secure location away from the computer or other password-protected device.

Explanation/Notes: Employees are discouraged from ever writing down passwords. Under certain conditions, however, it may be necessary; for example, for an employee who has multiple accounts on different computer systems. Any written passwords must be secured in a safe place away from the computer. Under no circumstances may a password be stored under the keyboard or attached to the computer display.

15-9 Plaintext passwords in computer files

Policy: Plaintext passwords shall not be saved in any computer file or stored as text called by pressing a function key. When necessary, passwords may be saved using an encryption utility approved by the IT department to prevent any unauthorized disclosures.

Explanation/Notes: Passwords can be easily recovered by an attacker if stored in unencrypted form in computer data files, batch files, terminal function keys, login files, macro or scripting programs, or any data files which contain passwords to FTP sites.

POLICIES FOR TELECOMMUTERS

Telecommuters are outside the corporate firewall, and therefore more vulnerable to attack. These policies will help you prevent social engineers from using your telecommuter employees as a gateway to your data.

16-1 Thin clients

Policy: All company personnel who have been authorized to connect via remote access shall use a thin client to connect to the corporate network.

Explanation/Notes: When an attacker analyzes an attack strategy, he or she will try to identify users who access the corporate network from external locations. As such, telecommuters are prime targets. Their computers are less likely to have stringent security controls, and may be a weak link that may compromise the corporate network.

Any computer that connects to a trusted network can be booby-trapped with keystroke loggers, or their authenticated connection can be hijacked. A thin client strategy can be used to avoid problems. A thin client is similar to a diskless workstation or a dumb terminal; the remote computer does not have storage capabilities but instead the operating system, application programs, and data all reside on the corporate network. Accessing the network via a thin client substantially reduces the risk posed by unpatched systems, outdated operating systems, and malicious code. Accordingly, managing the security of telecommuters is effective and made easier by centralizing security controls. Rather than relying on the inexperienced telecommuter to properly manage security-related issues, these responsibilities are better left with trained system, network, or security administrators.

16-2 Security software for telecommuter computer systems

Policy: Any external computer system that is used to connect to the corporate network must have antivirus software, anti-Trojan software, and a personal firewall (hardware or software). Antivirus and anti-Trojan pattern files must be updated at least weekly.

Explanation/Notes: Ordinarily, telecommuters are not skilled on security-related issues, and may inadvertently or negligently leave their computer system and the corporate network open to attack. Telecommuters therefore pose a serious security risk if they are not properly trained. In addition to installing antivirus and anti-Trojan Horse software to protect against malicious code, a firewall is necessary to block any hostile users from obtaining access to any services enabled on the telecommuter's system.

The risk of not deploying the minimal security technologies to prevent malicious code from propagating cannot be underestimated, as an attack on Microsoft proves. A computer system belonging to a Microsoft telecommuter, used to connect to Microsoft's corporate network, became infected with a Trojan Horse program. The intruder or intruders were able to use the telecommuter's trusted connection to Microsoft's development network to steal developmental source code.

POLICIES FOR HUMAN RESOURCES

Human resources departments have a special charge to protect employees from those attempting to discover personal information through their workplace. HR professionals also have a responsibility to protect their company from the actions of unhappy ex-employees.

17-1 Departing employees

Policy: Whenever a person employed by the company leaves or is terminated, Human Resources must immediately do the following:

- Remove the person's listing from the on-line employee/ telephone directory and disable or forward their voice mail;
- Notify personnel at building entrances or company lobbies; and
- Add the employee's name to the employee departure list, which shall be emailed to all personnel no less often than once a week.

Explanation/Notes: Employees who are stationed at building entrances must be notified to prevent a former employee from reentering the premises. Further, notifying other personnel may prevent the former employee from successfully masquerading as an active employee and duping personnel into taking some action damaging to the company.

In some circumstances, it may be necessary to require every user within the former employee's department to change his or her passwords. (When I was terminated from GTE solely because of my reputation as a hacker, the company required all employees throughout the company to change their password.)

17-2 IT department notification

Policy: Whenever a person employed by the company leaves or is terminated, Human Resources should immediately notify the information technology department to disable the former employee's computer accounts, including any accounts used for database access, dial-up, or Internet access from remote locations.

Explanation/Notes: It's essential to disable any former worker's access to all computer systems, network devices, databases, or any other computer-related devices immediately upon termination. Otherwise, the company may leave the door wide open for a disgruntled employee to access company computer systems and cause significant damage.

17-3 Confidential information used in hiring process

Policy: Advertisements and other forms of public solicitation of candidates to fill job openings should, to the extent possible, avoid identifying computer hardware and software used by the company.

Explanation/Notes: Managers and human resources personnel should only disclose information related to enterprise computer hardware and software that is reasonably necessary to obtain resumes from qualified candidates.

Computer intruders read newspapers and company press releases, and visit Internet sites, to find job listings. Often, companies disclose too much information about the types of hardware and software used to attract prospective employees. Once the intruder has knowledge of the target's information systems, he is armed for the next phase of attack. For example, by knowing that a particular company uses the VMS operating system, the attacker may place pretext calls to determine the release version, and then send a phony emergency security patch made to appear as if it came from the software developer. Once the patch is installed, the attacker is in.

17-4 Employee personal information

Policy: The human resources department must never release personal information about any current or former employee, contractor, consultant, temporary worker, or intern, except with prior express written consent of the employee or human resources manager.

Explanation/Notes: Head-hunters, private investigators, and identity thieves target private employee information such as employee numbers, social security numbers, birth dates, salary history, financial data including direct deposit information, and health-related benefit information. The social engineer may obtain this information so as to masquerade as the individual. In addition, disclosing the names of new hires may be extremely valuable to information thieves. New hires are likely to comply with any request by persons with seniority or in a position of authority, or anyone claiming to be from corporate security.

17-5 Background checks

Policy: A background check should be required for all new hires, contractors, consultants, temporary workers, or interns prior to an offer of employment or establishing of a contractual relationship.

Explanation/Notes: Because of cost considerations, the requirement for background checks may be limited to specific positions of trust. Note, however, that any person who is given physical access to corporate offices may be a potential threat. For example, cleaning crews have access to personnel offices, which gives them access to any computer systems located there. An attacker with physical access to a computer can install a hardware keystroke logger in less than a minute to capture passwords.

Computer intruders will sometimes go to the effort of obtaining a job as a means of gaining access to a target company's computer systems and networks. An attacker can easily obtain the name of a company's cleaning contractor by calling the responsible employee at the target company, claiming to be from a janitorial company looking for their business, and then obtaining the name of the company that is currently providing such services.

POLICIES FOR PHYSICAL SECURITY

Though social engineers try to avoid showing up in person at a workplace they want to target, there are times when they will violate your space. These policies will help you to keep your physical premises secure from threat.

18-1 Identification for nonemployees

Policy: Delivery people and other nonemployees who need to enter company premises on a regular basis must have a special badge or other form of identification in accordance with policy established by corporate security.

Explanation/Notes: Nonemployees who need to enter the building regularly (for example, to make food or beverage deliveries to the cafeteria, or to repair copying machines or install telephones) should be issued a special form of company identification badge provided for this purpose. Others who need to enter only occasionally or on a one-time basis must be treated as visitors and should be escorted at all times.

18-2 Visitor identification

Policy: All visitors must present a valid driver's license or other picture identification to be admitted to the premises.

Explanation/Notes: The security staff or receptionist should make a photocopy of the identification document prior to issuing a visitor's badge. The copy should be kept with the visitor's log. Alternatively, the identification information can be recorded in the visitor's log by the receptionist or guard; visitors should not be permitted to write down their own ID information.

Social engineers seeking to gain entrance to a building will always write false information in the log. Even though it's not difficult to obtain false ID and to learn the name of an employee he or she can claim to be visiting, requiring that the responsible employee must log the entry adds one level of security to the process.

18-3 Escorting visitors

Policy: Visitors must be escorted or in the company of an employee at all times.

Explanation/Notes: One popular ruse of social engineers is to arrange to visit a company employee (for example, visiting with a product engineer on the pretext of being the employee of a strategic partner). After being escorted to the initial meeting, the social engineer assures his host that he can find his own way back to the lobby. By this means he gains the freedom to roam the building and possibly gain access to Sensitive information.

18-4 Temporary badges

Policy: Company employees from another location who do not have their employee badges with them must present a valid driver's license or other picture ID and be issued a temporary visitor's badge.

Explanation/Notes: Attackers often pose as employees from a different office or branch of a company to gain entrance to a company.

18-5 Emergency evacuation

Policy: In any emergency situation or drill, security personnel must ensure that everybody has evacuated the premises.

Explanation/Notes: Security personnel must check for any stragglers that may be left behind in restrooms or office areas. As authorized by the fire department or other authority in charge of the scene, the security force needs to be on the alert for anyone departing the building long after the evacuation.

Industrial spies or sophisticated computer intruders may cause a diversion to gain access to a building or secure area. One diversion used is to release a harmless chemical known as butyl mercaptan into the air. The effect is to create the impression that there is a natural gas leak. Once personnel start evacuation procedures, the bold attacker uses this diversion to either steal information or to gain access to enterprise computer systems. Another tactic used by information thieves involves remaining behind, sometimes in a restroom or closet, at the time of a scheduled evacuation drill, or after setting off a smoke flare or other device to cause an emergency evacuation.

18-6 Visitors in mail room

Policy: No visitors should be permitted in the mail room without the supervision of a company worker.

Explanation/Notes: The intention of this policy is to prevent an outsider from exchanging, sending, or stealing intracompany mail.

18-7 Vehicle license plate numbers

Policy: If the company has a guarded parking area, security staff shall log vehicle license plate numbers for any vehicle entering the area.

18-8 Trash Dumpsters

Policy: Trash Dumpsters must remain on company premises at all times and should be inaccessible to the public.

Explanation/Notes: Computer attackers and industrial spies can obtain valuable information from company trash bins. The courts have held that trash is considered legally abandoned property, so the act of *Dumpster diving* is perfectly legal, as long as the trash receptacles are on public property. For this reason, it is important that trash receptacles be situated on company property, where the company has a legal right to protect the containers and their contents.

POLICIES FOR RECEPTIONISTS

Receptionists are often on the front lines when it comes to dealing with social engineers, yet they are rarely given enough security training to recognize and stop an invader. Institute these policies to help your receptionist better protect your company and its data.

19-1 Internal directory

Policy: Disclosure of information in the internal company directory should be limited to persons employed by the company.

Explanation/Notes: All employee titles, names, telephone numbers, and addresses contained within the company directory should be considered Internal information, and should only be disclosed in accordance with the policy related to data classification and Internal information.

Additionally, any calling party must have the name or extension of the party they are trying to contact. Although the receptionist can put a call through to an individual when a caller does not know the extension, telling the caller the extension number should be prohibited. (For those curious folks who follow by example, you can experience this procedure by calling the National Security Agency and asking the operator to provide an extension.)

19-2 Telephone numbers for specific departments/groups

Policy: Employees shall not provide direct telephone numbers for the company help desk, telecommunications department, computer operations, or system administrator personnel without verifying that the requester has a legitimate need to contact these groups. The receptionist, when transferring a call to these groups, must announce the caller's name.

Explanation/Notes: Although some organizations may find this policy overly restrictive, this rule makes it more difficult for a social engineer to masquerade as an employee by deceiving other employees into transferring the call from their extension (which in some phone systems causes the call to appear to originate from within the company), or demonstrating knowledge of these extensions to the victim in order to create a sense of authenticity.

19-3 Relaying information

Policy: Telephone operators and receptionists should not take messages or relay information on behalf of any party not personally known to be an active employee.

Explanation/Notes: Social engineers are adept at deceiving employees into inadvertently vouching for their identity. One social engineering trick is to obtain the telephone number of the receptionist and, on a pretext, ask the receptionist to take any messages that may come for him. Then, during a call to the victim, the attacker pretends to be an employee, asks for some sensitive information or to perform a task, and gives the main switchboard number as a callback number. The attacker later calls back to the receptionist and is given any message left for him by the unsuspecting victim.

19-4 Items left for pickup

Policy: Before releasing any item to a messenger or other Unverified Person, the receptionist or security guard must obtain picture identification and enter the identification information into the pickup log as required by approved procedures.

Explanation/Notes: One social engineering tactic is to deceive an employee into releasing sensitive materials to another supposedly authorized employee by dropping off such materials at the receptionist or lobby desk for pickup. Naturally, the receptionist or security guard assumes the package is authorized for release. The social engineer either shows up himself or has a messenger service pick up the package.

POLICIES FOR THE INCIDENT REPORTING GROUP

Every company should set up a centralized group that should be notified when any form of attack on corporate security is identified. What follows are some guidelines for setting up and structuring the activities of this group.

20-1 Incident reporting group

Policy: An individual or group must be designated and employees should be instructed to report security incidents to them. All employees should be provided with the contact information for the group.

Explanation/Notes: Employees must understand how to identify a security threat, and be trained to report any threat to a specific incident reporting group. It is also important that an organization establish specific procedures and authority for such a group to act when a threat is reported.

20-2 Attacks in progress

Policy: Whenever the incident reporting group has received reports of an ongoing social engineering attack they shall immediately initiate procedures for alerting all employees assigned to the targeted groups.

Explanation/Notes: The incident reporting group or responsible manager should also make a determination about whether to send a company-wide alert. Once the responsible person or group has a good faith belief that an attack may be in progress, mitigation of damage must be made a priority by notifying company personnel to be on their guard.

·····•••●●●•••·····

Security at a Glance

the following lists and charts provide a quick reference version of social engineering methods discussed in Chapters 2 to 14, and verification procedures detailed in Chapter 16. Modify this information for your organization, and make it available for employees to refer to when an information security question arises.

IDENTIFYING A SECURITY ATTACK

These tables and checklists will assist you in spotting a social engineering attack.

The Social Engineering Cycle

ACTION	DESCRIPTION
Research	May include open source information such as SEC filings and annual reports, marketing brochures, patent applications, press clippings, industry magazines, Web site content. Also Dumpster diving.
Developing rapport and trust	Use of insider information, misrepresenting identity, citing those known to victim, need for help, or authority.
Exploiting trust	Asking for information or an action on the part of the victim. In reverse sting, manipulate victim to ask attacker for help.
Utilize information	If the information obtained is only a step to final goal, attacker returns to earlier steps in cycle till goal is reached.

Common Social Engineering Methods

- Posing as a fellow employee
- Posing as an employee of a vendor, partner company, or law enforcement
- Posing as someone in authority
- Posing as a new employee requesting help
- Posing as a vendor or systems manufacturer calling to offer a system patch or update
- Offering help if a problem occurs, then making the problem occur, thereby manipulating the victim to call them for help
- Sending free software or patch for victim to install
- Sending a virus or Trojan Horse as an email attachment
- Using a false pop-up window asking user to log in again or sign on with password
- Capturing victim keystrokes with expendable computer system or program
- Leaving a floppy disk or CD around the workplace with malicious software on it
- Using insider lingo and terminology to gain trust
- Offering a prize for registering at a Web site with username and password
- Dropping a document or file at company mail room for intraoffice delivery
- Modifying fax machine heading to appear to come from an internal location
- Asking receptionist to receive then forward a fax
- Asking for a file to be transferred to an apparently internal location
- Getting a voice mailbox set up so callbacks perceive attacker as internal
- Pretending to be from remote office and asking for email access locally

Warning Signs of an Attack

- Refusal to give callback number
- Out-of-ordinary request
- Claim of authority
- Stresses urgency
- Threatens negative consequences of noncompliance
- Shows discomfort when questioned
- Name dropping
- Compliments or flattery
- Flirting

Common Targets of Attacks

TARGET TYPE	EXAMPLES
Unaware of value of information	Receptionists, telephone operators, administrative assistants, security guards.
Special privileges	Help desk or technical support, system administrators, computer operators, telephone system administrators.
Manufacturer/ vendor	Computer hardware, software manufacturers, voice mail systems vendors.
Specific departments	Accounting, human resources.

Factors That Make Companies More Vulnerable to Attacks

- Large number of employees
- Multiple facilities
- Information on employee whereabouts left in voice mail messages
- Phone extension information made available
- Lack of security training
- Lack of data classification system
- No incident reporting/response plan in place

VERIFICATION AND DATA CLASSIFICATION

These tables and charts will help you to respond to requests for information or action that may be social engineering attacks.

Verification of Identity Procedure

ACTION	DESCRIPTION
Caller ID	Verify call is internal, and name or extension number matches the identity of the caller.
Callback	Look up requester in company directory and call back the listed extension.
Vouching	Ask a trusted employee to vouch for requester's identity.
Shared common secret	Request enterprise-wide shared secret, such as a password or daily code.
Supervisor or manager	Contact employee's immediate supervisor and request verification of identity and employment status.
Secure email	Request a digitally signed message.
Personal voice recognition	For a caller known to employee, validate by caller's voice.
Dynamic passwords	Verify against a dynamic password solution such as Secure ID or other strong authentication device.
In person	Require requester to appear in person with an employee badge or other identification.

Verification of Employment Status Procedure

ACTION	DESCRIPTION
Employee directory check	Verify that requester is listed in on-line directory.
Requester's manager verification	Call requester's manager using phone number listed in company directory.
Requester's department or workgroup verification	Call requester's department or workgroup and determine that requester is still employed by company.

Procedure to Determine Need to Know

ACTION	DESCRIPTION
Consult job title/ workgroup/ responsibilities list	Check published lists of which employees are entitled to specific classified information.
Obtain authority from manager	Contact your manager, or the manager of the requester, for authority to comply with the request.
Obtain authority from the information Owner or designee	Ask Owner of information if requester has a need to know.
Obtain authority with an automated tool	Check proprietary software database for authorized personnel.

Criteria for Verifying Non-Employees

CRITERION	ACTION
Relationship	Verify that requester's firm has a vendor, strategic partner, or other appropriate relationship.
Identity	Verify requester's identity and employment status at the vendor/partner firm.
Nondisclosure	Verify that the requester has a signed nondisclosure agreement on file.
Access	Refer the request to management when the information is classified above Internal.

Data Classification

CLASSIFICATION	DESCRIPTION	PROCEDURE
Public	Can be freely released to the public.	No need to verify.
Internal	For use within the company.	Verify identity of requester as active employee or verify nondisclosure agreement on file and management approval for nonemployees.

Data Classification *(Continued)*

CLASSIFICATION	DESCRIPTION	PROCEDURE
Private	Information of a personal nature intended for use only within the organization.	Verify identity of requester as active employee or nonemployee with authorization. Check with human resources department to disclose Private information to authorized employees or external requesters.
Confidential	Shared only with people with an absolute need to know within the organization.	Verify identity of requester and need to know from designated information Owner. Release only with prior written consent of manager, or information Owner or designee. Check for nondisclosure agreement on file. Only management personnel may disclose to persons not employed by the company.

Security at a Glance

Responding to a Request for Information

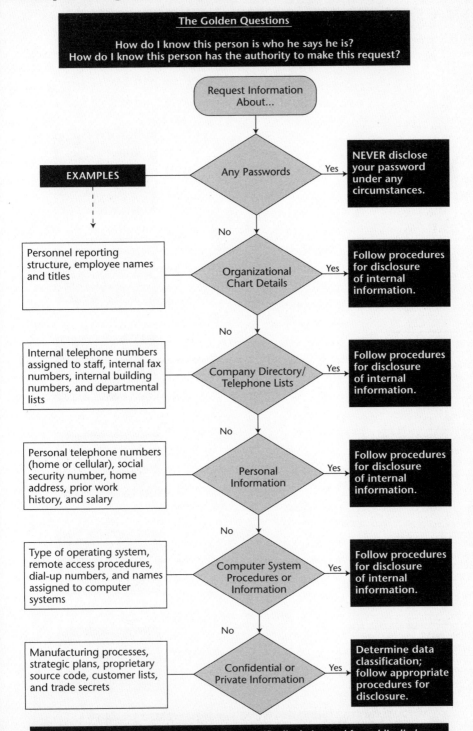

The Golden Questions

How do I know this person is who he says he is?
How do I know this person has the authority to make this request?

Request Information About...

EXAMPLES

Any Passwords — Yes → NEVER disclose your password under any circumstances.

No

Personnel reporting structure, employee names and titles

Organizational Chart Details — Yes → Follow procedures for disclosure of internal information.

No

Internal telephone numbers assigned to staff, internal fax numbers, internal building numbers, and departmental lists

Company Directory/ Telephone Lists — Yes → Follow procedures for disclosure of internal information.

No

Personal telephone numbers (home or cellular), social security number, home address, prior work history, and salary

Personal Information — Yes → Follow procedures for disclosure of internal information.

No

Type of operating system, remote access procedures, dial-up numbers, and names assigned to computer systems

Computer System Procedures or Information — Yes → Follow procedures for disclosure of internal information.

No

Manufacturing processes, strategic plans, proprietary source code, customer lists, and trade secrets

Confidential or Private Information — Yes → Determine data classification; follow appropriate procedures for disclosure.

All information is considered sensitive unless specifically designated for public disclosure.

Responding to a Request for Action

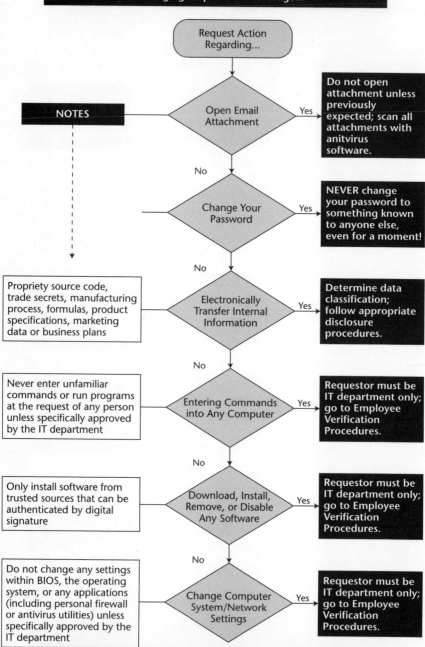

The Golden Rules

No Implicit Trust of Anyone without Verification.
Challenging Requests Is Encouraged.

Request Action Regarding...

Open Email Attachment — Yes → Do not open attachment unless previously expected; scan all attachments with anitvirus software.

No

Change Your Password — Yes → NEVER change your password to something known to anyone else, even for a moment!

No

NOTES

Electronically Transfer Internal Information — Yes → Determine data classification; follow appropriate disclosure procedures.

Propriety source code, trade secrets, manufacturing process, formulas, product specifications, marketing data or business plans

No

Entering Commands into Any Computer — Yes → Requestor must be IT department only; go to Employee Verification Procedures.

Never enter unfamiliar commands or run programs at the request of any person unless specifically approved by the IT department

No

Download, Install, Remove, or Disable Any Software — Yes → Requestor must be IT department only; go to Employee Verification Procedures.

Only install software from trusted sources that can be authenticated by digital signature

No

Change Computer System/Network Settings — Yes → Requestor must be IT department only; go to Employee Verification Procedures.

Do not change any settings within BIOS, the operating system, or any applications (including personal firewall or antivirus utilities) unless specifically approved by the IT department

All actions you take on the behalf of others may result in compromising your company's assets. Verify. Verify. Verify.

sources

CHAPTER 1

BloomBecker, Buck. 1990. *Spectacular Computer Crimes: What They Are and How They Cost American Business Half a Billion Dollars a Year.* Irwin Professional Publishing.

Littman, Jonathan. 1997. *The Fugitive Game: Online with Kevin Mitnick.* Little Brown & Co.

Penenberg, Adam L. April 19, 1999. "The Demonizing of a Hacker." *Forbes.*

CHAPTER 2

The Stanley Rifkin story is based on the following accounts:

Computer Security Insitute. Undated. "Financial losses due to Internet intrusions, trade secret theft and other cyber crimes soar." Press release.

Epstein, Edward Jay. Unpublished. "The Diamond Invention."

Holwick, Rev. David. Unpublished account.

Mr. Rifkin himself was gracious in acknowledging that accounts of his exploit differ because he has protected his anonymity by declining to be interviewed.

CHAPTER 16

Cialdini, Robert B. 2000. *Influence: Science and Practice, 4th edition.* Allyn and Bacon.

Cialdini, Robert B. February 2001. "The Science of Persuasion." *Scientific American.* 284:2.

CHAPTER 17

Some policies in this chapter are based on ideas contained in: Wood, Charles Cresson. 1999. "Information Security Policies Made Easy." Baseline Software.

Acknowledgments

FROM KEVIN MITNICK

True friendship has been defined as one mind in two bodies; not many people in anyone's life can be called a true friend. Jack Biello was a loving and caring person who spoke out against the extraordinary mistreatment I endured at the hands of journalists and government prosecutors. He was a key voice in the Free Kevin movement and a writer who had an extraordinary talent for writing compelling articles exposing the information that the government doesn't want you to know. Jack was always there to fearlessly speak out on my behalf and to work together with me preparing speeches and articles, and, at one point, represented me as a media liaison.

This book is therefore dedicated with love to my dearest friend Jack Biello, whose recent death from cancer just as we finished the manuscript has left me feeling a great sense of loss and sadness.

This book would not have been possible without the love and support of my family. My mother, Shelly Jaffe, and my grandmother, Reba Vartanian, have given me unconditional love and support throughout my life. I am so fortunate to have been raised by such a loving and dedicated mother, who I also consider my best friend. My grandmother has been like a second mom to me, providing me with the same nurturing and love that only a mother could give. As caring and compassionate people, they've taught me the principles of caring about others and lending a helping hand to the less fortunate. And so, by imitating the pattern of giving and caring, I in a sense follow the paths of their lives. I hope they'll forgive me for putting them in second place during the process of writing this book, passing up chances to see them with the excuse of work and deadlines to meet. This book would not have been possible without their continued love and support that I'll forever hold close to my heart.

How I wish my dad, Alan Mitnick, and my brother, Adam Mitnick, would have lived long enough to break open a bottle of champagne with me on the day this book first appears in a bookstore. As a salesman and business owner, my father taught me many of the finer things that I will never forget. During the last months of my Dad's life I was fortunate enough to be able to be at his side to comfort him the best I could, but it was a very painful experience from which I still have not recovered.

My aunt Chickie Leventhal will always have a special place in my heart; although she was disappointed with some of the stupid mistakes I've made, nevertheless she was always there for me, offering her love and support. During my intense devotion to writing this book, I sacrificed many opportunities to join her, my cousin, Mitch Leventhal, and her boyfriend, Dr. Robert Berkowitz, for our weekly Shabbat celebration.

I must also give my warmest thanks to my mother's boyfriend, Steven Knittle, who was there to fill in for me and provide my mother with love and support.

My dad's brother clearly deserves much praise; one could say I inherited my craft of social engineering from Uncle Mitchell, who knew how to manipulate the world and its people in ways that I never even hope to understand, much less master. Lucky for him, he never had my passion for computing technology during the years he used his charming personality to influence anyone he desired. He will always hold the title of the grand-master social engineer.

And as I write these acknowledgements, I realize I have so many people to thank and to express appreciation to for offering their love, friendship, and support. I cannot begin to remember the names of all the kind and generous people that I've met in recent years, but suffice it to say I would need a computer to store them all. There have been so many people from all over the world who have written to me with words of encouragement, praise, and support. These words have meant a great deal to me, especially during the times I needed it most.

I'm especially thankful to all my supporters who stood by me and spent their valuable time and energy getting the word out to anyone who would listen, voicing their concern and objection over my unfair treatment and the hyperbole created by those who sought to profit from the "The Myth of Kevin Mitnick."

I have had the extraordinary fortune of being teamed up with best-selling author Bill Simon, and we worked diligently together despite our different work patterns. Bill is highly organized, rises early, and works in a deliberate and well-planned style. I'm grateful that Bill was kind enough to accommodate my late-night work schedule. My dedication to this project and long working hours kept me up well into the early morning that conflicted with Bill's regular working schedule.

Not only was I lucky to be teamed with someone who could transform my ideas into sentences worthy of a sophisticated reader, but also Bill is (mostly) a very patient man who put up with my programmer's style of focusing on the details. Indeed we made it happen. Still, I want to apologize to Bill in these acknowledgments that I will always regret being the one, because of my orientation to accuracy and detail, who caused him to be late for a deadline for the first and only time in his long writing career. He has a writer's pride that I have finally come to understand and share; we hope to do other books together.

The delight of being at the Simon home in Rancho Santa Fe to work and to be pampered by Bill's wife, Arynne, could be considered a highlight of this writing project. Arynne's conversation and cooking will battle in my memory for first place. She is a lady of quality and wisdom, full of fun, who has created a home of warmth and beauty. And I'll never drink a diet soda again without hearing Arynne's voice in the back of my mind admonishing me on the dangers of Aspartame.

Stacey Kirkland means a great deal to me. She has dedicated many hours of her time assisting me on the Macintosh to design the charts and graphics that helped give visual authority to my ideas. I admire her wonderful qualities; she is truly a loving and compassionate person who deserves only the good things in life. She gave me encouragement as a caring friend and is someone who I care deeply about. I wish to thank her for all her loving support, and for being there for me whenever I needed it.

Alex Kasper, Nexspace, is not only my best friend, but also a business partner and colleague. Together we hosted a popular Internet talk radio show known as "The Darkside of the Internet" on KFI AM 640 in Los Angeles under the skillful guidance of Program Director David G. Hall. Alex graciously provided his invaluable assistance and advice to this book project. His influence has always been positive and helpful with a kindness and generosity that often extended far beyond midnight. Alex and I recently completed a film/video to help businesses train their people on preventing social engineering attacks.

Paul Dryman, Informed Decision, is a family friend and beyond. This highly respected and trusted private investigator helped me to understand trends and processes of conducting background investigations. Paul's knowledge and experience helped me address the personnel security issues described in Part 4 of this book.

One of my best friends, Candi Layman, has consistently offered me support and love. She is truly a wonderful person who deserves the best out of life. During the tragic days of my life, Candi always offered encouragement and friendship. I am fortunate to have met such a wonderful, caring, and compassionate human being, and want to thank her for being there for me.

Surely my first royalty check will go to my cellular phone company for all the time I spent talking with Erin Finn. Without a doubt, Erin is like my soul mate. We are alike in so many ways it's scary. We both have a love for technology, the same tastes in food, music, and movies. AT&T Wireless is definitely losing money for giving me all the "free nights and weekend" calls to her home in Chicago. At least I am not using the Kevin Mitnick plan anymore. Her enthusiasm and belief in this book boosted my spirits. How lucky I am to have her as a friend.

I'm eager to thank those people who represent my professional career and are dedicated in extraordinary ways. My speaking engagements are managed by Amy Gray (an honest and caring person who I admire and adore); David Fugate, of Waterside Productions, is a book agent who went to bat for me on many occasions before and after the book contract was signed; and Los Angeles attorney Gregory Vinson, who was on my defense team during my years-long battle with the government. I'm sure he can relate to Bill's understanding and patience for my close attention to detail; he has had the same experience working with me on legal briefs he has written on my behalf.

I have had too many experiences with lawyers but I am eager to have a place to express my thanks for the lawyers who, during the years of my negative interactions with the criminal justice system, stepped up and offered to help me when I was in desperate need. From kind words to deep involvement with my case, I met many who don't at all fit the stereotype of the self-centered attorney. I have come to respect, admire, and appreciate the kindness and generosity of spirit given to me so freely by so many. They each deserve to be acknowledged with a paragraph of favorable words; I will at least mention them all by name, for every one of them lives in my heart surrounded by appreciation: Greg Aclin, Bob Carmen, John

Dusenbury, Sherman Ellison, Omar Figueroa, Carolyn Hagin, Rob Hale, Alvin Michaelson, Ralph Peretz, Vicki Podberesky, Donald C. Randolph, Dave Roberts, Alan Rubin, Steven Sadowski, Tony Serra, Richard Sherman, Skip Slates, Karen Smith, Richard Steingard, the Honorable Robert Talcott, Barry Tarlow, John Yzurdiaga, and Gregory Vinson.

I very much appreciate the opportunity that John Wiley & Sons has given me to author this book, and for their confidence in a first-time author. I wish to thank the following Wiley people who made this dream possible: Ellen Gerstein, Bob Ipsen, Carol Long (my editor and fashion designer), and Nancy Stevenson.

Other family members, personal friends, business associates who have given me advice and support, and have reached out in many ways, are important to recognize and acknowledge. They are: J. J. Abrams, David Agger, Bob Arkow, Stephen Barnes, Dr. Robert Berkowitz, Dale Coddington, Eric Corley, Delin Cormeny, Ed Cummings, Art Davis, Michelle Delio, Sam Downing, John Draper, Paul Dryman, Nick Duva, Roy Eskapa, Alex Fielding, Lisa Flores, Brock Frank, Steve Gibson, Jerry Greenblatt, Greg Grunberg, Bill Handle, David G. Hall, Dave Harrison, Leslie Herman, Jim Hill, Dan Howard, Steve Hunt, Rez Johar, Steve Knittle, Gary Kremen, Barry Krugel, Earl Krugel, Adrian Lamo, Leo Laporte, Mitch Leventhal, Cynthia Levin, CJ Little, Jonathan Littman, Mark Maifrett, Brian Martin, Forrest McDonald, Kerry McElwee, Alan McSwain, Elliott Moore, Michael Morris, Eddie Munoz, Patrick Norton, Shawn Nunley, Brenda Parker, Chris Pelton, Kevin Poulsen, Scott Press, Linda and Art Pryor, Jennifer Reade, Israel and Rachel Rosencrantz, Mark Ross, William Royer, Irv Rubin, Ryan Russell, Neil Saavedra, Wynn Schwartu, Pete Shipley, Joh Siff, Dan Sokol, Trudy Spector, Matt Spergel, Eliza Amadea Sultan, Douglas Thomas, Roy Tucker, Bryan Turbow, Ron Wetzel, Don David Wilson, Darci Wood, Kevin Wortman, Steve Wozniak, and all my friends on the W6NUT (147.435 MHz) repeater in Los Angeles.

And my probation officer, Larry Hawley, deserves special thanks for giving me permission to act as advisor and consultant on security-related matters by authoring this book.

And finally I must acknowledge the men and women of law enforcement. I simply do not hold any malice towards these people who are just doing their jobs. I firmly believe that putting the public's interest ahead of one's own and dedicating your life to public service is something that deserves respect, and while I've been arrogant at times, I want all of you to know that I love this country, and will do everything in my power to help make it the safest place in the world, which is precisely one of the reasons why I've written this book.

FROM BILL SIMON

I have this notion that there is a *right* person out there for everyone; it's just that some people aren't lucky enough ever to find their Mr. or Ms. Right. Others get lucky. I got lucky early enough in life to spend a good many years already (and count on spending many more) with one of God's treasures, my wife, Arynne. If I ever forget how lucky I am, I only need to pay attention to how many people seek and cherish her company. Arynne—I thank you for walking through life with me.

During the writing of this book, I counted on the help of a loyal group of friends who provided the assurance that Kevin and I were achieving our goal of combining fact and fascination into this unusual book. Each of these people represents true and loyal value and knows he or she may be called on as I get into my next writing project. In alphabetical order: Jean-Claude Beneventi, Linda Brown, Walt Brown, Lt. Gen. Don Johnson, Dorothy Ryan, Guri Stark, Chris Steep, Michael Steep, and John Votaw.

Special recognition goes to John Lucich, president of the Network Security Group, who was willing to take time for a friend-of-a-friend request, and to Gordon Garb, who graciously fielded numerous phone calls about IT operations.

Sometimes in life, a friend earns an exalted place by introducing you to someone else who becomes a good friend. At literary agency Waterside Productions, in Cardiff, California, Agent David Fugate was responsible for conceiving the idea for this book, and for putting me together with coauthor-turned-friend Kevin. Thanks, David. And to the head of Waterside, the incomparable Bill Gladstone, who manages to keep me busy with one book project after another: I'm happy to have you in my corner.

In our home and my office-at-home, Arynne is helped by an able staff that includes administrative assistant Jessica Dudgeon and housekeeper Josie Rodriguez.

I thank my parents Marjorie and I. B. Simon, who I wish were here on earth to enjoy my success as a writer. I also thank my daughter, Victoria. When I am with her I realize how much I admire, respect, and take pride in who she is.

index

C

cable and pair number, 109
callback, 268
call blocking, 212
caller ID, 209–214, 222–223, 268, 278
callers, verification of, 21–22, 29, 334
call forwarding, 143–144, 145, 277–278
call trace feature, 279
candy security, 79
cell phone case study, 48–49
charts, organizational, 307
checks, bounced, 44
class-action suit case study, 225–228
Cleaner, The, 104
cleaning crews, security training of, 192
clearlogs program, 119
CNA (Customer Name and Address) bureau, 81–82
codes, security, 134–136, 138–140, 146
college records, as target, 124–128, 130
command shell, remote access to, 59, 60
computer administration policies, 292–302
computer operations policies, 302–304
confidence (con) man, 232, 234–235
Confidential data classification, 264, 274–275, 286, 318, 336
consistency, 248
console terminal, 184
contractor, accounts for, 281–282
corporate directory, as target of social engineers, 24–26
cost center number, 23–26
courtesy phones, 278
cracking tools, 310–311
credibility, gaining, 50
credit card numbers, 43–46, 52–53, 98–99
CreditChex case study, 16–22
criminal history record, 33
Customer Name and Address (CNA) bureau, 81–82
customers
  information on, obtaining, 36–38, 43
  protecting, 52–53

D

data classification
  Confidential, 264, 274–275, 336
  Internal, 265, 276, 335
  policy, 27, 28, 263–266, 272
  Private, 264, 275, 336
  Public, 265, 335
  terminology, 265–266
dead drop, 70, 216
deception
  social engineering use of, 7–8
  terrorists and, 9–10
  trust as key to, 41–44
defense in depth, 254
deleting files, 169

deniability, plausible, 225
deny terminate telephone service, 174–177
Department of Motor Vehicles (DMV), obtaining information from, 141–145
detention center case study, 173–179
dictionary attack, 70, 187–190
digital certificate, Web site, 102
direct connect telephone service, 174–176
directory
  company directory as target, 24–26
  on-line, 146
  Test Number Directory, 34–35
DMV (Department of Motor Vehicles), obtaining information from, 141–145
driver's license, 140, 155, 227
dual-homed host, 185
dumb terminal, 126
dumpster diving, 156–159

E

eavesdropping, on radio frequencies, 82
eBay, 97, 100
e-commerce, 98–99, 235
email
  address, disclosure of, 68
  attachment, 94–96, 298, 313
  dead drop, 216
  digitally signed, 269
  drops in foreign country, 205, 216
  generic addresses, 294–295
  links in, 96, 100–102
  usage policy, 255, 313–314
employee
  admitting an off-site, 171
  attacks from current or former, 110
  background checks, 324
  departing, procedures for, 169–171, 322–323
  disgruntled, 159–161, 222
  entry-level, attacks on, 195–208
  new employee as attack target, 61–64
  private information on, 307–308, 323–324
  verification, 273
  See also training
employee number, disclosing, 26–27, 29, 78–79, 91
employment agency, social engineering use by, 22–26
employment status, verification, 270, 334
encryption
  of backup and stored files, 227–228, 240–241, 297
  keys, 240–241
  password, 69–70, 188–189, 197
  voice message, 82
  Web site information, 102
entry, illegal, 149–156
enumeration, 186–187
espionage, corporate (industrial), 64–72, 157, 180, 225–242

receptionist
  policies for, 327–328
  social engineering attacks on, 162–165, 171,
    228, 233
reciprocation, 247–248
reminders, security, 130–131
remote access, 159–161, 216, 288–289, 292,
    293–294
Remote Access Trojan (RAT), 95
remote command shell, 59, 60
removable media, 311–312
reporting, security incidents, 75, 129, 304–305
requests
  for action, responding to, 338
  for information, 74–75, 90, 266–267, 337
revenge, 108–110, 220–222
reverse lookup, 32
reward program, 257–258, 261–262
Rifkin, Stanley Mark (social engineer), 4–6
risk assessment, 260–261
role-playing, in training, 246, 251–252

S

salary, discovery of, 166–167
scarcity, tendency to comply and, 249
screen saver password, 298, 312
screen shots, capture, 208
script kiddies, 7
Secure HTTP, 103
Secure ID, 85–87
secure sockets layer (SSL), 103–104
security
  candy, 79
  codes, 134–136, 138–140, 146
  through obscurity, 81–82
  speakeasy, 80, 116
  terminal-based, 182
security guards
  predictability of, 165
  social engineering attacks on, 195–199
  training, 207, 251
Sensitive data classification, 265
server
  dial-up access number for, 69, 71
  disclosing, 88, 125, 129
  locating, 164, 186
  proxy, 53
service providers, accounts with, 284
shoulder surfing, 221
shredders, 169, 306–307
signature card, bank, 136, 139
silent install, 204
social engineering
  head-hunter use of, 22–26
  methods, common, 332
  by parents, 10–11
  reverse, 60
  success rate of attacks, 245
  technology combined with, 173–193

terrorist use of, 10
  See also attack, social engineering
social engineers
  deception by, 7–8
  gender of, 42
  lingo knowledge, importance of, 32
  people skills of, 8, 26, 133
  rank, exploitation of, 52
Social Security Administration case study,
    112–116
social security number, 51, 113
social validation, 249
software
  antivirus, 103–104, 208, 298, 302, 310, 321
  authentication, 298–299
  downloading or installing, 309
  enumeration, 186–187
  malicious (malware), 95, 208
  silent installation, 204
  source code, obtaining, 83–89
  spyware, 203–205, 207–208
  surveillance, 199
  transfer to third parties, 276–277
  Trojan Horse, 59, 310, 321
source, burning of, 19
source code, obtaining, 198, 236–239
speakeasy security, 80, 116
SpyCop, 208
spyware, 203–205, 207–208
SSL (secure sockets layer), 103–104
sting, reverse, 133, 141
storage, on-line, 241
storage facility, attack on, 226–228, 240–241
stranger, cooperation with, 47, 73–74
student records, as target, 124–128, 130
switch, telephone, 142–143, 145, 211, 212
sympathy, exploiting, 77, 107, 115, 124, 236,
    239
system administrator privileges, 183, 184

T

technical support requests, 288
telecommuters, policies for, 321–322
terminal, 126, 182, 184
terrorists, deception and, 9–10
Test Number Directory, 34
thin client, 321
token, time-based, 85, 90
traffic ticket, beating, 217–220
training, 91, 206–207, 245–258, 286–287
  according to job profile, 73, 251, 253
  to challenge authority, 112
  cleaning crews, 192
  content of program, 253–255
  employees to be included in, 35, 39, 73
  establishing a program, 251–252
  goals, 249–251
  motivating employees, 249–250
  necessity for, 245–246

Index